SHOT FROM THE SKY

SHOT FROM THE SKY

AMERICAN POWs IN SWITZERLAND

CATHRYN J. PRINCE

NAVAL INSTITUTE PRESS
ANNAPOLIS, MARYLAND

Naval Institute Press
291 Wood Road
Annapolis, MD 21402

Library of Congress Cataloging-in-Publication Data
Prince, Cathryn J., 1969–
    Shot from the sky : American POWs in Switzerland / Cathryn J.
Prince.
    p. cm.
    ISBN 1-55750-433-4 (alk. paper)
    1. World War, 1939–1945–Prisoners and prisons, Swiss. 2. World
War, 1939–1945–Aerial operations, American. 3. Neutrality–Switzer-
land–History–20th century. 4. World War, 1939–1945–Switzerland. I.
Title.
    D805.S78P75 2003
    940.54'72494–dc21

                                                    2002153476

Printed in the United States of America on acid-free paper ∞
        10 09 08 07 06 05 04 03   9 8 7 6 5 4 3 2
                        First printing

Unless otherwise noted, all photographs are courtesy
of the Swiss Internees Association Inc.

For the airmen

CONTENTS

This book is about one of the great dark secrets of the Second World War. From 1943 until the end of the war, Switzerland shot down American aircraft and imprisoned the surviving airmen in internment camps. The Swiss military detained more than one thousand American fliers between 1943 and 1945. Conditions at the internment camps were adequate and humane for internees who obeyed their captors' orders and did not try to escape. These internees were held in vacant hotels in small mountain villages and were allowed to interact with the villagers. The internment experience was very different, however, for the hundreds of airmen who tried to escape: those who were apprehended were held in appalling conditions in special penitentiary camps. One camp in particular, the infamous Wauwilermoos, kept Americans in conditions as bad as those in some prisoner-of-war camps in Nazi Germany. Ironically, the airmen could not demand better treatment under the Geneva Accords (precursor of the Geneva Convention) because at that time the accords did not apply to prisoners held in neutral countries.

I moved to Lausanne, Switzerland, in 1995—not by choice, but because my husband, then a Swiss citizen who had come to the United States on a J1 visa, had to return to his home country for two years before he could be eligible for a green card. Six months after we married I left my job as a reporter for a Boston business newspaper, my family, and my friends to move to a place where I had previously spent all of two hours.

As our moving date approached, I contacted many U.S. newspapers and magazines to advertise my services as a stringer. Time and again I was answered with the same mantra: "Nothing happens in Switzerland, but here's my number if you want to keep in touch." Then, about a month before we were to leave, I met with editors at the *Christian*

Science Monitor who were eager to have a correspondent in Switzerland to cover both domestic affairs and the United Nations.

I must confess that I had no inkling of the complexities of Swiss society before I arrived. Switzerland had always seemed to me a bastion of multilingual and multicultural harmony content to remain uninvolved in European affairs. Almost immediately I learned how far from reality was this view. Soon after we arrived I began immersing myself in Swiss politics, meeting with key officials from Switzerland's political parties, trade organizations, and social groups. I was accredited to the United Nations in Geneva, and soon I was filing reports nearly once a week from a country where "nothing happens."

I saw European Union flags snapping in the breeze in the French-speaking part of the country. In German-speaking Switzerland, however, save for some of the larger cities, I witnessed much resistance to the notion of joining a greater Europe. The country was starting to question the value of neutrality at a time when the world was becoming increasingly interconnected. Not only did the Swiss argue about joining the European Union, but during my two years there they questioned what role to play in NATO and whether to allow NATO aircraft to overfly Swiss airspace to bomb targets in Bosnia-Herzegovina.

I had been in Switzerland for nearly a year when the first sparks of the Nazi gold crisis ignited and Senator Alfonse D'Amato of New York began taking the Swiss banks to task for their ignoble practices during the Second World War. Suddenly, journalists, particularly American journalists, were not held in great favor. I had, however, been diligently reporting the domestic affairs of Switzerland for some time and had cultivated a great many contacts. These people helped me as I reported the bank situation, but they proved even more important as I embarked on what turned out to be an extraordinarily compelling story.

It is because of my father, a physician, that I am deeply interested in Switzerland's actual role in World War II. He was a captain in the U.S. Air Force, served as a flight surgeon in Vietnam, and is a history buff. I mention these facts because they influenced the course of study I pursued. I have always been fascinated by the history of war and diplomacy and the role of aircraft in war, and when he recounted a story from one of his patients, I was finally able to embark on a project that would meld my interests.

The patient, David Disbrow, told my father that the only way he would ever return to Switzerland would be in a bomber. Disbrow had been a waist gunner in World War II. His plane crash-landed in Switzerland, and he was caught trying to escape and sent to a Swiss prison camp. He tried to escape again, and at the border Swiss guards shot one of the men accompanying him. That is the extent of the story Mr. Disbrow told my father. I was intrigued by this forty-five-year-old account, having never seen any reference to American airmen being interned in Switzerland during World War II. The ramifications of such a story—neutral Switzerland shooting down U.S. aircraft and interning U.S. servicemen—would be enormous if true, I thought.

I began my investigation by contacting Jürg Stüssi-Lautenberg, the director of the Swiss Military Archives and an excellent source of help and information. He had heard that American pilots had been interned in the country, but the Military Archives did not have the records I sought; they were in the Federal Archives. To help get me started, Stüssi-Lautenberg introduced me to Peter von Deschwanden, the mayor of Adelboden, whose own father, a physician, cared for many interned U.S. fliers during the war. Von Deschwanden met me in Bern, and we talked about what it was like when the Americans came to Adelboden. He agreed to take me to the village and introduce me to people who had known the Americans. Through him I met and interviewed many Swiss civilians and retired military personnel who had known the interned fliers. An octogenarian owner of a ski store recalled imprisoned Americans whizzing down the slopes and breaking legs in winter and hiking in the spring to scout for escape routes. American airmen constantly attempted to flee Switzerland, risking arrest and imprisonment in camps run by Nazi sympathizers.

Stüssi-Lautenberg also furnished me with a contact at the Federal Archives who helped me find my way through the hundreds of files pertaining to Switzerland's internment of American airmen during World War II. I spent months in the archives researching original source documents such as letters, photos, arrest papers, medical reports, and work releases. This material, according to some librarians, had not been examined in years, and never by an American.

When I returned to the United States in 1997, I began locating and interviewing the American airmen who were interned in Swiss camps. Robert Long, president of the Swiss Internees Association, was and continues to be an invaluable source; he answered countless questions, set up innumerable contacts, and provided me with documents and photographs.

This book brings to the public a part of World War II that has so far remained untold. For more than fifty years, an episode of World War II has remained on the periphery of history: neutral Switzerland shot and forced down disabled U.S. aircraft that entered Swiss airspace, captured the airmen, and interned them in camps throughout the country. Some histories of the war and memoirs mention the Swiss policy in passing, but virtually no secondary sources other than Swiss books and articles published in the ten years after the war mention the internment camps—and these sources tend to justify or whitewash what went on.

First-person accounts and unpublished sources describing the dreadful conditions of some of these camps, the Nazi sympathizers who ran them, and Switzerland's strong but hidden German sympathies form the base of this book, providing, for the first time, a comprehensive view of these events. This book records the stories of living witnesses, men I have come to know, and helps to set the record straight regarding Switzerland's role in World War II. It is a balanced account of Swiss policy, not an attempt to distort or sensationalize the events. The United States does not emerge blameless from this account: evidence suggests that the bombings of Basel, Schaffhausen, and Zürich in 1945, which resulted in civilian deaths, were acts of deliberate retaliation for Switzerland's involvement with Nazi Germany.

This book also examines the main argument the Swiss use to justify their wartime internment policy: that it satisfied international law. That may be true under some interpretations of international law, but the policy was applied in a grossly unfair manner: virtually no German airmen or troops were interned, and Nazi aircraft were allowed to land unharmed at Swiss airfields, refuel, and depart.

The story of the Swiss internment camps seems to have simply vanished over the past fifty years, submerged beneath the many worse atrocities of the war. The internees themselves were often misunderstood; some were accused of flying deliberately to Switzerland to avoid combat and were treated like deserters when they finally returned home. Others found that the U.S. military did not believe their accounts of the horrors of the penitentiary camps. This book will set the record straight.

ACKNOWLEDGMENTS

I will be forever grateful to the former internees for their willingness to trust me. Initially, many were hesitant to discuss their experiences because they had so often seen the facts distorted, but over time these men opened up and graciously shared their stories, some of which were extremely painful to recall. It has truly been an honor to come to know these heroes.

This book would not have been possible without the assistance of several people. From his first letter to me in 1996, Robert A. Long, president of the Swiss Internees Association Inc., was an invaluable source. He opened his archives and gave me access to all the association's records—photos, videos, and numerous notebooks—as well as providing me with crucial contacts.

Sig Robertson took the time to answer many questions, recounted escape stories, and loaned me books from his personal library.

George Michel gave so much to this book by patiently answering every question I asked, no matter how trivial it might have seemed. He not only searched out information that would further the book, he took the time to read the draft. In the process, he and his wife, Colleen, became cherished friends. During our visit to Wisconsin, the Michels welcomed me and my family with open arms.

In Switzerland, Jürg Stüssi-Lautenberg of the Military Archives in Bern introduced me to Peter von Deschwanden, a connection that set me on course. Dr. von Deschwanden spent a great deal of time introducing me to the people of Adelboden and Wauwilermoos, and to veterans of Switzerland's World War II army. Geoffrey von Meiss, an officer and a true gentleman, gave me the Swiss Air Force perspective and introduced me to Martin Andrews.

I must mention Richard Z. Chesnoff and Joseph L. Galloway, who pointed me in the right direction when I sought a publisher. I am grateful to the U.S. Naval Institute Press for publishing this piece of World War II history and not letting it slip silently into the past; and to Melinda Conner for her thoughtful and careful editing.

When I began this venture I did not know where it would lead. All I knew was that the story of these men should not go untold. So I take this opportunity to thank my parents, my first teachers, for their endless encouragement and for instilling in me the values of responsibility and perseverance. My parents read draft after draft and gave me wonderful, and honest, feedback. This book would never have come about if my father had not given me the idea. Throughout my life he has taught me the importance of duty. He is my moral compass. When I decided on journalism as my career, my mother often took to the road with me to track down information. She is the color of my life.

My children were troopers throughout this process. They are truly my fresh air.

And above all I thank Pierre, my husband. He literally took the journey with me, from tramping around Münsingen on a rainy afternoon (the day before we moved back to the States) to flying to Racine, Wisconsin, with our two small children. His fresh ideas, suggestions, and constant support gave me the courage to stick with this book. Never once did he waver in his belief for this project. He is my anchor, my most dear and trusted friend, and the love of my life.

SHOT FROM THE SKY

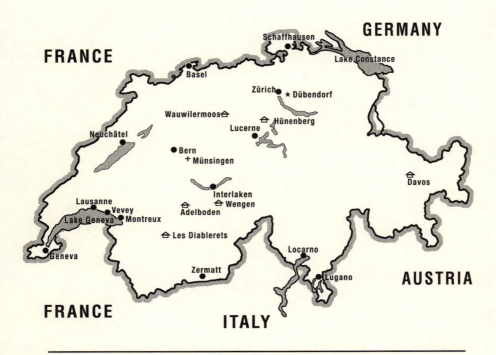

FRANCE

GERMANY

Schaffhausen

Lake Constance

Basel

Zürich ★ Dübendorf

Wauwilermoos⊟

⊟ Hünenberg

Lucerne

Neuchâtel

● Bern

✚ Münsingen

Davos ⊟

Interlaken

Lausanne

⊟ Wengen

● Vevey

Adelboden

Lake Geneva ● Montreux

⊟ Les Diablerets

Locarno

Geneva

Zermatt

Lugano

AUSTRIA

FRANCE

ITALY

SWITZERLAND IN WORLD WAR II

1

SWITZERLAND ON THE BRINK

The Swiss, remaining neutral, during the great revolutions in the states all around them, grew rich on the misfortunes of others, and founded a bank upon human disasters.

CHATEAUBRIAND, French author and diplomat

Belligerents are forbidden to move across the territory of a neutral Power troops or convoys, either of munitions of war or supplies.

ARTICLE 2, HAGUE CONVENTION 1907

Tiny Switzerland lies locked inside Western Europe, surrounded by Austria, France, Germany, and Italy. Throughout the centuries its mountain passes have presented an attractive path for advancing armies and foreign kings who often tried—and failed—to bring the small country under their domination. World War II would be no different. This time, however, Nazi Germany would succeed, effectively counting Switzerland as part of its empire. Germany had no need to physically occupy Switzerland, for that nation's leaders guaranteed that the Reich was favored in all ways over the Allies. To understand how this situation came to pass one must examine the changing nature of Swiss armed neutrality.

• • •

One night in 1291, free peasants from the cantons of Uri, Schwyz, and Unterwalden gathered on the Rütli Meadow on the shore of Lake of Lucerne. With the moonlight as their beacon, they pledged to unshackle their lands from Habsburg servitude and rise together against any future threat to their sovereignty. Out of this oath Switzerland was born.

Freedom did not come easily. Time and again soldiers would swoop into Switzerland trying to wrest control for one foreign monarch or another. One of the first challenges to the infant alliance came in 1315 when about twenty thousand Austrian knights sent by the house of Habsburg clashed with about fourteen hundred peasants from the three founding cantons in the Battle of Morgarten. Equipped only with halberds and pikes, the vastly outnumbered peasant warriors emerged victorious, more determined than ever to defend their independence.[1] Only in 1515, when the Swiss were soundly defeated at Marignano, Italy, did the country change its strategy. Forced by the defeat to realize that it lacked the requisite unity to pursue either a uniform foreign policy or a clear-cut military strategy, the state turned inward, aspiring instead to neutrality.[2] This new tactic spared Switzerland from most of the European conflicts that swirled about it.

The idea of pursuing neutrality as an official policy seems to have first germinated in 1481 at the Diet of Stans. The Swiss monk Niklaus von der Flüe advised the Swiss Confederation to stay nonaligned, arguing that denying others a casus belli might deter foreign aggression and ensure unity in that country of many tongues. While foreign armies were barred from marching through Switzerland as early as 1638, official international recognition took a bit longer.[3] The Treaty of Westphalia of 1648, which ended the Thirty Years' War, first recognized Swiss independence and separation from the Holy Roman Empire.[4]

In 1674 the Swiss Diet declared the absolute neutrality of Switzerland as a political principle. Though Switzerland remained uninvolved in combat for nearly a century, its mountain passes continued to tempt armies marching across the Continent. In May 1797, Napoleon invaded. The French essentially subjugated the Swiss, taking some cantons without firing a shot. After Austria and Britain made peace with France in 1802, Napoleon withdrew his forces; however, Switzerland remained under Napoleonic control.

Finally, in 1815, after the emperor's defeat at Waterloo, the Congress of Vienna organized a committee dedicated to consider the matter of Switzerland. It was in Vienna that a Swiss diplomat named Pictet de Rochemont advocated the theory that Switzerland pursued neutrality not for its own sake, but for the sake of others. The presence of a neutral state in the heart of Europe, he insisted, would serve the interests of all nations on the Continent. The cantons of Geneva, Valais, and Neuchâtel were thus added to the Swiss Confederation with the guarantee that Switzerland would remain neutral. Austria, France, Great Britain, Prussia, and Russia jointly declared the "formal and authentic acknowledgment of the perpetual neutrality of Switzerland."[5] Thus the Treaty of Vienna enshrined Swiss neutrality.[6] Consequently, Switzerland, which had removed itself from the possibility of actual combat, put itself in position to become a fount of information, a broker of prisoner exchanges, and a palace of spies during the two great conflicts that would sweep across Europe nearly one hundred years later.

But this time, having learned an important lesson during the Napoleonic Wars, Switzerland would not rely on other countries to respect its neutrality. On 20 August 1817, the country organized a standing army requiring universal male service and establishing uniform standards.[7] The model remains in effect today. Unlike most other European nations, the Swiss Army requires its soldiers, men aged eighteen to forty-eight, to be on call for short stretches each year rather than serving one short stint at age eighteen. The soldiers are actually liable for call-up in a national emergency until they are sixty years old. The few exemptions to this rule are usually reserved for the physically disabled, with those men, until recently, being required to pay a special tax.

Until the latter part of the 1800s the cantons had little to do with each other save for mutual defense pacts. It was not until 1848, following a civil war, that the cantons renewed their alliance and modern Switzerland emerged.[8] In its modern form, Switzerland's neutrality, really a pragmatic creation, has never been passive or weak; by necessity it has always been supported by force of arms. This stratagem was codified into law in the first decade of the twentieth century. In 1907, at the invitation of President Theodore Roosevelt, delegates from several countries gathered at The Hague for a peace conference whose participants signed the "Convention Respecting the Rights and Duties of Neutral Powers and Persons in War on Land." Perhaps the most fundamental tenet of the 1907 Hague Convention is the maxim that neutral territory is inviolable: "The fact of a neutral Power repelling, even by force, attacks on its neutrality cannot be considered as a hostile act."

In international law neutrality means a country will refrain from participating in a war between other states and will observe strict impartiality in its relations with the warring nations.[9] Yet, as it pertains to Switzerland, this concept of neutrality showed a remarkable unevenness in practice during World War II. Although obliged by international law to intern combatants of all belligerents, Switzerland routinely freed Germans, even going so far as allowing German officers to take leave in Davos.

• • •

Most Swiss were terrified by the Nazis and saw Germany as a threat to their nation's security. As the seeds of National Socialism began to bloom in the early 1930s, newspapers in Basel, Zürich, and Bern openly denounced the Führer. However, given the proximity of their country to Germany and their kinship with the German-speaking world, it can hardly be a surprise to learn that some prominent Swiss citizens greeted the rise of Hitler with open joy and longed to be taken into the fold of the Third Reich.[10]

The degree to which Switzerland aligned itself with Germany was determined by its government. The focal point of the Swiss government is the Federal Council, a seven-person executive. A joint session of Parliament elects the members to represent the seven departments of state: Foreign Affairs, Interior, Justice and Police, Military, Finance, Agriculture and Industry, and Posts and Railways. The Council is led by a president, with the title rotating among the seven members. No constitutional powers are bestowed on the president. The president holds no veto power, no qualifications to conduct diplomacy, and no authority to choose fellow councillors. The president is president in name only.

In theory, the Council should have communally decided Switzerland's response to the rise of the Third Reich. But one man, Marcel Pilet-Golaz, had an inordinate part in determining Swiss foreign policy. Pilet-Golaz, who was president of the Federal Council for nearly the duration of the war, would emerge as a Swiss Neville Chamberlain, pushing and prodding the government and industry toward appeasement.

During the Second World War the Swiss split their sympathies between the belligerents in much the same way that they had during the First World War: the German-speaking cantons felt a strong kinship for

Germany both intellectually and economically, while the French- and Italian-speaking cantons looked toward France and Italy. Germany had long dominated Europe's intellectual arena, and German-speaking Swiss in particular had long admired a German presence in aspects of life ranging from painting to politics. Unsurprisingly, the German-speaking people of Switzerland consolidated their hold on the country's affairs during World War I. The German-speaking majority in Parliament ensured the appointment of Gen. Ulrich Wille as commander of the armed forces. (In Switzerland, a general is elected only during wartime.) General Wille, who was from the German part of Switzerland, had a reputation for supporting Prussian militarism, and under his leadership the army performed intelligence operations for the Germans. While they stopped short of condoning the utter violation of Belgian neutrality during World War I, most German Swiss cantons continued to believe in German ideals, a faith that helps explain Switzerland's conduct a few decades later.[11]

The willingness of the Swiss government to work for the Germans during World War II also stemmed from powers the executive branch had usurped during World War I—powers jealously guarded even after hostilities ceased. In 1914, Parliament surrendered much of its authority to the executive branch, to an extent unusual even under wartime conditions. The growing lack of openness in the political system this engendered laid the ground for fascism, but it took the Nazis' rise to power in 1933 to give it full bloom. It was then that various "fronts" began to spread and gain in importance. These fronts appealed to right-wing conservatives and lower-middle-class elements that wanted to remodel the state and society in the fashion of their neighbor. Hans Frick, for example, of the National Front, insisted that "the exhausted forms of parliamentary democracy must be replaced. . . . Everywhere parliamentary government is in a degenerate state and must . . . disappear. That farce of so-called popular elections must be stopped."[12] And Robert Tobler exulted in the rise of the Third Reich: "Germany! The national uprising thrills everyone who desires to see a renewal of his people. It gives joy to everyone who is capable of recognizing in it a product of his own native soil. It excites the young Swiss observers" (*Basler Nachrichten,* 1 June 1933).

Certainly few other small countries have seen such a disproportionate concentration of far-right organizations as Switzerland saw during the Nazi era. German nationalism had taken root in Switzerland in the 1920s, and by 1939 there were forty thousand known Nazi sympathizers in a population of 4.2 million Swiss. In Basel alone there were four thousand registered Nazi Party members. Well into the war, on 4 October 1942, some fifteen thousand German Nazis living in Switzerland held a rally in Zürich's Oerlikon Stadium.

Germans living in Switzerland and local sympathizers alike actively promoted Nazism. Whereas none of the native Swiss organizations won a politically significant following, they did represent an appreciable threat. The groups published books, magazines, and newspaper articles and tried to seduce the Swiss leadership into adhering to Nazi principles.[13] "A comprehensive policy that understands the signs of the times will ensure Switzerland becoming a living channel by which the two Axis powers to the north and south are connected. . . . The geographic circumstances designate our country as the natural link between north and south. Would it not be a sign of global vision to realize the possibilities open to us, and to take our future into our own hands?" asked Rolf Henne in the 16 October 1937 issue of *Die Front*.

Of the many groups to surface, the Schweizerischre Vaterlandischer Verband, or SVV, had the distinction of being the earliest. Founded by Dr. Eugen Bircher in 1918, the SVV worked to curtail Jewish emigration to Switzerland during the 1930s and 1940s. Its members included the highest-ranking army officers, politicians, bankers, and industrialists of Switzerland. Among his dinner companions Bircher often enjoyed the company of other senior government members or sympathizers including Marcel Pilet-Golaz, president of Switzerland in 1940; Giuseppe Motta, a former president; Eduard von Steiger, a friend of Himmler who headed the Justice and Police Department and served as president in 1945; Minister of the Interior Philipp Etter; Gen. Henri Guisan, commander of the Swiss Army; Col. Karl Kobelt, the head of the Ministry of Military Affairs; Walther Stampfli, who coordinated the whole of Swiss industrial production to accommodate Nazi Germany's needs when he was minister of economic affairs; and Dr. Ernst Weber, president of the Swiss National Bank.[14]

The Bund Der Schweizer in Grossdeutschland (League of the Swiss in Greater Germany), or BSG, likewise dedicated itself to collaborating with Nazi Germany. Of all these organizations, however, the best organized and strongest was the National Front, a party that closely followed its Nazi German cousin in costume, terminology, and behavior, and had about twenty-five thousand members at its peak. The existence of these groups allowed Swiss children to join in many of the same activities found in Germany, from Hitler Youth for boys to a Bund deutscher Mädel for girls.

Perhaps the Swiss branch of the National Socialist German Workers' Party in Davos best illustrates the Reich's sway over internal Swiss organizations. Wilhelm Gustloff, known among his followers as the Swiss Führer, founded the chapter in 1932.[15] The party was openly Nazi; its members wore uniforms and met in headquarters adorned with swastikas. Gustloff, a government meteorologist, allowed the Germans to become directly involved in every aspect of the party's management. But Gustloff did not live to see the Reich he so idolized wreak havoc on Europe. On 4 February 1936, David Frankfurter, a Jewish medical student from the University of Bern, assassinated the party leader. (After Frankfurter served the maximum sentence of eighteen years in jail, he immigrated to Israel.) At the time of Gustloff's death, nearly fifty Nazi chapters thrived in the northern part of the country alone.

The Swiss federal government refused the party permission to appoint a successor to Gustloff. Now leaderless, the organization was ripe for the German legation in Bern to manage its activities in every respect and promote Nazi propaganda throughout Switzerland. Berlin funded the Workers' Party, whose ranks swelled to 130,000 members, enabling the official Nazi Party of Germany to exert complete control over German citizens residing in Switzerland. The Swiss government did not close down the Workers' Party until May 1945, one week before Germany itself surrendered to the Allies.[16]

. . .

Not all Swiss were Nazi sympathizers. Many influential Swiss citizens spoke out against the ominous stirrings of their neighbor. In a 10 May 1934 speech, Minister of Finance Jean Marie Musy warned that Switzerland must not allow Germany to play a role in its government:

"Switzerland will either remain a democracy or cease to be Switzerland." Given the collaboration that would come to pass, Musy's speech was keenly prescient.

The danger was obvious and imminent. Just two years earlier, in 1932, Ewald Banse, a Nazi military theorist and geographer, published *Raum und Volk in Weltkriegen* (Space and people in world war), in which he argued that the only means to wage war against France would be to attack through Belgium and the Netherlands in the north and Switzerland in the south.[17] According to Banse, Switzerland's importance from a military point of view lay in its location. Because its terrain is mostly highlands, however, with only a few very small plains, it would be hard for a foreign power to invade and occupy Switzerland.[18] Moreover, a foreign power would find the character of the German-speaking Swiss both a help and a hindrance to a successful occupation: "The character of the German Swiss . . . like the old German character, is grounded in common sense and is of a very independent spirit, enterprising, tough and reserved. Its ruling features, however, are a calculating materialism, unlimited self-reliance and a tendency to criticism, not to say faultfinding. The latter tendency is directed mainly towards their German kinsfolk across the Rhine, and reminds of the pelican which pecks its own breast."[19] In other words, Banse was suggesting that if the character of the Swiss from the German-speaking region could be tamed, the Third Reich would find Switzerland easy to invade and conquer.

Hitler became chancellor of Germany on 30 January 1933, and about ten months later, on 14 October 1933, Germany pulled out of the League of Nations. Switzerland had joined the league in 1920. Within five years of Germany's exit, Switzerland too left the world organization. The league's failure to prevent aggression and the return of the world to regional alliances led the Swiss government, under the persuasion of Giuseppe Motta, to leave the organization in May 1938, ostensibly to reinforce its neutrality. In fact, the government wanted to avoid having to join in any sanctions the league might impose against violators of the covenant—that is, Germany.

Taking not only Banse's words but the aggressive posturing of Germany to heart as well, the Swiss military prepared to rearm and defend the nation against any incursions into its territory. Still abiding by the Hague Convention and with a nod from the Federal Council, Defense Minister Rudolf Minger secured increased appropriations for armaments after a steady decline in military spending following World War I. Parliament approved a credit of 15 million francs ($4.5 million) as a first installment of a multiyear budget of 100 million francs ($30 million).[20] The Federal Council provided funds for rifles, machine guns, and artillery on 16 November 1933, and an additional 82 million francs were earmarked for the military on 14 December 1933. More than 1 billion Swiss francs would be spent on arms by the end of 1939.[21]

General fortification began in earnest in 1934 during the presidency of Giuseppe Motta, who feared that a strong Germany would ignore Switzerland's neutrality and invade, just as it had overrun neutral Belgium in 1914. To repel the threat, the army repaired the dilapidated World War I–era earthworks and constructed tank traps (some can still be seen) from the fortress of Sargans near Austria to Basel, through the Jura Mountains, and east to Geneva. Natural obstacles such as the Alps, Lake Constance, and the Rhine River were factored into the defense plans.

But Germany too had been busy. While most countries had reduced their military expenditures because of the global economic depression, Germany had been building up its armed forces, initiating a program that quickly tipped the balance of military power throughout the world.[22] Even before 1933 the Germans had begun testing the limits imposed by the Treaty of Versailles. German army officers, for example, committed minor violations such as apprising themselves of the latest developments in air, armored, and chemical warfare. In 1935, Germany rearmed, brazenly violating the treaty. The Swiss government, no longer trusting that fortification alone could repel an invasion, initiated a series of surreptitious meetings with French Army officials to plan for military cooperation should Germany attack. The French were quite willing. With the Maginot defenses ending at the Swiss border, France needed a strong Switzerland at its back and stood ready to lend support with its own troops should the Germans attack.

This was not the first time Switzerland had entertained the possibility of military cooperation with France.[23] In both 1848 and 1849 there were those in the Swiss military who considered joining with their French counterparts to intervene on the side of the liberals in Italy. Precisely because Switzerland had forged such contacts in the past, it did not consider this overture to France to be in conflict with its rights and duties as a neutral nation under international law. One week before the fall of France, the Germans would discover the documents outlining the intention of Switzerland and France to cooperate at La Charite-sur-Loire. Foreign Minister Joachim von Ribbentrop reportedly wanted to exploit the find, but the German government decided to squirrel away the papers for future use.[24] The Reich never dealt this card, however; there was no need. The Swiss government proved to be a willing Nazi puppet.

Responding to Germany's reoccupation of the Rhineland on 7 March 1936, Switzerland sped up the construction of blockhouses along its northern border. When Italy invaded Ethiopia in 1936, breaking with the Western powers, Germany took the opportunity to break the Peace Treaty and Locarno Treaty of 1925, which called for the demilitarization of the Rhineland. As Germany tripled its forces along the Swiss frontier, air raid drills regularly echoed across the Alps.

Fear of a German occupation further intensified after the Anschluss on 13 March 1938. The Nazis showered Switzerland with photographs and newspaper articles showing the welcome they received in Austria. Soon after that, Field Marshal Goering produced a map of the Reich that included most of Switzerland. Three-quarters of the Swiss were German speakers considered to be *Volksdeutsh*, or ethnic Germans, in the eyes of their neighbor, and thus were legitimate targets for some sort of annexation or incorporation into the German Reich.[25]

Germany's swift destruction and occupation of Poland in 1939 propelled Switzerland to take even stronger actions. On 30 August Parliament granted the Federal Council full and unlimited authority to run the country. No longer would the government explain and justify its decisions to the public.[26] Also on that day, acting within the mandate of the Swiss Constitution, the Swiss Parliament, by a vote of 202 to 27, elected sixty-five-year-old Henri Guisan general, a position he would hold for the war's duration. Guisan hailed from the canton of Vaud, spoke fluent Swiss German and French, and had been a full-time officer for only nine years when he was elected. Under his command the Swiss Army mobilized; 435,000 troops were charged with the dual mission of repelling a German invasion and protecting their country's neutrality.

On 30 January 1939 the Swiss government announced the power to mobilize the militia without further notice. Antiaircraft batteries rolled into position in Zürich, Schaffhausen, and Basel. Mines had been laid under all bridges and roads leading into Switzerland, and twenty-four-hour surveillance of these roads and bridges commenced. Most households were equipped with gas masks, and the frontier reserves had been called out to guard the German border.[27] The Germans were not the only ones massing troops along the Swiss border. The French had put about six divisions along their frontier in case the Germans plowed through Switzerland.

The situation grew ever graver in the months leading up to the fall of France. After conquering lands to the east, Germany turned an eye westward and began massing troops along the Swiss border.[28] On 26 March 1939 as many as 200,000 Germans were reported around and beyond Lake Constance. The Swiss federal government authorized the Military Department to call up all men aged 36–48 for six days of training. At the time Guisan assumed the rank of general, the Swiss militia included men aged 20–60; elite troops were men aged 20–36, reserves were men aged 36–48, and the Home Guard comprised men aged 48–60.

On 18 April 1940 the Federal Council and General Guisan issued joint orders for total resistance.[29] The Swiss were well aware of the various invasion routes the Teutonic armies were considering that spring.[30] One plan called for the Germans to outflank the French Maginot Line, a chain of underground forts, by going through Switzerland rather than Belgium. Both the Maginot Line and Germany's Siegfried Line ended near Basel in the northwest. This point, the Dreiländerecke, or "Three-Country Corner," was considered the most vulnerable point of the Swiss defenses. If the Germans used this plan, the German armies would march through the old Austrian border between Ragaz and the eastern end of Lake Constance, then Appenzell and St. Gallen. If they made it east of Zürich, they would continue to Lake Zürich and the Limmat River. Once past this obstacle the Germans would be at the Swiss Plateau, or Mittelland, which extends one hundred miles southwest to Lake Geneva.

Guisan conceived the "redoubt" strategy to combat the expected invasion. The strategy called for soldiers to plant explosive charges on bridges and along mountain passes; if the Germans came, the charges would be detonated and wide swaths of the country abandoned. Once the bridges and mountain passes had been destroyed, the Swiss army would hunker down in geographically defensible areas in the hope of stopping the German Panzers from rolling into the central part of the country. Basel was considered expendable. Fortifications were built at the Gempen Plateau south of Basel, an inviting invasion route for either side to outflank the other's frontal defenses. Additional fortifications were constructed from the plateau to Sargans and the Limmat River and Lake Zürich, all of which faced northeast toward Germany. Part of the country would be sacrificed to save the whole.

At the same time, the country's infant air force was poised to defend Swiss skies. A network of 221 observation towers spanned the country ready to alert Swiss fighters and antiaircraft guns to potential airspace invasions. The service would report 6,501 violations of Swiss airspace by the end of the war.[31]

On the brink of World War II it would have been easy for Hitler to order the obliteration of Switzerland—or, as he called it, the "pimple on the face of Europe."[32] After all, Germany, after six years of Hitler, boasted more than four thousand of the world's most modern aircraft, and the armed forces had a tactical advantage the world was about to witness. The twenty-one years of economic depression that had gripped much of the world after World War I had left Switzerland's armed forces diminished. The country had no mechanized forces, and its artillery and air force were still in the initial stages of modernization, leaving the army with 120-mm artillery guns dating from 1882. Of Switzerland's twenty-one military aviation units, five lacked aircraft and could not be immediately deployed.

• • •

The Swiss Air Force was first formed on 31 July 1914 as the Fliegertruppe, and many of its pilots served with the French Aviation Militaire during World War I. On 19 October 1936 the air arm was reorganized and renamed the Schweizerische Flugwaffe, becoming an autonomous, equal-status service under the Swiss Military Department. At the start of World War II the Swiss Air Force was not well equipped to face either of the warring sides. With the exception of the Messerschmitt Bf 109E, most of its fighters fell below the world standard. The main fighter in Swiss service was the Morane Saulnier MS-406, license manufactured in Switzerland. Ironically, the Swiss purchased additional Bf 109E-3 fighters from Germany in May 1940 just weeks before a period of brief but intense dogfights between the two countries erupted. At the onset of the war, and throughout hostilities, the air force vigilantly patrolled Swiss airspace, slowly increasing the number of its airplanes as it incorporated French and German equipment.[33]

In the months preceding the Wehrmacht's attack on Belgium, the Netherlands, and France, Germany had led the Allies to believe that it would strike through Switzerland to bypass the Maginot Line. Performing a carefully choreographed ruse, German troops marched toward the Swiss border by day only to draw back at night. So convincing was this deception that French general Maurice Gamelin diverted nineteen French divisions to the Swiss border thinking that no less than thirty elite units were about to encircle his right wing. The French kept most of their forces south of the Maginot Line in anticipation of a German thrust through Swiss territory south of Basel against Belfort and Lyon. In actuality there were only thirteen German units patrolling the area, all of them reserves. The hoax succeeded.

Just before first light on 10 May 1940, when the German offensive against France began, Swiss antiaircraft guns fired at a German bomber flying over Basel. In the west, twenty Luftwaffe planes engaged French fighters over Delémont as Swiss antiaircraft guns fired. Bombs dropped by the Luftwaffe landed in northern Switzerland, damaging railroads.[34] Meanwhile, a Swiss squadron of pursuit planes tangled with the Luftwaffe and a Swiss Me-109 from Olten shot down a German Heinkel-111 twin-engine bomber that had flown near Solothurn in the region of Brugg.[35] At the time, 300,000 Swiss soldiers stood their ground on the Winkelried Line facing Germany.

On 12 May 1940 French and Swiss intelligence officers reported heavy concentrations of German troops, about 700,000 in all, marching south. The officers, who had been operating in the Black Forest just above the Swiss border, also reported that bridging materials were clearly visible on the other side of the Rhine. Still apprehensive that the Germans would strike between Basel and Lake Constance on their way to France and that Italy would attack Ticino, the Swiss Army braced itself for an assault.[36] It never came. Instead the Germans fell into position at the Maginot Line's junction with the southern Belgian border and crossed through the Ardennes Forest in Luxembourg. Seven Panzer divisions crossed the Meuse River where the French had not anticipated an attack, overwhelming the French 9th Army. By the end of the day on 15 May the Germans had broken through, leaving Britain's Northern Army virtually cut off at Dunkirk. The British began evacuating the men, with the Panzers in hot pursuit. Then, with no apparent reason, the tanks ground to a halt on 24 May 1940. The last British troops stepped off the mainland on 2 June, and on 5 June the Germans began pushing southward.

During the autumn of 1940 Germany and Italy made plans to divide Switzerland. Germany would get the northern four-fifths of the country, and Italy would get the area south of a line from Lake Geneva and east to Ticino. Just after the Axis surrounded Switzerland, orders came from the high command of the German army to prepare an invasion of Switzerland. During this time panic seized the citizens of Basel and its environs, and civilians fled from the Wehrmacht's anticipated path.

The remaining vestiges of Swiss political opposition to Hitler rapidly collapsed after the outbreak of the war. Indeed, almost immediately following the Nazi invasion of Poland, the Swiss turned toward a pragmatic stance of neutrality combined with appeasement. While the military worked to build up the country's strength, some in the government did not bother to mask their sympathies. Marcel Pilet-Golaz, a pro-German sympathizer, became president of the Federal Council in 1940. That event combined with a desperate fear of Blitzkrieg prompted Switzerland to give Germany virtually unfettered access to its airspace, an access that would be in stark contrast to Switzerland's treatment of Allied planes a few years later.[37] Once the United Kingdom and France had declared war on Germany, German planes began flying over Swiss airspace as a matter of routine, usually at night, during bad weather, or above cloud cover.

By the end of 1939, Swiss airspace had already been invaded 143 times, and whether out of powerlessness or political sympathy, not once did the Swiss Air Force react. The imbalance of power had led to an agreement between Bern and Berlin that declared a five-kilometer zone extending inward from Switzerland's borders off-limits to Swiss fighters, effectively giving the Luftwaffe an exclusive and privileged entrée to Swiss airspace. Through this one act Switzerland willingly relinquished sovereignty over its own territory. The no-fly-zone agreement was briefly interrupted during the spring of 1940 when the German offensive toward the west commenced and the Luftwaffe attacked Holland, Belgium, Luxembourg, and France. On 10 May, the day that offensive began, Swiss fighters received permission to operate within the five-kilometer restricted zone. This led to the most significant engagements—from 1 June through 8 June—between the Swiss Air Force and the Luftwaffe. During the French campaign of 1940, Germany violated Swiss airspace countless times and the Swiss pilots pursued Luftwaffe planes into French airspace.

On 21 April 1940 the crew of a Luftwaffe Dornier Do-17Z-3 apparently mistook Basel-Birsfelden airfield for a German field and landed. The Swiss held the plane briefly but quickly responded to pressure from Germany and freed the crew and aircraft.[38] On 16 May 1940 a Heinkel bomber returning from a raid south of Paris became disoriented and breached Swiss airspace. Two Me-109s from Swiss Fighter Squadron 21 attacked the aircraft; two crewmen were wounded and bailed out. The plane crashed, hit by Swiss antiaircraft fire over Zürich. On the ground the pilot and remaining crewmen tried to flee after crashing but were taken by Swiss troops. They were later returned to Germany.

On 1 June 1940 a German bomber formation crossed Swiss airspace over Lake Neuchâtel. Swiss fighters attacked. One He-111 crashed into the woods, killing its five crewmen, after losing control. That same day, Fighter Squadron 6 met with a flight of twenty-four German planes attempting to cut across Swiss territory near Basel. On 2 June a French fighter shot down another Heinkel over Switzerland. A gunner was killed; the rest of the crew was briefly interned. On 4 June twenty-nine German planes, Heinkels escorted by Me-110s, engaged twelve Swiss fighters over the Frei Mountains. In the ensuing air battle two Me-110s were downed and a Swiss Me-109 was lost.

The aerial skirmishes reached their peak on 8 June when thirty-six German Me-110s and twenty-four Swiss Me-109s faced off inside Swiss airspace over the Jura Mountains. Six German Me-110s attacked a Swiss observation plane, causing it to crash and killing its crew. That same day two squadrons of fifteen Swiss fighters confronted twenty-eight German Me-110s over Swiss terrain. Three German planes crashed, one after being hit by Swiss antiaircraft fire. Another Swiss Me-109 went down. This battle prompted Hermann Goering, head of the Luftwaffe, to threaten Switzerland with retaliatory bombing raids against Swiss towns and farms.[39] So furious was Goering with this streak of Swiss combativeness that he instituted Operation Wartegau, which sent German terrorists to blow up Swiss aircraft and other civilian targets. Operation Wartegau did not enjoy a long run. On 16 June, seven German and two Swiss saboteurs from Berlin were arrested en route to blow up the Altdorf munitions plant and the Payerne and Dübendorf air bases.

On 17 June German Panzers reached the Franco-Swiss border, closing Switzerland's last overt geographic passageway to the free world. The dogfights ended once and for all. On 20 June, the Swiss and German authorities concluded an agreement forbidding Swiss Air Force pilots to engage in air combat with German warplanes over Swiss territory.

Now surrounded, Switzerland had three choices: side with the Nazis, side with the Allies, or split its stocks of precious precision products between the two factions in the hope of getting at least some coal, iron, and oil from Germany and foodstuffs, oil, iron, and coal from the Allies. Switzerland essentially chose to aid and abet the Axis and began providing economic aid for Germany's war engine.[40] This was an attractive arrangement for Germany, which could always crush Switzerland's independence when it no longer needed to use the rails parallel to the St. Gotthard and Simplon Tunnels. And as Edgar Bonjour wrote in his 1946 book *Swiss Neutrality,* "the well-stocked markets of Switzerland and her practice of free trading were among the reasons why Germany supported Swiss neutrality." In a word, it was to Germany's benefit to keep Switzerland free.[41]

Yet the existence of a free Switzerland continued to gnaw at some in the German high command. In the spring of 1943 the Wehrmacht formulated yet another invasion plan, this one called Fall Schweiz (Case Switzerland). Invasion headquarters were set up in Munich, and Hitler himself examined the merits of the strategy. SS Gen. Walter Schellenberg, head of the foreign intelligence service, likewise appraised the preparations. Despite strong support from Himmler and the SS, the plan never came to fruition, due in part to strong opposition from economic advisers who saw the especially lucrative advantages of keeping Switzerland unoccupied.

· · ·

In January 1940 Marcel Edouard Pilet-Golaz, a supporter of the Nazi movement who called for an "authoritarian democracy," became Switzerland's foreign minister and president. From the time he assumed the presidency until November 1944, Pilet-Golaz dominated Swiss foreign policy and therefore all dealings with Nazi Germany. Normally the Swiss presidency rotated annually, but Pilet-Golaz manipulated a change in procedure and clung to the title until 10 November 1944, when the Council forced his resignation. Like Neville Chamberlain and Henri Pétain, the Vaudois Pilet-Golaz sought appeasement. By no means was he a solitary proponent of these views. He enjoyed the support of a majority of the Federal Council, many of the principal diplomats in Germany or German-occupied countries, senior officials in the Political Department, and some of the best-known officers in the Swiss armed forces.

During his years as president Pilet-Golaz pursued policies designed to bring Switzerland closer into step with the German "New Order." He pledged a broad economic collaboration with Germany. When the Germans expressed concern about the number of skilled Swiss workers immigrating to the United States, he offered advice on the best ways to staunch the flow. Pilet-Golaz also made certain that Swiss industry worked diligently for Germany and substantially augmented its exports, chiefly arms and ammunition. During 1943, as the bombing of the Reich increased, Germany turned to the safer factories of Switzerland for production.[42]

In June 1940, to quell German irritation, Pilet-Golaz ordered two-thirds of the nation's forces demobilized. That same month, on the twenty-fifth, he delivered a radio address peppered with the language of Nazi Germany in which he advised his fellow Swiss citizens to prepare for a new future—a German future.[43] Convinced that the "New Order" was near, Switzerland's pro-German groups melded into one organization, the Nationale Bewegung der Schweiz (National Movement of Switzerland), or NBS, under the direction of Dr. Rolf Henne, a former member of the National Front, and Leo Keller. The new group stepped up its propaganda campaign and had even more frequent contact with Nazi Germany. During the war Keller frequently traveled to Germany and met with Heinrich Himmler to find ways to politically integrate Switzerland into the Third Reich. An SS training organization came to Switzerland, courtesy of Keller's ministrations, to meet with Pilet-Golaz.

The accord for mutual economic cooperation signed on 9 August 1940 further demonstrated the extent to which Switzerland would accommodate Hitler's Germany. The agreement arranged for coal and steel shipments from the Third Reich in exchange for food, aluminum, machines, arms, and munitions from Switzerland. Such actions on the part of the Swiss government outweighed any position the military could take and gave credence to the far right throughout the war.

On 15 November 1940 more than 170 pro-Axis Swiss citizens presented the "Petition of the 200" to Foreign Minister Marcel Pilet-Golaz and the Federal Council. Among the petition's eight demands were stipulations that the Federal Council should inform its populace of the fine work being accomplished by the Third Reich, stop anti-Nazi remarks in Swiss newspapers, prohibit those deemed enemies of the Reich from seeking asylum in Switzerland, and completely integrate the Swiss economy with the Berlin-Rome Axis. Although the Federal Council publicly rejected the petition, it tacitly went about implementing many of the demands. Germany soon had the entire Swiss industry at its absolute disposal; massive credit, arms and munitions, airplanes, vehicles, locomotives, precision machinery, shoes, food, and chemicals were among the items available. The Swiss built factories throughout Germany to facilitate the war effort, and the Germans conducted quality control inspections in some Swiss ball-bearing and precision instrument factories.

Additionally the Federal Council exercised a great deal of censorship concerning the fate of Europe's Jews. On 27 June 1941 the Swiss government ordered the Swiss press to suppress the fact that Germans had killed at least two thousand Jews within twenty-four hours at Bialystok, Poland. But Germany wanted even more. The German government demanded that the Swiss press cease attacking its policies, and the German press attaché in Bern insisted that *Der Bund,* a leading anti-German paper of the time, fire its editor. While the Swiss government did not yield to this particular demand, it did give in to others such as lifting the ban on importing Nazi newspapers.

The Swiss armed forces collaborated with Germany as well. The Medical Service of the Ministry of Military Affairs dispatched medical teams to the eastern front to assist the Wehrmacht wounded, despite Switzerland's professed neutrality. The first of four such teams went to the eastern front on 15 October 1941. The second team, which comprised eighty doctors, nurses, and aides, left for the front on 8 January 1942. Dr. F. Merke led a third team of Swiss surgeons and physicians on 18 June 1942, followed by a fourth team under the leadership of Dr. Howald on 9 March 1943. Dr. Eugen Bircher, a full colonel in the Swiss Army, orchestrated the missions.[44]

Not only were the medical personnel ordered not to aid wounded Russians, they were also ordered to keep secret all they had witnessed. The secret got out. Defying orders, Rudolf Bucher, a physician who had participated on one of the missions, began speaking publicly about the atrocities he had observed, including the extermination of Jews in the Smolensk area. The military affairs minister, Col. Karl Kobelt, ordered Bucher to cease speaking about what he had seen or risk legal action. The reprimand did not satisfy the Federal Council. Bucher was dishonorably discharged from the military on 14 March 1944, exemplifying the lengths to which the Swiss government was willing to go to conceal German atrocities.[45]

On 25 July, in an act loaded with symbolism, General Guisan called for a meeting of officers on the Rütli Meadow at which he openly called for his army and fellow Swiss citizens to defend their heritage. The meeting caused a furor in Germany.[46] Yet not even Guisan emerged from the war with his reputation unsullied. At one point the general, one of several senior government officials belonging to the SVV, wrote to government officials suggesting that Switzerland align itself more closely with Hitler.

• • •

Throughout World War II German war matériel flowed freely across Switzerland in contravention of Article 2 of the 1907 Hague Convention, which said that "belligerents are forbidden to move across the territory of a neutral Power troops or convoys, either of munitions of war or supplies." Four rail links connected Germany, France, and Italy; two of those traversed Switzerland. At the center of these lines, piercing the Alps, were the ten-mile-long St. Gotthard Tunnel and the twelve-and-a-half-mile Simplon Tunnel in Switzerland. Because both the Germans and Italians had helped finance the building of the St. Gotthard, they were permitted to haul freight and passengers through the tunnel at no charge.

In 1909 the agreement between the three countries was expanded to allow Italy and Germany the use of all Swiss railways for any purpose except the transportation of war matériel.[47] Nevertheless, the Germans used the St. Gotthard and Simplon Tunnels throughout the war to supply Italy and North Africa with war matériel. This was a significant departure from centuries of prohibiting military transit along the Alpine passes. After the Thirty Years' War Switzerland had decided "to grant to none the right of passage through Swiss territory, and to prevent anyone from doing so with all their might."[48]

• • •

And so, as the 1930s drew to a close, the pro-Nazi elements won out against those who wanted to resist at all costs. This small pro-Nazi element had a disproportionately large influence on the treatment of U.S. airmen interned in the country from 1943 to 1945.

By the time World War II exploded, the notion of Swiss neutrality had reached mythic proportions. In fact, Switzerland's "religion" of armed neutrality was a sham; all the while the government was putting forth the image of a Swiss people prepared to keep the Wehrmacht in abeyance armed with little more than rifles, the Federal Council was privately pursuing close ties with the Third Reich. This contradictory posturing goes a long way toward explaining why the Swiss interned and mistreated Allied airmen during the war while freeing Luftwaffe airmen.

2

THE POLICY OF INTERNMENT

How neutral can you be? You just wanted to land there and kiss Mother Earth and they're shooting at us.

LARRY LAWLER, 385th Bomb Group,
549th Bomb Squadron, 8th Air Force

POWs are to be treated at all times with humanity and protected against acts of violence, insults and public curiosity.

GEN. HENRI GUISAN

World War II was the first truly comprehensive air war, and violations of neutral territory, as defined by law, thus included airspace violations. In January 1943 the Allied air campaign intensified the aerial bombing raids into Germany. Allied infringements of Swiss airspace increased concomitantly. Heavy bombers flew round-the-clock sorties over German-occupied areas; the British bombed under the cover of darkness while the Americans did their bombing by day. In 1944, as the Allies began to achieve air superiority, the U.S. Army Air Force was responsible for the majority of airspace violations over Switzerland.

Switzerland's close proximity with many important German targets made it an attractive alternative to Germany or German-occupied territory for disabled Allied planes seeking safe ground on which to land. But choosing Switzerland as a sanctuary was not always the wisest course. Once Switzerland chose to define its obligations as a neutral country (according to international law) to include armed opposition to territorial and airspace violations, its military shot down and forced down crippled Allied planes that had entered Swiss airspace because they were unable to return to their bases in England. Swiss fighters or antiaircraft guns attacked at least twenty-one American bombers and forced them to land. Nearly all of these attacks occurred inside Swit-

zerland at relatively low altitudes near Swiss air bases. The majority of
the U.S. bombers attacked displayed clear signs of disability: the propellers of at least one engine feathered, or windmilling; lowered landing gear (an international sign of distress); smoke and flames; damaged wings, fuselage, and control surfaces (such as vertical stabilizers,
rudders, and movable control surfaces); or leaking gasoline from ruptured fuel lines or a damaged fuel tank.

• • •

On 13 April 1944, the *Wichita Witch,* a B-17G bomber with the 447th
Bomb Group, 709th Bomb Squadron, 8th Air Force, attempted to land
with one engine out after being severely damaged by flak while on a
mission to Augsburg, Germany. The crew had already thrown all their
guns and ammunition overboard. As they were trying to maneuver
into position to land at Dübendorf airfield, Swiss fighters attacked and
shot down their damaged aircraft. The pilot, 2d Lt. Harold L. Kreuzer
of Wichita, Kansas (hence the name of the plane), ordered the crew to
bail out. The plane crashed at Siebnen, at the southern end of the Zü-
richsee. Fishermen rescued the copilot, 2d Lt. Lawrence P. Koenig.
Soon afterward the crew found themselves the subjects of an extensive
interrogation, after which they were escorted to internment camps.
Not a word was ever uttered about why Swiss fighter planes had shot
down a hapless aircraft seeking sanctuary.

At least Kreuzer's crew survived. Not all were so fortunate. On 24
April, the B-17G *Little Chub,* with two engines out, prepared to crash-
land in Switzerland. As the plane plunged to one thousand feet, three
Swiss fighters suddenly attacked. Six Americans died when the plane
went down.[1] Swiss guns resulted in the deaths of at least twenty British
and sixteen American airmen; if questionable cases are included, the
numbers rise to twenty-six British and twenty-three U.S. airmen. Other
fliers were so gravely injured by Swiss fire or by crash landings that
they later died.

To further maintain the face of neutrality, Switzerland adopted the
policy of internment outlined in the Hague Convention of 1901. Once
the airmen landed, they were sent for the duration of the war to internment camps where the Swiss were to provide shelter, food, and medical care. The servicemen's own government would be responsible for

paying for these services. After Switzerland began its internment policy, 1,516 American fliers (if escapees from POW camps in Germany, or evadees, are taken into account, the number is actually 1,740) and 13,500 other foreign military personnel were confined on Swiss soil. Unlike the American airmen, however, whose circumstances forced them to seek a safe place to land, the majority of the latter group had intentionally sought refuge in Switzerland. Between 1939 and 1945 more than 100,000 refugees lived in Switzerland. In September 1944 there were 12,809 military internees: 1,036 were American, 78 were English, and 4 were German.

• • •

World War II was not the first time Switzerland had hosted soldiers from foreign countries seeking protection. On 2 February 1871, under a pale winter dawn, an army of eighty-three thousand men and eleven thousand animals trekked through knee-high snow toward the Swiss border town of Les Verriers. With the crushing force of the Prussian Army behind them, refuge in Switzerland seemed the only option for these men of France's Eastern Army.

Days before France declared war on Prussia on 19 July 1870, Switzerland had staked out a neutral position. Five divisions stood ready to protect Swiss territory from invasion in the tense weeks before the fighting began. Once the yearlong war commenced, however, the Swiss, no longer worried about foreign invasion, demobilized many of the troops. Gen. Hans Herzog, the commander of the Swiss Army, had even taken a leave of absence.

When Sedan and Metz fell in January 1871, Switzerland once again called up the troops. It now appeared that the Prussian army would push the bedraggled French Eastern Army into Switzerland. Until recently the French troops had been under the command of Gen. Charles Denis Sauter Bourbaki. But Bourbaki had attempted suicide on 26 January 1871 after losing several battles, and Gen. Justin Clinchant, commander of the French XX Corps, had assumed command. Cut off from all supply routes, the French force stumbled toward the frontier, a short but grueling ten-mile march away.

Adhering to an agreement between France and Switzerland, the soldiers surrendered their arms and ammunition as they crossed the border. It took nearly two days for the contingent to cross, a massive passage immortalized in a mural that now hangs in Lucerne. The Swiss promised that all confiscated weapons, ammunition, and other war matériel would be returned to France once the French government had paid all costs relating to the internment of the troops. The arrival of the exhausted soldiers presented a daunting challenge for the Swiss in terms of food, clothing, and shelter. Realizing that it would be easier to attend to the men in small groups, the Swiss government divided the French soldiers among various cantons, housing them in schoolhouses and churches. Food was rationed. The government recommended that living accommodations "be, whenever possible, heatable, and in any case dry, and have windows and doors which close well." The villages and towns were to "supply at least 20 pounds of straw per man, to which 5 pounds more was to be provided every 5 days." Thus the incident of Bourbaki's army, as the affair became known, set a precedent of sorts for combatants seeking refuge in Switzerland.

The Bourbaki affair also highlighted the fact that although Swiss neutrality, as understood by international law at the time, seemed to have covered all the bases—trade with belligerents, asylum for political and religious refugees, etc.—there still was no consensus governing the internment of foreign troops. Indeed, in 1673 the Diet had resolved unanimously "that if fugitives from any army should come, they should be refused admittance, be they who they may." Part of the reason for the lack of a formal policy may have been concern that harboring foreign combatants would provoke a belligerent nation to attack.[2]

When the subject of giving refuge to foreign soldiers arose in 1848, the Federal Council insisted that internment of troops in flight should be regarded as a "free right of the neutral state and not as an obligation incumbent upon it," and that the cost of lodging and feeding the internees should be borne by the state to which the troops belonged. The Brussels Conference of 1874 adopted this policy and confirmed it in the two Hague Conferences of 1874 and 1907. Consequently, international law under the Hague Convention allowed neutral countries to intern foreign combatants: "A neutral Power which receives in its territory troops belonging to the belligerent armies shall intern them, as far as possible, at a distance from the theater of war. It can keep them in camps and even confine them in fortresses or places assigned for this purpose." The parties to the convention also recognized the right of Switzerland to repatriate internees before hostilities ended, provided a guarantee was given that the repatriates would not fight in the same war.[3] Hence the policy Switzerland carried out during World War II was technically legal. It was the application of the policy that is questionable.

The idea that foreign combatants might find themselves on Swiss soil became a concern in Switzerland as early as 1939. And Swiss apprehensions became reality in a remarkably uncanny event. The Germans had choked off the 45th French Army Corps along the frontier between Belfort and Switzerland. Like Bourbaki before him, their commandant, Gen. Brunislaw Pruger-Ketling, refused to surrender. Instead the corps, which included a great many Polish soldiers, requested permission to cross into Switzerland. President Marcel Pilet-Golaz granted safe passage, and over the course of two days, from 19 June through the evening of 20 June 1940, the 45th Corps, now in a miserable state, entered Swiss territory. But here ends any similarity with the crossing of 1871.

This time, the soldiers were taken to internment camps, and all arms confiscated by the Swiss were handed over to the Germans. Theoretically the weapons were French property, but Germany controlled France through the Vichy government. And so the Swiss began a double standard—interning only enemies of the Reich. As for the 45th Corps, only the eleven thousand Polish soldiers had to remain in the camps. All the French were repatriated in February 1941.[4]

The arrival of General Daille's corps prompted the Swiss military to establish regulations regarding combatants seeking protection. The task fell to the newly created Federal Commission of Internment and Hospitalization (FCIH), which had been established in 1940 to handle the influx of foreign servicemen and refugees. The FCIH divided the refugees into two groups. The Swiss Police Department had jurisdiction over civilian refugees, and the army was responsible for military personnel.

At the outbreak of the war there were seven thousand Jews in Switzerland. They had begun arriving by the thousands in 1933, when Hitler rose to power. It was not a perfect haven for them. Jews had long been discriminated against in Switzerland. Until 1879 they were allowed to live in only two towns in the entire country, Lengnau and Endingen in northeastern Switzerland. Over the course of the war some twenty-seven thousand Jews found shelter in Switzerland. The Jewish Swiss community and other organizations were charged a head tax to support them. Many more Jews had been turned away at the border because of a J stamp in their visas that Germany had mandated in 1938 at the urging of Dr. Heinrich Rothmund, head of the Swiss Justice and Police Department. In 1942 about thirty thousand were denied entry; some were even arrested and delivered into the clutches of the Germans or the Vichy government.[5]

By the end of the war Switzerland had taken in 300,000 refugees and foreign military internees representing every fighting nation in Europe. Most civilian refugees had to live in small work camps and work either in the camps or in the surrounding countryside helping to offset the loss of the farmhands who were mobilized together with their horses to defend Switzerland. By June 1942 one hundred internment camps had been constructed across the country.

Many foreign enlisted men were required to work during the duration of their internment as well, and so joined the refugee brigades in clearing swampland, farming, and repairing roads. At first the Swiss had wanted to put the American internees to work on road gangs. The American government greeted this proposition with a loud protest, insisting that the airmen, who were either officers or noncommissioned officers, were not liable to forced labor under the Geneva Accords. This was one of the rare times the Swiss heeded such protests. However, under U.S. orders, some airmen were detached to the American legation in Bern to help support a staff stretched thin by the imprisonment of Americans.

Originally the Internment and Hospitalization Commission seemed intent on treating both civilian refugees and military internees as equitably as possible, with certain differences designated for military internees based on rank and the circumstances of their arrival in the country. Eventually, however, the commission strayed from its original pledge. Conditions varied from camp to camp and were especially difficult in the Wauwilermoos penitentiary camp in Lucerne. The conduct displayed toward Jewish refugees showed that religious affiliation was indeed a consideration. And the repatriation of Luftwaffe airmen further demonstrated the dramatic departure from the policy set forth in June 1940.

The same month that Germany conquered France, General Guisan wrote a memorandum outlining provisional instructions pertaining to the internment of combatants.[6] First and foremost, "POWs [as the memo called internees] were to be treated at all times with humanity and protected against acts of violence, insults and public curiosity." As the chapters that follow will show, many American internees did not enjoy this protection. According to the memo, internees were to live under the same conditions as Swiss troops: housed in clean buildings or barracks properly sheltered from the elements and with sufficient heat and light. The camps were to be cloistered in places where there were already barracks or in vacant hotels. A Swiss officer would command each sector or camp, but POWs could choose their own building, floor, and room chiefs.

Because the men would be living in close quarters, prevention of epidemics was a priority—at least on paper. Each camp would have enough water for showers, a place for exercise, and an infirmary. There would be monthly health inspections to check for tuberculosis and venereal disease. Many of these policies were followed in the regular internment camps of Adelboden, Wengen, and Davos. Few were followed in the penitentiary camps of Wauwilermoos and Les Diablerets.

Acknowledging that a significant reduction in trade with other countries had diminished the country's food supplies, the FCIH proclaimed that internees would be able to purchase sundries at local prices in camp canteens in order to supplement their rations. The commission also appeared to recognize that boredom would be a major problem for the internees. Libraries were to be organized in each camp and intellectual and sporting pursuits encouraged. In the end, most of the classes and libraries that were organized were done at the initiative of the internees, although in some cases the International Red Cross provided professors and books. The internees would also have the right to practice their religion.

From the outset the Swiss authorities made it clear that instituting order among the internee population was a priority and decreed that POWs would be subject to the same rules and orders as soldiers in the Swiss Army. One day a month would be set aside for a lecture on camp rules. Furthermore, in an effort to prevent fighting between soldiers from the different belligerent nations, no national signs, flags, or other ornamentation would be permitted on the face of any building. Combatants would also be separated by country; Allied and Axis soldiers were not to be mixed.

The FCIH also endeavored to govern relations between the internees and the Swiss civilian population, in essence holding the position that there should be minimal contact between the two groups. In fact, however, Americans and other nationalities mingled with Swiss citizens, went to their homes for meals, and in some cases even married Swiss women.

The POWs were authorized to receive individual packages containing food and other articles designed to improve their situation. Many of these packages never reached their intended recipients; instead, Swiss guards enjoyed their contents.

The FCIH also allowed the internees to communicate with relatives back home: "Within a week after his arrival in his sector of internment, and also in the case of sickness, each prisoner will be able to address his family [in their native language] with a postcard informing them of his capture and health status." Many airmen were grateful to be allowed to send a telegram just after landing. That way their families knew of their internment before the missing-in-action telex from the War Department arrived. The commission subjected all correspondence from internees to censorship—German censorship, as it turned out. Many former internees have saved these swastika-stamped letters.

Most Swiss government officials now refer to the soldiers kept in Switzerland during World War II as internees. During the war, however, there never was any consensus on how to refer to them. A letter from a Lieutenant Colonel Chauvet to a Colonel Combe, for example, noted: "Included is a map representing the internment camps and prisoner of war camps."[7] In an 11 November 1944 letter, Major Imer wrote that Allied pilots shot down over Lake Constance should not be considered POWs in the strict sense. Even though half of Lake Constance lies in Germany, the men not taken prisoner by Germans were just "regular" military internees. This distinction became important for the U.S. fliers after the war, particularly those seeking benefits from the U.S. Veterans Administration afforded to other prisoners of war.

Internees were forbidden to escape. Efforts to head off escape attempts included forbidding internees to use public telephones at post offices or telephone booths. Internees needed authorization to dine in restaurants; attend theaters, cinemas, and sporting events; and go to public gatherings. They also needed permission to use bicycles and visit private homes in the respective villages of their internment. Internees not imprisoned in penitentiary camps were allowed to drink alcohol.

Guisan's memo also discussed punishment for POWs, suggesting that any POW charged with a violation had the right to a defense of his choice and the right to appeal. In practice the Swiss clearly violated these rules. Many Americans were held without trial before being sent to serve long sentences in various penal camps.

Had only this document survived the war, later generations might have looked on internment in Switzerland as a prolonged stay in summer camp with slightly more stringent rules. But fortunately, a truer picture of the complexities of what internment meant has surfaced over the years. Surely internment for some Americans was the clichéd life in a gilded cage; but the reality of camp life for many others was not.

Despite the evidence to the contrary, there are to this day Swiss who insist that their government upheld the law of neutrality during World War II. They claim that Switzerland did not exhibit preferential treatment of a military nature for any of the war's participants. There was, they say, "no granting of free passage for troops, no release of interned soldiers before the end of the war, no state-owned weapons sales to the war's leaders."[8] These Swiss argue that Switzerland complied in every respect with the requirements and duties of a neutral power. That is not the case.

The policy of interning downed Allied fliers for the duration of the war was pursued in large part to avoid antagonizing Germany, even when it became clear that the Axis would be defeated.[9] The U.S. government tried to convince Switzerland to cease its pro-German policies. In a letter to the U.S. legation in Bern on 6 December 1943, Secretary of State Cordell Hull pushed the legation to protest the internment of Americans, which removed highly trained crews from their combat units and lost valuable equipment. Bombsights, navigational equipment, and crews' clothing were all confiscated if not destroyed.[10] Many German airmen, on the other hand, at the behest of President Pilet-Golaz, were quickly repatriated after crossing into Switzerland. The Swiss avoided violating the Hague Convention by employing a legal loophole in which they classified German aircrews landing in transports or trainers as "confused non-combatants." Their aircraft were refueled and the airmen were directed to return to Germany—that is, if they were not sent to the Luftwaffe rest and relaxation facility at the Schatzalp Hotel in Davos.

One of the most notorious examples of favoritism occurred in the spring of 1944. Wilhelm Johenen was a German night fighter pilot who held a command position in the Luftwaffe. He had flown into Switzerland from Hagenau, south Germany, and landed at Dübendorf on 28 April 1944. Johenen remained in Switzerland only a few days before being repatriated. The borders also remained open to Germans sent by the Reich to stir up pro-Nazi zeal throughout the country.[11]

There were other nuances to the policy of internment, some of them inherent in the law itself. The Hague Convention did not apply to servicemen who crossed into Switzerland after escaping a German or an Italian prisoner-of-war camp. According to Article 13 of the convention: "It has long been a rule of international law that a prisoner of war escaping and taking refuge in a neutral state is free, but it was not settled whether the neutral state could restrain him from rejoining his army if he subsequently wished to do so." Switzerland chose to detain these "evadees," but afforded them more freedom to move about the country than other internees.

Over time, internees learned the different categories and had a general understanding of how they would be treated according to each. Word made it back to the fighting forces as well. On 13 April 1944, for example, the crew from the *Lassie & ?*, 390th Bomb Group, 571st Bomb

Squadron, 8th Air Force, landed in Switzerland with two engines slightly damaged, a badly shot-up fuselage, and a ruptured fuel tank. Aware of the different treatments afforded evadees and internees, 1st Lt. Donald L. Cooper and his copilot, 1st Lt. Robert Cockrum, concocted a plan before landing. After crossing Swiss airspace they circled over Dübendorf and landed in a large meadow at Langenzinggen. The ten crew members high-tailed it to a nearby forest and hid.

Their plan might have succeeded had officers in the Swiss Air Force not noticed a discrepancy between the number of aircrews they had processed that morning and the number of aircraft that had landed. Thirteen aircraft and 130 crewmen had arrived that day, making it one of the busiest yet (fourteen bombers would land on 24 April), but one crew remained unaccounted for.

After searching everywhere, Swiss soldiers finally found the crew hiding in the forest. With straight faces Cooper's crew, hoping to be classified as evadees, insisted that they had just escaped from a German POW camp, crossed the Rhine, and found safety in Switzerland. The interrogation officer, Capt. Geoffrey Von Meiss, was not about to swallow that tale; not only were the airmen still wearing their flight suits, they were bone dry. Finally tiring of the game, Von Meiss summoned an American official to Dübendorf. After a brief but pointed discussion, Cooper and his crew confessed.[12]

• • •

According to the 1929 Geneva Accords, which governed the treatment of captives, servicemen taken as prisoners or internees were required to furnish the belligerent government that had captured them with only their name, rank, and serial number. As was their prerogative, since Switzerland had not signed the accords, the Swiss broke this rule. On their arrival in Switzerland, all airmen were asked to complete a Red Cross form that also requested their home address, date of birth, education, parents' names, and parents' occupations. Before being transferred to an internment camp, aircrews were taken to an interrogation center where enlisted men and officers were separated and handed forms seeking information of a classified nature. This aroused the suspicion of many airmen, who could not understand why neutral Switzerland wanted this information and feared that it would be passed to the Germans—as perhaps it was. A recalcitrant airman would sometimes be handed a completed questionnaire with the forged signature of one of his crewmates. Sometimes the interrogation ended with an invitation to what, in wartime, was considered a sumptuous banquet. The Americans were told that it was just an informal gathering of airmen. In reality, the U.S. fliers were separated and seated between Swiss intelligence officers.[13]

S.Sgt. Alfred V. Fairall, of the 44th Bomb Group, 68th Squadron, 8th Air Force, landed in Switzerland on 18 March 1944. He later recalled: "I was then interrogated by the Swiss, that is to say, we filled out papers as to our mother and father's name and our home address and our civilian profession. They also requested information as to the strength and location of our squadron and group, which we refused to fill in, in fact laughed at them."[14]

The recollections and testimony of Allied airmen interned in Switzerland during World War II make it clear that Switzerland treated internees from different countries in different ways. And while Switzerland did not come close to matching the behavior of the Germans and Japanese, who committed grievous crimes against prisoners of war, in many respects it did not uphold the law and even abused its position of neutrality.

3

FOLLOWING THE SILK ROAD

Fortunately, ahead of us we could see an opening in the overcast. We went for broke and went down through it. By the grace of the greater power that looks over those who are dumb enough to fly combat, we came out in a valley.

PENROSE REAGAN

In addition to firing upon a plane which was obviously in distress and which made no hostile maneuvers, the Swiss fighter aircraft apparently attacked the American machine in contravention of instructions issued by the Swiss military authorities.

U.S. LEGATION, BERN

If you ask them, the men of the U.S. Army Air Force will say that they were simply doing their jobs each time they went aloft—nothing more. And when in the course of carrying out their missions their planes were too damaged to make it back to England, some pilots decided to land in a neutral country, hoping eventually to get back to England to fight another day. They did not realize that they might be imprisoned for the duration of the war. And they most certainly did not expect the military forces of a neutral country to fire at them—particularly when their planes were clearly in distress. What neutral country would try to kill men seeking safety? The world had turned upside down.

George Michel was born in Saginaw, Michigan, on 10 June 1924. His father, Jacob, was the son of German immigrants from the Volga Deutsch colony in Russia; his mother was a lifelong resident of Saginaw. Jacob Michel had no formal schooling beyond the seventh grade; he had to quit school to help support his family. Although Jacob worked hard and provided a good living for his own family, there was no money for his son George to go to college, which he was determined to do.

In June 1942 Michel graduated from Arthur Hill High School, named for one of the area's many lumber barons, and won a place at the General Motors Institute of Technology in Flint, Michigan. He alternately spent one month in school and one month at a GM factory gaining experience and earning enough money to cover his school expenses. Then, one afternoon in March 1943, the mailman delivered a selective service postcard to the Michel residence. His mother brought the postcard to his school in Flint, her face streaked with tears.

Like all draftees, Michel was tested to determine his place in the army. He scored well on his night vision test and so was sent to gunnery school. "We had to practice out of the back of a pickup truck. I never had a gun in my hand before that," Michel said. George Michel was on his way to becoming a radio operator/gunner in the U.S. Army Air Force.

. . .

Like George Michel, most of the American airmen and warplanes interned in Switzerland during World War II were attached to the U.S. 8th Air Force based in England.[1] This was because the Eighth conducted the largest number of operations in the European theater; it flew 26.2 percent of the 2.4 million sorties flown by the USAAF and dropped about 40 percent of the two million tons of bombs.[2] In numbers of both men and units, the 8th Air Force was one of the most highly decorated military organizations. Collectively, its members were awarded fourteen Medals of Honor, 220 Distinguished Service Crosses, and 817 Silver Stars.[3]

The 8th Air Force lost twenty-six thousand men in action, and more than twenty-eight thousand of its men became prisoners of war. In one week alone, from 8 October to 14 October 1943, more than one hundred heavy bombers were lost in combat: fourteen bombers and three fighters were lost on an 8 October mission to Bremen, Germany; six went down on a mission to Anken, Germany, on 9 October; thirty bombers and one fighter were lost on a 10 October mission to Münster, Germany; and sixty bombers and one fighter went down on the 14 October mission to Schweinfurt, Germany.[4]

England, France, and Germany first recognized the potential role aviation could play in combat during World War I. In that conflict, airplanes primarily carried out observation missions—but the idea to use them to drop bombs quickly followed.[5] Subsequently, many countries began pursuing the concept of an air service apart from their other military branches. Even so, as the United States resumed an isolationist policy after the Armistice was reached on 11 November 1918, many in the upper echelons of the government dismissed the idea of a separate air service. The leaders of the Army Air Service persisted in their efforts for recognition, and finally, in 1926, the service gained representation on the General Staff—although not yet a separate branch.

In 1931, in order to fulfill an agreement with the navy for coastal defense, military strategists determined that they needed a highly specialized aircraft, one with a range of five thousand miles, a bomb load capacity of two thousand pounds, and a top speed of two hundred miles per hour. Such a bomber would give the Air Service the ability to execute long-range reconnaissance and bombardment actions. Boeing produced the first B-17 prototype in 1935.[6] Convinced that this and other aircraft would be instrumental in the war he knew was about to erupt across Europe, President Franklin D. Roosevelt pushed for a separate air arm.[7] In March 1942 the Joint Chiefs of Staff was organized and Gen. Henry "Hap" Arnold was appointed commanding general of the Army Air Force.

At the start of World War II, most of the world's air forces still flew biplanes. But the pace of fighting quickly gave rise to swifter, sleeker, and more serviceable aircraft. Soon the single-engine single-wing fighter characterized air forces the world over. At first the German and Japanese fighters were lords of the skies, but as the war pressed on, newer British, American, and Soviet models ascended to supremacy. For one thing, their range was significantly extended. Early in the war, Allied bombers sometimes crashed because they ran out of fuel, and fighter planes lacked the range to fly much past the coast of France. The bombers were easy prey for the Luftwaffe fighters waiting just at the point where the American fighters had to turn back.[8] Improved design and auxiliary fuel tanks allowed fighters such as the P-51 Mustang and P-47 Thunderbolt to escort bombers much longer distances.[9]

Bombers were likewise improved. At the start of the war, two-engine bombers were the standard of all air forces, and they continued to be used in varying modifications by all air forces during the war. New developments introduced a four-engine bomber, produced mostly by the United States and Great Britain, that could fly faster and carry a heavier load than two-engine bombers. These new bombers bore the burden of the strategic bombing offensive, hauling and dropping loads of high-explosive and incendiary bombs on German and Japanese cities, factories, and other installations.[10]

The original B-17, which earned the nickname Flying Fortress, was sixty-eight feet long and eighteen feet high. It had four 750 horsepower engines and could attain a speed of 230 miles an hour at fourteen thousand feet. Fully loaded the bomber weighed twenty-one tons. It was armed with five .30-caliber machine guns. Superchargers that forced compressed air into carburetors allowed the bomber to reach top speeds of more than 300 miles per hour at operational altitudes. The B-17 was slower than its successor, the B-24, but could fly higher, which was a comfort to the crew when it meant escaping German flak. The B-17 was armed with a .303-caliber gun in the nose and .50-caliber machine guns on the waist.

By 1943 the B-17 had been significantly modified to meet the challenges of daylight bombing: it was lengthened to seventy-four feet and raised to nineteen feet, and a long, rising tail section with a rear gunner's turret was added. The modified plane had four 1,200-horsepower engines and could fly 325 miles an hour at twenty-five thousand feet. The fully loaded aircraft weighed approximately 30 tons and was armed with nine .50-caliber machine guns and a single .30-caliber machine gun. One of its treasures was the Norden bombsight, designed by C. L. Norden for the navy. Under ideal conditions, that precision instrument allowed bombs to be delivered on target from thirty thousand feet. So valued was the bombsight that crews often jettisoned it or shot .45 slugs through the vital parts if they had to parachute or crash-land, to prevent it from falling into enemy or even Swiss hands.

The other principal bomber in the Eighth's arsenal was the B-24 Liberator from Consolidated Aircraft Corporation. The B-24 had a greater tactical range than the B-17 but had a harder time flying in formation. The prototype first flew in December 1939. The Liberator was heavily armed; .50-caliber machine guns extended in all directions:

from the nose turret (lacking on the original D model), which was manned by the bombardier; the top Martin turret located directly behind the pilot and copilot, which was manned by the engineer; the bottom or ball turret; the two waist guns; and the tail turret. The B-17 was developed under prewar conditions and had conveniences that were not designed into the B-24, which was brought out under the pressures of an imminent war. Each B-17 crew member had a place to sit, for example; B-24 waist gunners on long missions had to use .50-caliber ammunition boxes as seats.

These winged weapons served the U.S. Army Air Force well in its objective to take out the military and industrial targets that fed the German war beast. Bomber crews would destroy both the industrial facilities essential for physically conducting the war and the enemy's will to fight by destroying morale on the home front. Using the British Isles as a base from which to bomb specific enemy targets, the 8th Air Force weakened the armies and war machine of Germany before Allied soldiers stepped on French soil. Nevertheless, the effective range of Allied bombers was between six hundred and seven hundred miles, and there was still some difficulty in reaching much of German-controlled Europe from air bases in Britain and North Africa. This made the strategic advantage of a landing in Italy and the seizure of airfields in the Foggia area imperative.[11]

Unlike the British Royal Air Force, which confined its actions to night bombing runs, the USAAF engaged in daylight bombing, a costly strategy. Indeed, effective daylight bombing raids had so far remained elusive for both sides. The RAF had soundly defeated German attempts to bomb England during the day, but it had likewise failed in its own efforts at daylight bombing missions. In February 1942, Brig. Gen. Ira C. Eaker arrived in England with a skeleton staff of six and, despite resistance from the British, zealously pursued the implementation of daylight bombing.

Hindrances to daylight raids were plentiful. Clouds were perhaps the greatest "bête noire" for pilots. In order to maintain wing position it was vital to continuously watch the plane on whose wing one was flying. This became impossible when clouds reduced visibility to near zero. And until the advent of radar bombsights, which could identify land features through clouds, the lead bombardier could not locate and track targets if clouds obscured the mark.

Flying in tight formation gave the bombers the best defense against German fighters. However, assembling the formation could frazzle the nerves of the most experienced crew. It could take nearly an hour for even a small group of bombers to reach their assigned positions. During this time the lead planes flew on a racetrack course around a radio "buncher" beacon while the following planes moved into position by successive cutoffs across the "infield." Each pilot had to choose his best route to optimize his approach to position while simultaneously avoiding the other planes attempting the same thing. Planes whizzed past above, below, to the right, and to the left. In a normal assembly, four to six crossings would be required to catch up with the leaders and move to the designated formation spot. Needless to say, there were many close shaves and some midair collisions, and the Germans interfered whenever they could.

"The Luftwaffe had successfully destroyed American bomber formations in the early months of the war by bombing them from above. They dropped heavy anchor chains into the formations entangling the bombers' propellers and destroying their engines. They later refined their technique by having the Luftwaffe bomb from above with short-fused bombs that would explode at the bombers' altitude," recalled Siegvart Robertson, the pilot of the B-24 *Georgia Peach* of the 392d Bomb Group, 576th Bomb Squadron, 8th Air Force.[12]

Capt. Lester Kotlan, who flew thirty-five missions with the 487th Bomb Group, 838th Bomb Squadron, 8th Air Force, said that flak gave him and his B-17 crew the most trouble: "They laid down an asphalt road."[13] "We were well behaved boys, but we were crazy doing those missions," said Larry Lawler. "We were clay pigeons going on with six thousand pounds of bombs at a speed that felt like ten miles an hour. The Germans would just pick us off. We were American Kamikazes. On my first three missions to Berlin, the flak was so thick you could walk on it."

The close-formation daylight bombing strategy was severely tested on 17 August 1943 and again on 14 October 1943 when Eaker sent swarms of B-17s to strike two crucial targets in Germany: a ball-bearing plant in Schweinfurt and a Messerschmitt plant in Regensburg that was responsible for 30 percent of the German single-engine fighter production. Nearly six hundred American aviators perished during the two days and two missions that constituted this raid.[14] Nonetheless, the United States persisted with daylight bombing, eventually overcoming the Germans.

By the time Operation Overlord began, Gen. Dwight D. Eisenhower had replaced General Eaker with Lt. Gen. Carl A. "Tooey" Spaatz as commander of the U.S. Strategic Air Forces in Europe (the 8th and 15th Air Forces). Spaatz was a graduate of West Point who transferred to the Air Corps in 1915. In 1918, with the rank of major, he commanded an air squadron on the Western Front and had three enemy kills to his credit. In 1940 he was posted to the United Kingdom as a military observer, and when the United States entered the war he organized the air forces destined for combat in the European theater.[15]

One of the other personalities in the top ranks who helped shape the nature of the Mighty Eighth was Gen. James Doolittle, whose combative spirit characterized the unit's determination to forge ahead no matter what. Not even the loss of more than six thousand men in combat in the 2d Air Division could change that attitude.[16]

The 2d Air Division was inaugurated on 7 June 1942, exactly six months after the Japanese attack on Pearl Harbor. The division had five bombardment wings, which were in turn divided into fourteen separate bombardment groups, all based in England. Five fighter groups were also part of the division. Between its first bombing mission on 7 November 1942 and its last on 25 April 1945, the division flew a total of 95,946 sorties in 439 operational missions. Its crews claimed 1,079 enemy fighters destroyed in combat at a cost of 1,458 B-24s lost in action.[17]

Born on 14 December 1896 in Alameda, California, Doolittle had secured his place as a hero and public figure long before America entered World War II. He served in the Army Air Corps in World War I. In April 1942 he planned a bombing raid on Tokyo and led sixteen B-25s from the deck of the aircraft carrier USS *Hornet*, a feat that caused Americans' morale to skyrocket and for which he received the Medal of Honor. He returned from that mission and in September 1942 arrived in the United Kingdom as a brigadier general to command the 12th Air Force. After a stint in North Africa he went back to England to build up the 8th Air Force and push the fighters to go on the offensive.

· · ·

The distinction of being the first Allied aircraft to land in Switzerland falls to a British Mosquito PR-IV based at Benson, Oxfordshire, England. Pilot G. R. Wooll and navigator Sgt. J. Fielden were returning from a reconnaissance flight to Venice on 24 August 1942 when the engine overheated. The airmen landed at Bern-Belp airfield, a small airstrip used today mostly for recreational and small business flights. They were sent back to the Allies soon afterward in exchange for two Germans and one Italian.[18]

The first Americans to be interned in Switzerland did not land at all–they were shot down just outside the border and guided into Switzerland by the French underground.[19] Granted evadee status, the men were soon allowed to return home.

The saga of the interned U.S. airmen officially began on 13 August 1943 when the first American Liberator crash-landed in Switzerland. The bomber, a B-24 nicknamed *Death Dealer*, was on detached service to the 9th Air Force. It was part of a group of 114 B-24s en route to destroy the Messerschmitt fighter factories at Wiener-Neustadt near Vienna. Although the Liberators were outfitted with extra gas tanks in their bomb bays, they carried only enough fuel to reach their target and return to their base in North Africa. The mission was without serious incident for pilot Alva Geron's crew until they turned for home.[20]

On its previous mission *Death Dealer* and most of its crew had participated in the Ploesti oil fields raid. On the return leg of that mission the plane ran into heavy flak. Paul Daugherty, the gunner, was mortally wounded. Geron turned over control to his copilot and went to give morphine to Daugherty, who had a gaping flak wound in his chest. "Lieutenant can you pray?" asked Daugherty. "Will you say a prayer for me?" Geron gathered the gunner in his arms and prayed. The gunner squeezed Geron's hand and slumped in death. One of *Death Dealer*'s engines had been shot out. Then another failed. The crew threw out everything possible to stay aloft. A conference via intercom was called to discuss a possible water landing, but the men stayed with the bomber, unwilling to leave Daugherty behind to sink at sea. They landed in Libya with five minutes of gas left. Daugherty was buried in the desert.

Three weeks later, *Death Dealer* lost its number three engine en route to Wiener-Neustadt; the number two engine was destroyed by flak over the Messerschmitt works. Two engines short and trailing smoke, the bomber fell behind the formation. Geron tried but could not maintain altitude. He told the navigator to find a heading that would take them to Switzerland. But there was a slight problem: "None of our maps showed details of the Swiss interior," Geron explained; "no cities, no mountains, particularly—so as we approached the cloud cover concern developed about the heights of mountains and the possibility of encountering them in our flight path. We had no maps of the area except those in our escape kits. We knew generally which direction to take and later Bob Simpson, our navigator, gave us a heading after consulting his escape kit map."

After passing Lake Constance the plane circled Swiss territory searching for a place to land. Swiss terrain, with its numerous mountains and lakes, was largely unknown to Allied bomber crews, so crippled Fortresses and Liberators would search for the natural landmarks they did know about, such as Lake Constance. If no airfield could be located, the pilots would look for any flat piece of land, open field, or unused road. Geron found such a field and landed with wheels down. The crew, uncertain whether they were on neutral ground, began detonating charges to destroy the plane. Curious villagers and soldiers began approaching the smoking bomber. Most fliers forced to land in Switzerland recall that no matter how deserted the landing strip, no matter how improvised the landing, Swiss soldiers in full battle dress and brandishing bayoneted rifles or machine guns always seemed to spring up from nowhere and immediately surround the plane.

Geron's crew asked the small crowd where they were and discovered they had landed in a small village in western Switzerland. The men were taken to the Wil railway station and sent on to the Dübendorf aerodrome near Zürich. This was the last time they were together. Geron was later part of a group of seven Americans exchanged for seven German aviators. Gunner Sgt. Richard G. Ryan made an unsuccessful escape attempt from Adelboden and was sent to the penitentiary camp of Wauwilermoos. Dressed in civilian clothing, Ryan escaped from Wauwilermoos and crossed into France. It had long been thought that the Nazis caught and shot Ryan, but he escaped and now lives in Salem, Massachusetts. Some of the other crew members worked at the American legation or the American Red Cross.

Death Dealer too ended up at Dübendorf, but in a rather altered state. The fire-damaged Liberator was disassembled and carted off in trucks bound for the railway station at Wil. After the Swiss Air Force finished examining it, the Liberator remained stored in a hangar at Kloten until 1945, when it was scrapped.

• • •

As the Allied air campaign increased in intensity, the U.S. 8th Air Force was assigned the lion's share of the bombing missions over southern Germany. Aircrews caught in dire circumstances—attacked by the Luftwaffe or about to run out of fuel—often tried to find safety in Switzerland, only to be shot down and imprisoned. "The consensus was that if you went to Switzerland you'd be safe. Nothing was ever said that there was a possibility that you'd be shot at over Switzerland," recalled Leonard Schutta.[21]

Some aircrews landed in Sweden; 327 aircraft from belligerent countries landed there between 1939 and 1945—most had been damaged and were unable to continue, but some had simply gone astray. Of the 327, 140 were American, 113 were German, and 58 were British. The most landings, 160, were in 1944, the year that the Allied air forces' bombing of industrial targets in Germany and German-occupied lands intensified. Nearly all the men interned in Sweden were repatriated before the war ended. The first aircraft to land in Sweden was a Polish RWD carrying thirteen refugees; the second was a German He-60. Both landed in September 1939. The first British aircraft to force-land in Sweden was a Swordfish Mark 1, in September 1940. During the first years of the war airmen were repatriated on a "one-for-one" basis—one German airman for one British airman. In July 1943 the first USAAF aircraft arrived, the *Georgia Rebel* of the 535th Bomb Squadron, 381st Bomb Group, 8th Air Force, based at Ridgewell, England. During 1943 seven American bombers landed in

Sweden. Their numbers increased throughout 1944.[22] The decision to land in a neutral country did not come easily. "It was an option of last resort to avoid capture, and no one violated this concept," said John E. Rosenberg, who flew with the 392d Bomb Group, 576th Bomb Squadron, 8th Air Force.[23] It was done only when "battle damage to the plane and/or crew prevented flying to Allied airspace."

Allied war departments had been informed that Swiss aviators would approach any single aircraft violating Swiss airspace and order it to land by means of green flares and the lowering of landing gear (if speed permitted). Foreign aircraft were to answer with a return flare. Foreign military aircraft flying in formations of two or more would be attacked without warning. Such an attack actually occurred early in March 1944 when Swiss fighters shot down one U.S. bomber and forced another to land at Dübendorf.[24]

Swiss antiaircraft fire wounded a crew member on Ralph Jackson's plane, which flew with the 44th Bomb Group, 67th Bomb Squadron, 8th Air Force. During interrogation Jackson recounted how he objected to Swiss authorities about the Swiss gunners firing at them. The Swiss officer seemed "proud we were hit, saying they were supposed to hit us."

Nearly all Swiss Air Force attacks on American bombers took place far inside Switzerland at relatively low altitudes near Swiss air bases. A Swiss fighter pilot and Swiss flak gunners destroyed a disabled American bomber on 24 April 1944 as it attempted to land at Zürich Dübendorf. Capt. Robert Cardenas witnessed the incident. Cardenas had been a pilot on a B-24 that was shot down over Nazi-occupied Europe. Despite head wounds he evaded capture and entered Switzerland, where he was interned. The incident with *Little Chub,* mentioned in chapter 2, was typical of such attacks. *Little Chub,* severely damaged by enemy antiaircraft and fighter fire, was losing altitude and barely maneuverable when Swiss fighters approached it one minute after it crossed Lake Constance and entered Swiss airspace. The plane twice circled the Zürich area before heading to the southern end of Lake Greifen, where two Swiss fighters attacked it. Their fire immediately killed two crewmen—the bombardier, 2d Lt. Jesse L. Greenbaum, and the left waist gunner, S.Sgt. Richard M. Sendleback—and wounded the navigator, 2d Lt. Charles D. Wallach. The plane caught fire and lost altitude. It was down to five hundred feet before the pilot, 1st Lt. Everett L. Bailey, recovered and gave the bail-out order. Bailey did not have enough time to open his parachute. The three men in the back bailed out into a tempest of Swiss antiaircraft fire. The ball turret gunner, Sgt. Anthony T. Melazzi Jr., and the tail gunner, Sgt. Sidney J. Pratt, were killed. The aircraft crashed into the Greifensee. The body of 2d Lt. James E. Burry, the copilot, remained entombed in the plane until it was raised in 1953. Wallach survived the crash and was interned along with Sgt. Raymond A. Newall, the engineer; Sgt. William J. Silag, the radio operator; and Sgt. Richard R. Hollingsworth, the right waist gunner. The U.S. legation chastised the Swiss Political Department for the incident, which killed three officers and three noncommissioned officers.[25] "In addition to firing upon a plane which was obviously in distress and which made no hostile maneuvers, the Swiss fighter aircraft apparently attacked the American machine in contravention of instructions issued by the Swiss military authorities," stated the letter from the legation. "In this instance the Swiss fighter aircraft attacked the American plane after the latter had answered the green rocket signal of the Swiss planes with a like signal. That the American plane was in distress was also evidenced by the fact that its left front wheel had been shot off and right wheel and tail wheel were down. The attack is considered to have been unjustifiable and the Legation has, in consequence, been directed to lodge a formal energetic protest." The terse Swiss response declared only that the American aircraft ignored orders to land.[26]

. . .

On 6 September 1944 the 8th Air Force mounted an attack against Stuttgart, Germany. Clouds painted the skies as 338 B-17s massed overhead searching for their target, a cluster of factories. Calamity marked the mission. The lead planes could not identify the target beneath the cloud cover; some groups flew past the city, and formations began to unravel. The Luftwaffe downed thirty-three Flying Fortresses. Twelve bombers plummeted into the icy waters of the English Channel, too severely damaged to make it home. Of the several bombers that tried to reach Switzerland only four succeeded; *Raunchy* was one of them.

Pilot Sam Turner struggled to keep his Flying Fortress aloft. It had lost three engines over Stuttgart, and the ball turret gunner, Sgt. Joe Maloney, lay dead, cut down by enemy fire. Vance Boswell, the navigator, remembered that as they flew over Friedrichshafen at three hundred feet the plane had only one functioning engine. They had to land. Lake Constance, whose waters lap against the shores of Switzerland, Austria, and Germany, was the only possible landing site.

The bomber broke in half on impact. Swiss and German patrol boats rushed toward the plane. The Swiss patrol boats beat the Germans to the scene by a few seconds and took the nine battered Americans to shore. The accident left Boswell sightless in his left eye and without the use of his left arm. Shrapnel pierced Turner's chest. And for a month, until the Swiss could raise the plane from 230 feet below, Sergeant Maloney's body lay entombed in the *Raunchy*. The American internee camp at Adelboden was named in his honor.

German patrol boats were always a serious threat to aircrews trying to land in Lake Constance. On 20 July 1944, on a mission to Friedrichshafen, Germany, 2d Lt. Howland J. Hamlin, a B-24 pilot, ordered his crew to bail out over Lake Constance five minutes after flak damaged their plane, *Hell's Bells*. The crew parachuted out over the lake. Sgt. Donald W. Anderson landed on Swiss soil and was interned. Swiss fishermen were able to rescue Sergeant Tonnesson. The fishermen nearly saved 2d Lt. George T. Hunter Jr., the bombardier, but German patrol boats chased them away. Hunter, entangled in his chute, drowned before the Germans pulled him from the water. The Swiss later retrieved the body of Sgt. John A. Boardsen from the wreckage. Reports indicate that the Germans opened fire and killed the other five crew members: 2d Lieutenant Hamlin; 2d Lt. Richard V. S. Newhouse, the copilot; Sgt. Aaron C. Slaughter, the radio operator; Sgt. Raymond C. Ertel, the ball turret gunner; and Sgt. Ronald W. Charrington, left waist gunner.[27]

• • •

Several years ago, Norris King, a right waist gunner on the B-17 *Sugarfoot*, journeyed back to Switzerland to pay homage to his lost comrades. "I have gone to the place where our plane hit the ground and where my seven crew members were killed. I have since learned that it was Swiss antiaircraft fire that blew our plane to bits," King said.[28] *Sugarfoot* had been flying over a heavily fortified Swiss area close to the German border on 1 October 1943. It was the twenty-sixth mission for the North Africa–based crew. The target this time was an aircraft factory in Augsburg, but inclement weather forced the 99th Bomb Group to turn back. On their way home a group of Luftwaffe fighters attacked.

"The ship shook and shuddered throwing us to the floor in the waist as machine gun bullets and cannon fire passed just above us and lodged in the tail," said Marion "Dale" Pratt, the left waist gunner.[29] "We believe our tail gunner was killed at that time. The fighters left and antiaircraft fire began. Swiss officers told us later the antiaircraft fire was Swiss." An explosion rocked the front of the aircraft, which nosed down. King and Pratt were pinned to the top of the ship. The plane bucked and leveled out, throwing the two gunners back on the floor. Equipment and ammunition flew around. Pratt saw the waist window with the gun off the mount.

"I summoned my strength and rolled toward the window, placed my foot on the edge and shoved myself out into space," Pratt wrote in his memoirs. "As I left the ship something hit me across the shoulder and head which sent me spinning like a top. As the spinning slowed I pulled the ripcord and nothing happened. With gloved hands I clawed at the edges while falling, my back to the ground." Then something white appeared. Pratt grabbed it and pulled: "A swish and loud bang was followed by a terrible jerk sending pain through my body. My chute had opened and I was alive and thanked God in prayer. There was a peaceful quiet in comparison to the din of the previous minutes." Pratt saw parts of the ship floating down and a major portion of the plane heading toward a mountain. He saw one chute below and assumed it was King's. *Sugarfoot* disintegrated as he watched.

King too barely escaped the crashing airplane. Stunned by flying debris in the waist, he tried and failed three times to get out the upper waist window. Then he saw the lower window and jumped. Barely clearing the ship, he pulled his ripcord and was jerked upright. Almost immediately afterward he found himself tangled in tree limbs. "Joe Carroll, the radioman; Dale Pratt, the left waist gunner; and myself were able to bail out," recalled King, who received a mild brain concussion during the crash. "The other seven crew members went down with the wreckage. We were picked up by the Swiss and taken to a hospital in Bad Ragaz where Joe and I spent three weeks. Our care was excellent, and we even had a visit from Henri Guisan, the Swiss General."

Joe Carroll was at his gun in the radio room when the shooting started.[30] Like King and Pratt, he too was hurled about the aircraft. Debris lacerated his face. At one point during the tumultuous descent the life raft broke loose and pinned him. He was able to free himself and open the door to the bomb bay. The bombs had already been dropped and the bomb bay doors were open. He bailed out. After he cleared the ship his chute blossomed upward.

Later in the hospital the three learned that none of their crewmates had survived.

"That was our 26th mission," Pratt wrote. "We each lost seven of the finest friends any of us ever had." At the time *Sugarfoot* went down there were about eighty American airmen interned in Switzerland. All attended the funeral in Bad Ragaz on 5 October. Thirteen fliers were buried that day.

• • •

April 1944 had been the most difficult month yet for the 8th Air Force, despite the addition of six new heavy bomber groups. During that month the Eighth lost outright or could not repair 422 heavy bombers. The sortie loss rate rose to 3.6 percent from March's 3.3 percent. The 15th Air Force lost 214 heavy bombers, up from 99 in March. Of those lost in April, fifty-two crews—one out of every eight planes lost—landed in a neutral country: twenty in Sweden and thirty-two in Switzerland. This was a large increase from the period 30 December 1943–29 February 1944, when only five crews had landed in neutral countries. Most of the crews lost in April had been part of deep penetration raids, and all landed because they knew they could not make a safe landing in England. On 11 April the Eighth had its second worst casualty total of the war. It lost sixty-four planes; nine were interned.[31]

Less common, but no less deadly, were incidents along the Swiss-Italian border. Jack C. Falk, a bombardier with the 446th Bomb Squadron, 331st Bomb Group, 8th Air Force, went down there.[32] Falk's B-25, the *Spiders' Frolic Pad,* crashed on 21 March 1945 near Lugano, Ticino. After flak destroyed the right engine, Herman Everhart, the thirty-two-year-old pilot, could not maintain altitude over the Brenner Pass and ordered the crew to get out. Falk and Sgt. Elvin Scheetz, the engineer, bailed out as the bomber headed toward Lake Como. Everhart bailed out while the townspeople of Ponte Tresa watched. The Swiss standing on the shore waved their arms, frantically signaling Everhart to their side of the border. But just as the young pilot touched down, someone on the Italian side—an SS officer or an Italian fascist—opened fire. Everhart died in Italy, just feet from the Swiss border.

The Swiss-Italian border also claimed part of *Rowdy Dowdy's* crew. On 25 April 1944 the B-24 Liberator took off from its base in Manduria, Italy, to bomb a bridge at Ferrara on the outskirts of Varese. Morris Sipser, of the 720th Bomb Squadron, 450th Bomb Group, later wrote about the mission.[33] "The morning of our briefing we found our mission pleasantly amusing—the sending of such a large group to bomb a bridge. I understood that this specific bridge had been a regular target of our group but the damages, however successful, were quickly repaired. In good humor we participated in this mission which was known to be a 'milk run.' An easy flight to add to your bombing record."

The milk run curdled. After takeoff one of the right engines began to sputter. Sam Houston, the pilot, said he could fly the ship on three engines if need be, and so off they went. Almost immediately after it joined formation the plane began to lag behind. Several other planes of the group also began falling behind, and the group leader instructed the stragglers to make their own formation.

"The formation was a poor one and the escorts were now beginning to leave us," Sipser recalled. "As we approached Varese, fighters appeared. We hoped they were ours but we soon learned they were German Me-109s. Firing began and from where I sat at the bombardier's position I saw several of our planes in real trouble. Many parachutes appeared. Firing was intense: there seemed to be a number of enemy planes, perhaps five or six. We were being hit and it appeared to me that we were the focal point of concentration."

Rowdy Dowdy listed sharply. Houston shouted that a second engine had been hit and damaged and ordered the crew to bail out. Sipser, on the flight deck, did not hear the signal. Wes Urquhart, the copilot, turned to Sipser and told him to jump. All of a sudden the flight engineer screamed. The tail gunner, Sgt. George K. Monroe, could not leave his position because of hydraulic failure. The ball turret gunner, Sgt. Benjamin H. Roderique, left his gun and went to aid the rear gunner, joined by the engineer, Sgt. Albert V. Lattimer. "I then took over the ball turret," Sipser wrote. "We were still falling, still being attacked; and in my new position I just kept firing away."

The copilot asked Sipser to locate their position. He studied his maps. "No planes were visible. The terrain we were crossing was mountainous. Sam dove for a heavy cloud formation and I could see very little except that we were flying quite low and at peak level. We all saw a lake on the other side of the mountain." The map showed a lake in Geneva and a similarly shaped lake in Germany.

"We landed in the late morning unaware of our pilot's intent to blow up the ship if we were in German territory," Sipser wrote. "As we approached the landing strip, I saw crowds of people who seemed very friendly and who appeared to be cheering. We landed in Geneva. There we learned that four of our crew had bailed out in northern Italy and became POWs."

• • •

Initially, airmen with the 8th Air Force had to complete twenty-five missions before being rotated back to the United States. The number was later increased twice, first to thirty and then to thirty-five. Fifty missions, each one lasting at least ten hours, were required of the airmen flying with the 15th Air Force out of Italy. During the summer of 1944 the percentage of aircraft lost per sortie dropped for the 8th Air Force, declining from 3.6 percent in April to 2.2 percent in May, to 1.1 percent in June, when the Eighth flew numerous missions, and rising slightly to 1.5 percent in both July and August. This lower loss rate meant a significant increase in crews' chances of completing their tours of duty.[34] On the other hand, combat tours in Europe had been increased from twenty-five to thirty missions, and even at a loss rate of

1.5 percent per sortie, a crew member still had a 36 percent chance of being killed in combat before completing his required missions.

Mission days started early. Crews could be roused as early as 2:00 A.M. They reported to breakfast and a general briefing about an hour later. "The bicycle ride with no lights in nearly pitch darkness from the Quonset barracks to the mess hall was considered by some to be the most dangerous part of the mission. We made it O.K. to find the usual powdered scrambled eggs, toast and jam," remembered Russell K. Sherbourne, a second lieutenant with the 491st Bomb Group, 853d Bomb Squadron, 8th Air Force.[35]

If the mission was to be a lengthy one, the crews were often given a treat to start the day off right—real fried eggs, and sometimes even oranges. On the morning of George Michel's ill-fated flight to Munich, the chow line inched forward. One of Michel's crewmates, waist gunner Frank Kintana, went up to investigate the reason for the slow pace. "And then we started to do some thinking along a different channel," Michel recalled. "You see, Frank reported that the cooks were frying eggs and we only got them on long hauls. It was almost a cinch that on a big raid we'd get an extra special breakfast; you know, kinda fattening us for the kill."[36]

Navigator James Hewlett, who had been a fire fighter in the U.S. Forest Service in southern California before the war, remembered those breakfasts too.[37] "I shall always remember the Quonset huts where we lived and slept with other combat fliers. And those early mission wakeup calls—then that nervous appetite facing those powdered egg, powdered milk breakfasts. And at the pre-mission briefings, we could usually tell the hazardness of the mission by the strength of the groans that we heard when the 'target' curtain was pulled."

After the joint briefing each crew member attended a briefing for his assigned task. Then the crew would suit up, donning their gear in layers. Cold-weather attire called for undershorts, undershirts, and long underwear followed by a wool olive drab shirt and pants and then a heated suit, which included heated boots and gloves. Over that went a one-piece wool coverall, then the flying suit and the Mae West life preserver, and finally the parachute harness. Gunners wore silk gloves under heated gloves so their hands would not freeze to the weapons.

After getting dressed, the fliers went to the equipment room to get flak suits, flak helmets, and oxygen masks. When everyone was ready, the crew was taken to the plane and the bombardier would furnish them with emergency rations—usually candy for energy—and escape maps, silk squares encased in small rubber containers.

The first mission meant different things for different airmen. Whatever their impressions, however, most thought about two things: whether they were up to the task and the pure relief on landing on the ground after it was finished. "Our first mission was on 11 June 1943 to bomb a bridge near Monte Forte, France. . . . We bombed through the clouds so I didn't get a visual confirmation from my spot by the open bomb bay doors," said George Michel, who was based in Wendling, England. "We started out on the mission when it was still my birthday, 10 June, back in Saginaw, Michigan, so I have fun saying that that was quite a birthday present that year."

Michel stayed by the bomb bay bulkhead during the bomb run portion of the six-hour mission, his hand on the emergency lever that could move the bomb bay doors back to the full open position in case they crept even the slightest bit toward a closed position. It was important that the bomb bay doors stay open so the bombs would not jam up in the bay. The bomb run itself was nearly uneventful, but "on the return leg of that mission," Michel said, "somewhere over the English Channel, I sent a radio message that reported a man coming down in a parachute, right through the bomber stream. What had happened we never found out. There was no plane going down. The only thing to hope for was that the British air/sea rescue crew got out to pick him up before the cold water of the Channel killed him."

Norris King recalled his first mission as a tapestry woven of confusing and fearful images. King, who was born in Kansas on 24 December 1923, enlisted in the Army Air Corps after high school. During World War II he was based in North Africa. "It was around the first of June 1943. Each crew member was assigned to his position. When we got to about twelve thousand feet we were hooked up to oxygen, to [the] intercom system and to the heated suit, so couldn't move around much. As we got closer to the target we were at about eighteen thousand feet to twenty-five thousand feet and it was very cold. The oxygen mask would freeze to your face. There was nothing pleasant about a combat mission and I was always scared, more so when being shot at."

. . .

Flying Fortresses could withstand tremendous damage and remain airborne, but there were times when aircrews had to bail out or crash-land. Since German POW camps were notorious for their harsh treatment of Allied servicemen, most crews tried to reach a neutral country such as Switzerland. But finding Switzerland on an Allied map could be tricky. What crews knew about their options and what they had in the way of maps regarding Switzerland are still points of contention among former aircrews. Apparently, some knew where to go and some did not. "We had been briefed and given maps of Switzerland," Michel said. "This was an option that was specifically mentioned to the pilot and navigator. Before we took off, there was a delay and I remember a couple of the crew members doing their versions of Swiss yodeling which the pilot immediately ordered them to stop. We definitely were told about options in Switzerland."

All airmen were issued escape kits that contained handkerchief-sized maps printed on silk, a knife, a compass, concentrated chocolate, dextrose pills, water purification pills, and foreign currency. Some fliers remember that Switzerland's borders were printed on the escape map of Europe, which some called the silk road.

The silk road came in handy for 2d Lt. James Hewlett.[38] His final mission, on 21 July 1944, was to bomb Oberpfaffenhofen, Germany, the site of Dornier-Werke GmbH, where both the Do-217N-2 night fighter and the Do-335A-1 twin-engine fighter were manufactured. On the 24 April 1944 mission, one of the first over Oberpfaffenhofen, bombers were sent to bomb an underground assembly line building jet engines for the M-262 twin-jet fighter. The underground complex still operates today, producing aircraft under the name Fairchild Dornier.

Hewlett's plane lacked enough fuel to make it back to England after the bomb run, so the pilot asked for a heading to Switzerland. "I looked through my maps; I did not have a map of Switzerland," said Hewlett. "I used my escape map as best I could and gave Andy a general heading for Switzerland. When we were over what I had calculated to be Switzerland, and when we found a break in the clouds below, we started to let down. Getting below the cloud base, we circled for one and a half hours over what we believed was Switzerland, searching for an airfield that would take a B-24. We didn't find one. Since fuel was getting low, the possibility of parachuting was becoming imminent. By now, we had started referring to the crude, small scale, cloth maps of Europe that were in our escape kits." Hewlett and the crew bailed out, with most landing near the small village of Gonten. Their waist gunner was killed when his chute failed to open completely.

Apart from regarding Switzerland as an emergency airfield of sorts, the aircrews had many misconceptions about those who landed there and what happened to them. Some thought that aircrews deserted there, landing in perfect condition with full fuel tanks. Many airmen were under the impression that they would be permitted to return to their own lines, or at least travel freely about the country. Others believed there were American military personnel on the ground ready to greet incoming bomber crews and repair their aircraft. As those who were forced down on Swiss soil quickly learned, the reality was far from the paradise they had imagined. Many airmen were quite surprised and disappointed to learn they would be detained for the length of the war.

Interned aircrews were sent to one of three internment sites in remote Alpine villages: Adelboden, Davos, or Wengen. Captured planes were stored at Dübendorf, the Swiss Air Force headquarters near Zürich. The Swiss, ever eager to discover all they could about American aircraft, dissected, inspected, and flew many of the bombers. They test-fired the .50-caliber machine guns to learn about the angle and range of fire in preparation for attacking foreign bombers that refused to land. The superchargers, engines, and other equipment were given to private factories and universities for analysis. Fuel and parachutes were examined and compared with similar products from the Swiss aviation industry. A B-24 Liberator, stripped of its national markings, even starred in a Swiss propaganda film depicting the cunning and agility of Swiss fighters as they intercepted the Liberator and forced it to land.[39]

• • •

On 11 July 1944 the Allies dispatched 1,176 bombers and 795 fighters to bomb Munich. Twenty of the bombers were shot down and 131 were damaged; 193 airmen went missing in action, 19 were wounded in action, and 12 were killed in action. Four fighters were shot down.

Munich was a deep penetration raid that required more than eight hours of flying time from takeoff to landing. It was a mission fraught with peril. Even with the extra gasoline carried in the internal wingtip tanks, planes had run out of gas in the landing pattern on the downwind leg of the final approach. A gasoline gauge for each of the four main tanks that fed the engines helped B-24 crews monitor the fuel level. But the glass tubes actually sampled only one location in the tank, making the observation strongly dependent on the plane's altitude. Readings were therefore often grossly inaccurate.

The Munich raid was George Michel's final mission. That day the *Georgia Peach*, the last to take off and in low squadron, flew in the exposed position commonly known as Purple Heart corner.

On the approach to the target, the assistant engineer, who flew in the right waist position, reported that the number four engine (outboard on the starboard side of the plane) had developed a serious oil leak. Instruments showed a drop in oil pressure on that engine. At the same time, the copilot, 2d Lt. Vincent C. Willis, tried to increase engine RPMs and found that the prop governor was stuck. Manipulating the RPM switch on that engine finally got oil to flow through the governor, and things seemed to be stabilized.

By this time, 2d Lt. John S. Gates, the navigator, advised the crew that they were at the initial point of the bomb run to the marshalling yards of Munich. When the crew reached the target, they found the target completely covered by clouds and that the German radar and flak gunners hadn't been confused by the chaff that had been dumped out of the waist windows at the initial point (I.P.). Chaff (the British called it "window") was the Allies' answer to German flak: slivers of metal foil that would jam German radar and render flak ineffective. It came in bundles and was released when crews spotted flak. In the early stages of the air war, crews reported that chaff was effective; they could see the drop in altitude of the flak bursts. But not this time. The crew of the *Georgia Peach* found flak bursts right at their altitude and right in their flight path, filling the bright blue sky like deadly balloons.

The *Georgia Peach* made its bombing run and dropped its thousand-pound bombs on the marshalling yards. No sooner were the bombs away than the lead and deputy lead planes were hit and went down. At the same time, the number four engine on the *Georgia Peach* started to windmill. Sig Robertson, the pilot, could control the engine's RPMs for only short periods before they started speeding up again and vibrating the daylights out of the plane. Engine number three (the inboard engine on the starboard side) had apparently been hit by flak over the target, and the assistant engineer reported that it was heating up and ready to burn. Instruments confirmed this, so power had to be cut back on that engine as well. Two engines were out on the same side of the aircraft. With only two good engines the *Georgia Peach* could not keep up with the formation.

Robertson gave everyone a chance to voice his opinion as to what to do: bail out or stick with the aircraft and try to find Switzerland and a place to land. "To a man, we decided to stay with the plane," said Michel. "Who in his right mind would have wanted to jump into the clouds, not knowing what lay below and, at the same time, remembering what you had just dropped on Munich's marshalling yards. No doubt that there would be some very angry Germans waiting to 'welcome' you."

Robertson recalled that the crew "went through a wide range of emotions" during that mission. "Intense fear looking at the flak over the target and knowing we had to go through it. When hit, we lost control in spite of our efforts to keep the bomber level. . . . Finally, we were all alone. It was quite fearful to realize what was about to happen. Fear took over until the engineer and I decided we couldn't go home. Then there was no more fear. Total resignation without emotion. Just do what you had to. The men who suffered the most were the ones who had nothing to do. To observe and not participate was excruciating."

Robertson decided to attempt to land in Switzerland. The crew began throwing out anything that was not tied down. Machine guns, ammunition, fur-lined flying suits, chaff boxes, and fire extinguishers all went out the waist gun windows. The debris rained down.

Robertson had told Michel to radio for Swiss fighter support to guide them to a landing field. Four P-51s escorted them to the Swiss border. "The leader then flipped up his wing and away they flew. We sure could have used some close support right then. The 51s had been so close it was possible to make out the name of the leader's plane: *Hurry Home Honey.*"

Once they found themselves over Swiss airspace the crew faced the deadly problem of Swiss antiaircraft guns and one further problem caused by the fact that the pilot, being very anxious to get the Swiss to stop shooting flak at the plane, dropped the wheels without going through the normal procedure of notifying the crew in the nose that this was going to happen. A fierce wind tore through the open nose-wheel door, scattering navigator John Gates's maps. But even worse, as the nose wheel dropped out, so did Gates. In his scramble to pull himself back into the plane, Gates grabbed at his chest chute, which was also about to drop out, and in so doing pulled on the ripcord and spilled the chute. This eliminated the possibility of the crew bailing out, as there were nine men but only eight usable chutes; but a safe landing seemed unlikely because Gates was unable to find the map showing possible landing points in Switzerland. Gates finally found the map, and the deliberations began. "The glider field at Altenrhein was the best solution that the pilot and copilot had to work with," Michel said; ". . . and it did work."

Should an aircraft land in enemy, or foreign, territory, the crew was also required to try and destroy all sensitive equipment and documents. Michel almost blew his plane up while trying to destroy the "flimsies" that had secret codes and information that he, as the radio operator, was responsible for. "Supposedly the rice paper that the data was printed on could be eaten," Michel said. "But as the plane had been surrounded and the Swiss were making very definite motions for us to get out of the plane, I ended up with a mouth full of what must have looked like a cow trying to chew its cud. And I still had a lot of destroying to do." Michel built a fire on the flight deck intending to burn the rest of the pages. Robertson, the pilot, yelled at him to extinguish the fire while Michel kept trying to get him to eat some of the pages. "His big flying boot came over my shoulder as I was kneeling on the flight deck and put out the fire PDQ. Then he said: 'Look!' Behind me at the bomb bay bulkhead I could see fuel leaking out of the gas tanks that had been damaged somehow in the landing. If the vapors had gotten to my fire, that would have been the end of all of us."

Michel succeeded in demolishing the IFF set, removing the knob from his radio set Morse code key (which he still has). He crawled out of the plane through the open bomb bay section. There he found Frank Kintana, the waist gunner. Kintana had "charged his .50 caliber machine gun and was going to start shooting at the troops that were closing in on the plane. . . . [T]heir forest green uniforms and helmets that were the spitting image of German helmets as far as we were concerned . . . were enough to get Frank ready to take out a few of them." Fortunately, Joe Burdett, the other waist gunner, was able to stop Kintana.

• • •

On 9 August 1944, nearly one month after the *Georgia Peach* landed in Switzerland, American pilots were issued orders not to "abandon their planes over Swiss territory where they might endanger Swiss life and property," and, further, were told that they "should make desperate efforts to land planes or be sure they crash in one of the many Swiss lakes or in isolated places in the high mountains."[40] Of course, the directives were sometimes ignored out of sheer necessity. On 19 July, for example, a crippled bomber abandoned by its crew crashed into the Château Weyden, home of Max Huber, the president of the International Red Cross. *Marking Time,* a twelve-page weekly published by English evadees in Switzerland, gave wide attention to the incident in the 21 July 1944 issue: "U.S. Bomber falls on Château. Home of head of I.R.C. in flames. Eyewitnesses reported that the four-engine bomber appeared to hover before crashing. One wing of the aircraft remained on the roof, the engine and the other wing fell to the ground, and the roof timbers took fire. The roof was destroyed and one tower demolished. The crew had parachuted out before the plane crashed. Five airmen were unhurt, but two were wounded and one died. The château, which burned for days, contained valuable art treasures, many of which the firemen were able to carry out to safety."

• • •

Fortunately for George Michel and his crewmates on 11 July, it was possible to avoid houses, châteaux, and other buildings. They found a small grass-covered airfield, really no more than a dirt strip, jutting into Lake Constance. Engineers pumping mud from Lake Constance had built the strip at Altenrhein between 1927 and 1928. The runway was about six hundred meters by one hundred meters and was marked on both sides by a ditch filled with yellow gravel. It had been certified for light single-engine aircraft only, not the heavy bombers that would land there during the war.

Pilots choosing to land at this field in Altenrhein had to be exceptionally careful because German-occupied Austria lay just across the Rhine. The river, a slip of a stream at that point, is all that separates the two countries, so planes had to land short and stand on the brakes. Moreover, the Germans had rigged a damaged B-24 on a similar field on their side to lure Americans to the wrong side of the border. Whenever Americans were about to land, the Germans shot green flares. Aware of the trap, Robertson landed with caution. The plane stopped two hundred meters shy of German territory.

"To put it mildly, it was like a dream," Michel recalled of the landing. "The first words we heard in English as the Swiss soldiers marched us away from the plane were, 'For you the war is over!'" After Swiss soldiers secured the landing area, Robertson's crew was taken to a facility in Altenrhein and interrogated. Immediately classified as military internees, the men were confined to two floors of a guarded building. English-speaking Swiss officers stayed with them at all times. During the standard interrogation the crew offered only the officially sanctioned information: name, rank, and serial number. The navigator, who spoke fluent German and could understand conversations between their Swiss captors, soon realized that the Swiss had shot at their clearly disabled bomber deliberately in retaliation for the accidental bombing of Schaffhausen by other members of the 392d Bomb Group some weeks earlier. "The 392d Bomb Group didn't have a lot going for it as far as the Swiss were concerned," Michel recalled. The Swiss interrogators were trying to find out if anyone on the crew had been involved in the bombing of Schaffhausen because they wanted to take legal action of some kind. Robertson's crew refused to furnish anything other than their names, ranks, and serial numbers.

"We had been warned in England if we couldn't get our landing gear down we would be considered an enemy and they would shoot at us," said Sig Robertson, who returned to his native Savannah, Georgia, after the war to practice maritime law and customs law for more than twenty-five years. "We didn't have our landing gear down. But they knew there was no question we were in trouble. One engine was out and that the other was smoking. It was a matter of pride with them I guess."

After the interrogation ended, the Swiss Red Cross allowed the men to send telegrams to their families notifying them that they were interned in Switzerland and safe. Michel has remained grateful to the Swiss Red Cross for that act of kindness because the telegram reached his parents before the one from the American government stating that he had been reported missing in action.

• • •

James Mahaffey, navigator on the *Battlin' Cannon Ball/Super Ball*, flew his final mission on 18 March 1944 when his crew was sent to bomb the aerodrome in Landsberg, Germany, a few miles west of Munich.[41] The crew completed the bomb run without problems. Just past Munich, however, a horde of FW-190s—twenty-five were later reported —closed in tight. "I was up in the astrodome calling out the fighter attacks when the bombardier, Dick Davis, called to me on the interphone, 'Jim you better get down on your gun. Fighters coming in at one o'clock.' I did, just as a burst of fire went past where my head had been seconds before and knocked out the pilot's controls. We also lost our hydraulic pressure, fuel lines, and number one and two engines."

With one wing low, "Woody," the pilot, exchanged places with Russ Ward, the copilot, to assume the flight controls. "A rather hairy situation," Mahaffey said. "With gas lines out and two engines gone we knew we would never make it back to England. So we set our course for Switzerland. Enemy fighters all around. Just before we were hit, a plane ahead of us had blown up and we flew through some of its debris. That will always be engraved in my memory."

The lone bomber no longer had the protection afforded by a group, and the enemy fighters swarmed around it. The crew prayed and prepared to use the escape hatch. Then, for some reason, the yellow-nosed FW-190s departed just as Lake Constance came into view. Suddenly another plane intercepted. It looked like an Me-109, a German fighter.

"Should we fire at him? No, no. He's wagging his wings and waving to us. As he slides in next to us, we can see the Red Cross on his fuse-lage. It's a Swiss Air Force fighter flying up to escort us down. With that the war was over—almost," Mahaffey said he remembered thinking. Mahaffey also recalled that the bombardier could not destroy the bombsight even after pounding it on the floor. So he dropped it out through the escape hatch at about eight thousand feet.

"On coming to a stop at Zürich's Dübendorf airfield, we were imme-diately surrounded by armed guards, searched, and taken into inter-rogation. We gave the usual name, rank, and serial number routine. It didn't matter, the Swiss knew all about us. Then we were taken to a Swiss resort hotel at Neuchâtel for two weeks of quarantine. We had a spaghetti dinner and that night we celebrated our good fortune by drinking all the wine and champagne we could hold."

...

Clinton O. Norby, born in Salt Lake City, Utah, would fly only two mis-sions over Europe. Norby was the flight engineer and top turret gunner on *Touchy Tess* of the 351st Bomb Group, 509th Bomb Squadron, 8th Air Force. "Before we reached Holland, the navigator (Brown) in-formed the gunners that we could test fire our guns out over the North Sea," Norby remembered. "Right after that, we picked up our fighter cover. They never flew too close to us but we could follow them by their contrails. This, to me, was a very beautiful sight, as the trails were above us, to our right and left and below us."[42]

After test-firing their guns the crew donned their flak suits, except for Genetti and Norby, who could not wear the protection in the turrets because of the cramped space. Designed to protect the men from shrapnel, the suits covered just the trunk of the body, leaving the arms and legs exposed. Helmets were also worn. One of Norby's duties was to verify that the bomb bay doors were open after the bombardier called on the intercom to say he had opened them. The procedure called for Norby to check them with a hand crank to make sure they were fully open and the stops were making contact. To crank the doors apart, Norby had to lie on his stomach with his upper body in the bomb bay and his lower body on the base of the upper turret, in the rear part of the flight deck. "This is the first time I had ever had to crank the doors open, and I never realized how hard they were to crank," Norby recalled. "When they were about a third of the way open I heard an explosion and the bomb bay filled with black smoke."

The wires that led to the bomb shackles dangled and smoked. Someone shook Norby's feet, and he crawled back into the cockpit. There stood Brown, the navigator and first-aid man, between the pilot and copilot. "The sight almost turned me sick. Brown was wearing his flying helmet and oxygen mask but not his flak helmet. All across his forehead was blood; it was running down over both eyes and the bridge of his nose and then onto his oxygen mask. The blood was freezing and building up over his eyes so he could not see. Brown also had a number of head wounds, which were bleeding and looking very messy with blood running down his neck in front of his ears and behind the ears. Brown was such a mess; I didn't know what to do."

Brown told Norby to sprinkle sulfa powder on his wounds and dress them with a compress bandage. Then the crew began to inventory the aircraft's damage. The plane sustained most of the damage on the left side; the flak had shattered the pilot's windshields, both front and side. The rest of the formation had left them behind, and no fighter support would be coming–the radio was not working. The number three engine had stopped. The number two engine had to be feathered. Engines one and four had oil leaks. Eventually both of those engines would freeze up and there would be no power left for flying. The flight controls were damaged. The oxygen system was also broken, but the plane was losing altitude so fast that it hardly mattered.

All the while the pilot, copilot, and navigator were frantically trying to determine their location. Then someone called on the intercom. Four enemy fighters were outside at three o'clock high. Norby climbed into the top turret and turned on the power, gun switch, and gun sight. He hand-charged the guns. "Then for some reason, I looked out at nine o'clock high and saw the four fighters. I called on the intercom that the fighters were at nine o'clock and not three o'clock as reported. It turned out there were four at each position. They were out of range of our guns. The eight fighters were going into what is called a pursuit curve. I was so afraid that my knees were actually knocking together."

Norby tried in vain to fire his guns as the enemy planes neared. He recognized some of the approaching aircraft as German Me-109s with yellow noses. Then a surprising thing happened. "When the enemy planes came closer and still didn't fire on us, I wondered why they had a red square with a white cross painted on the fuselage. This was not a German marking but still they had Me-109s and some other type of plane that we didn't recognize (later on we found out they were Swiss Moran fighters). By now the eight planes were above, below, at our sides, in front, and in back of us. The one in front put his landing gear down, which was a signal for us to do the same and follow him. However, our landing gear would not go down." The plane crashed. The impact gravely injured the pilot, Charles Abplanalp. He died shortly afterward.

"When I first saw the soldiers, all I could think of was that we were in Germany. Their uniforms looked German; they all talked German; and they were men in their fifties or above, which fit the idea that they were members of the home guard and too old for regular service." The resemblance in dress and comportment between Swiss and German soldiers confused many new arrivals.

Louis Joseph, a right waist gunner on a B-17 with the 447th Bomb Group, 710th Bomb Squadron, 8th Air Force, was certain he had landed in Germany when Swiss soldiers first approached his downed plane. "Upon landing I do remember the bombardier rushing around the craft checking that the items to be destroyed or disabled had been taken care of by us," said Joseph.[43] "I looked out and saw this vehicle approaching with men and bristling with arms. I thought we were in 'Der Deutschland' and really a sense of hidden fear swelled within me as the Swiss looked exactly as the Nazis to me. The fear arose from lack of information. They were armed to the hilt. We were ordered to throw out our gear, and the pile looked like a dark-colored igloo."

Donald Sellar was fooled as well.[44] Sellar, born in Worcester, Massachusetts, in 1921, had always wanted to fly. He volunteered for the navy but failed the eye exam. Determined to fly, he considered going to Holy Cross, where they were testing men to become glider pilots. However, to qualify one had to first be rejected by the Air Corps. To his surprise, Sellar qualified for the Air Corps in 1942 and was attached to the 385th Bomb Group, 550th Bomb Squadron, 8th Air Force, and sent to England.

"I remember being in a Quonset hut the first night there with other officers (pilot, navigator, bombardier) and four other officers from another crew. They were telling us how rough it was and the next day another officer came in and was telling us how lonely we would be for awhile, that two crews, one which was in our hut, had been shot down."

On his sixth mission, to bomb the Messerschmitt plant in Augsburg, Sellar's bomber was shot down. "We had dropped our bombs and turned left and the AA guns from Munich got us. We were really shot up by flak over Munich and only had about thirty seconds to decide to go into Switzerland. The Swiss really shot at us, when we crossed into their airspace. No one expected that. They didn't like us. Two weeks before we were shot down the United States had bombed Schaff-hausen. I had thought it was a mistake at the time; now I'm not so sure. The Swiss AA was shooting at us even though we had dropped our wheels. Swiss fighters came up (we thought they were Red Cross planes first) and we landed at Dübendorf."

After they landed, a big touring car filled with soldiers toting Tommy guns approached. The crew had no idea what a Swiss soldier looked like. The first thing they heard was, "For you the war is over." At first they thought the navigator had made a mistake and they had landed in Germany.

• • •

Leon Finneran, 457th Bomb Group, 748th Squadron, 8th Air Force, bailed out over the Alps on 12 July 1944 after two engines sustained flak damage. He was the only member of his crew interned in Switzer-land. The crash killed the pilot, copilot, navigator, and bombardier, and Germans captured the radio operator and the three gunners.[45]

"Kerr, the pilot, rang the 'bail-out' bell," Finneran later recalled. "The four in the back bailed out. A third engine began to throw oil. I suggested it was time to bail out as in a break in the clouds I saw we were below the peaks. I went to the nose hatch; Lindskoog was there also. The hatch looked small for me and the chute. I took off a boot and Lindskoog told me I'd break my foot landing. I left the other boot on and jumped. The chute opened and I heard the plane crash. I then saw I was headed for the side of a mountain. I tried to control direction but it was useless. The chute caught on the side of the mountain and slammed me against the side."

When Finneran regained consciousness, he still had the parachute's D ring clenched in his fist. He struggled to release the chute. He sat high on a mountain with snow all around. The clouds had dissipated, and he could see his ship burning across the valley. "On one side was a three- to four-thousand-foot sheer drop. On the other side was snow all the way down to the valley below." Finneran braced his back against the mountain and crab-walked across the snow. He made it to the valley and broke into a barn, where he slept out the night. The next morning he consulted his map and compass and started out again. Before long he found a cabin. "I'd had plenty to drink from numerous streams but no food. In the cabin were canned goods but I could not read the labels, so I remained hungry. My head hurt and I could walk only short distances without resting. I found a knife in a drawer and bunks with straw. I took the knife and laid down in a lower bunk. I was awakened by voices and the door opened. Three men entered dressed in uniforms. I thought they were German. I dropped the knife and showed my hands and said, 'I am an American.' They pointed to their uniform buttons showing the Swiss red field and white cross. They gave me cheese, wine, and raw bacon. One who was over fifty years old gave me his shoes and socks and another gave me his jacket. I was only two hundred yards from the German border." A few days later Finneran attended a funeral for Kerr, Levine, and Schilling. Lindskoog's body was recovered later and buried.

• • •

The nose art and nicknames of World War II's bombers have been celebrated in magazines, movies, and museum exhibits. No exception was one B-17 of the 401st Bomb Group, 615th Bomb Squadron. This Flying Fortress sported two names, *Umbriago* and *Freckles*. Painted on the pilot's side of the nose section, *Freckles* was depicted as a Rita Hayworth–type girl wearing a bathing suit. *Umbriago*, with a large head of

Jimmy Durante, was painted on the copilot's side of the nose. Flying inside the doubly named plane on 31 July 1944 to bomb Munich was one Penrose W. Reagan.[46]

Mishap marked the flight from the start. A tail wheel blew on take-off. The number two engine soon began throwing oil. Rather than drop their bombs and go around the target, 1st Lt. Jay Ossiander decided to fly across the target through heavy flak with three engines. Then the number two engine would not feather; it just kept going back into high pitch. Soon it lost all of its oil and seized. The violently rotating propeller stripped the gears in the engine until it rotated freely with considerable vibration.

By this time *Freckles/Umbriago* straggled behind the other Fortresses, which had gone ahead to bomb the target. Until they lost the formation Reagan's plane had been flying in Purple Heart corner. He saw a B-17 from another bomb group explode about four hundred yards off to his right. Then the propeller on the number three engine failed. Maintaining altitude was nearly impossible now because two of the propellers had frozen in the high-pitch position. This produced a lot of drag. The severe vibration set up by the two windmilling propellers added to the difficulty. Clearly the plane would not make it back across the English Channel. As the situation deteriorated they set a course for Yugoslavia. It soon became obvious that this too was futile, and the pilot set a course for Switzerland.

"When we came across the Alps it was completely overcast and we had no idea what was under the overcast, although we could see peaks around us through the overcast," Reagan said. "Fortunately, ahead of us we could see an opening in the overcast. We went for broke and went down through it. By the grace of the greater power that looks over those who are dumb enough to fly combat, we came out in a valley." The crew, still with no idea where they were, hurriedly began throwing equipment out of the aircraft. At about twelve hundred to fifteen hundred feet off the deck someone warned that there were Me-109s at nine o'clock.

"I popped back into the upper turret and swung my guns on them. At this time the closest 109 flipped its wings up so we could see the Swiss cross, then proceeded to drop his wheels and motioned for us to follow him. The fighters took us to Dübendorf airfield at Zürich where we landed. It was then that we found out one of our main landing gear tires had been shot out. This tire, plus the tail wheel tire that blew on takeoff, made the landing a bit dicey since the aircraft wanted to ground loop. However, control was maintained and the powers that be smiled on us again."

. . .

Peter Lysek, 456th Bomb Group, 747th Bomb Squadron, 15th Air Force, participated in thirty combat missions in the European theater. On 20 July 1944 enemy action disabled his plane, *Bear Baby,* but the entire crew bailed out and landed safely in Switzerland. The boy from Summerdale, Alabama, would later be awarded a citation from Lt. Gen. Ira Eaker.[47]

The morning of his final mission Lysek had an early reveille at about 3:00 A.M. The target that morning was Friedrichshafen. After the briefing the crews went to their assigned airplanes. As aerial engineer Lysek was responsible for checking the plane and making sure everything was in top shape for combat. "As the officers came back from briefing we talked about the target. And were sort of jittery about it. Before takeoff I told the pilot I felt very uneasy about the whole deal as I never did before," Lysek later wrote in his wartime log. The fourth plane to take off that morning, *Bear Baby* led the 704th Bomb Wing.

It took forty-five minutes for the bombers to get in formation. After about an hour and a half Lysek began to transfer the fuel out of the auxiliary tanks into the main fuel cells. He also checked the flight instruments. He put on his oxygen mask as he went back through the bomb bay to his gun station in the waist of the ship. Climbing to high altitude, *Bear Baby* neared the northern coast of Italy.

As the plane crossed over the snow-covered Alps of north Italy, the navigator, 1st Lt. Abraham Thompson, called over the interphone indicating the Brenner Pass below. "For the first time in combat I snapped on my parachute, although we still had another half hour to the target. As we neared Germany I put on my flak suit. May seem strange, but seems like something kept telling me we were going to be shot down," Lysek wrote.

Yet everything seemed quiet as the bombers passed the mountains and the land leveled out into Germany—quiet except for a half dozen Luftwaffe fighters. But there was no incident. Lysek could now see Lake Constance. Just beyond lay Friedrichshafen. The bombardier, Thomas J. Athanassion, opened the bomb bay doors and the plane began the bomb run. The flak started bursting a little ahead and a little above the aircraft. Then it got closer. "The next thing we knew the ship rocked from a burst under no. 2 engine," Lysek recalled. About a minute after the first hit the ship sustained two more direct hits, one in the bomb bay. The other, between the fuselage and the number three engine, tore two great holes in the fuel tank. Gasoline poured out as if from a faucet, covering the bombs and center of the ship with raw gasoline. The gasoline quickly covered the crew in the waist and started to travel up to the cockpit. Lysek gave the alarm to the pilot, William E. Newhouse. "With nearly a shaky voice I called again that we had a direct hit in the bomb bay and that gasoline was covering everything."

The pilot ordered the bombs dropped immediately. The bombardier hit the target. Newhouse recognized the danger the gas leak posed but ordered the men to stay aboard the ship until they cleared the Swiss border. He assured his crew they would make it to Switzerland. He also ordered the men to cut all the switches and feathered all the propellers except number two, which would not feather; it had been hit by flak.

"Everyone expected the ship to explode any second," Lysek said.

It would have if the pilot had not ordered all the switches cut off or if another close burst of flak had ignited the gasoline and fumes. As it crossed the lake, *Bear Baby* dropped down from twenty-one thousand feet to fourteen thousand feet. The crew began bailing out with a final word of good luck from the pilot.

"We started to hit the silk. No one seemed to be too much afraid," Lysek recalled. First went the tail gunner, S.Sgt. William E. Key; then the ball gunner, S.Sgt. Jefferson B. Brown. "Then it was my turn. If ever I thought I would croak of heart failure it was then," Lysek said. "Just before I jumped I tucked my G.I. shoes under my harness. Thank god. Later I sure needed them for walking. As I was ready to go, I put my feet over the escape hatch, which the wind blew back up, to my face. Seeing that wouldn't do I crawled over the hatch. And hesitated for a moment nearly losing my nerve. But through my mind flashed the thought of seeing so many of the ships in the same conditions we were in explode. And the fellows inside didn't have the chance a snowball did in hell. So, here was my 50-50 chance to live or die. I fell out head first."

The airstream from the ship turned Lysek for a few loops. Gritting his teeth, he pulled the ripcord and waited for the chute to open. "But no dice. Nothing was happening. And that ground was coming up fast. I didn't even have the sensation of falling. I dropped the ripcord. Pulling at the parachute trying to get it open. After a few tugs it flowered out above me. And what a beautiful flower I'll never see again to my dying day." He had dropped from fourteen thousand feet to four thousand before his chute opened. Lysek saw other bombers in formation dropping bombs on the target. He saw the flashes. He heard the noise. Then he saw *Bear Baby* crash and explode and a column of black smoke rise to the skies.

• • •

According to American records, 166 U.S. aircraft entered Switzerland between August 1943 and April 1945. The Swiss listed 167 U.S. aircraft entering Switzerland. The difference, as noted by Roy Thomas in his book *Haven, Heaven, and Hell,* is a P-47 lost on 4 February 1945. The Swiss list includes this aircraft and its pilot. The U.S. records do not.[48]

The last American aircraft to arrive in Switzerland landed on 20 April 1945, Adolf Hitler's birthday. *Princess O'Rourke,* a B-17G of the 301st Bomb Group, was with the 15th Air Force on a mission to bomb strategic points along the Brenner Pass.[49] Flak over the target damaged the Fortress, and the ship fell behind the rest of the formation. Swiss fighters intercepted the plane on its way and escorted it to Dübendorf. Three weeks later, Germany surrendered and the war in Europe ended.

4

LIKE ANGELS FROM THE SKY

Courage! he said, and pointed toward the land,
This mounting wave will roll us shoreward soon.
In the afternoon they came unto a land
In which it seemed always afternoon.
"The Lotos-Eaters," ALFRED, LORD TENNYSON

The strange thing about internment in Switzerland was that the fliers, most of whom had been under the tension of combat for quite some time, found themselves virtually plucked out of the air and plunked into a state of enforced idleness under conditions that fluctuated between privilege (by war standards) and privation.

By the end of the war a network of 768 camps for nearly 300,000 refugees and other foreign military personnel laced Switzerland. The sites for most of the military internment camps, principally situated in villages, were selected for their remoteness amid natural boundaries such as mountains, rivers, and ravines. While facilities in these camps were minimal and confining, and armed guards were present twenty-four hours a day, life there was relatively civilized.

"We were ultimately sent to Adelboden. While there I was always treated well and enjoyed first-class facilities at the Nevada Palace Hotel. It was very nice compared to the tents we lived in in North Africa," said Norris King, a waist gunner on the B-17F *Sugarfoot*.[1]

"First-class" in this case meant unheated rooms, few opportunities to bathe, scanty meals, and little support from the U.S. government. Yes, there were opportunities for recreation. And yes, there were good times, even jovial times. The American airmen were resilient and resourceful, able to create fun and make the best of their situation. But ultimately the men in Adelboden were prisoners in what amounted to a mile-long prison. In time the fairy-tale background, complete with snow-capped peaks and cowbells ringing in the distance, took on an almost sinister aspect.

There were also American internees in Sweden. Like those in Switzerland, they were quartered in guest houses and health spas in villages in central Sweden: Rättvik, Korsnäs, Älvdalen, Loka, Gränna, and Mullsjö. Unlike Switzerland, however, there were very few restrictions on the American airmen except for a 10:00 P.M. curfew. Many of the crews in the Swedish camps worked with Swedes in aircraft maintenance units. Perhaps the most important difference was that Sweden repatriated American aviators as soon as possible, usually when there was room on a courier plane, and Switzerland did not.

In Switzerland, time yawned endlessly before the fliers, who tried to fill their days and create some structure in their lives. After breakfast the internees often gathered outside for exercise. Those eager to keep their minds sharp spent the rest of the morning attending a variety of classes that included history, language, and math. The afternoon and evening were left open. The captives' quarters in all the village camps were within walking distance of the ski slopes and walking paths. Most villages also had ice rinks or skating ponds. Internees could ski, ice skate, play baseball or ice hockey, walk, or simply while away the time in one of the local restaurants or bars–if they had money. And they took advantage of opportunities to meet and mingle with the local inhabitants.

"I remember at Christmas time, the local children were invited to our hotel to see the movie *Snow White and the Seven Dwarfs*. And I also remember loading a sled with gifts and taking it to a less fortunate family. I feel we were well accepted by the people of Adelboden. I was happy not to be flying combat missions and living in tents in North Africa," recalled King.

By the time King arrived in Switzerland, the camp system was well organized and running more or less smoothly. A post exchange and club system had been established. On credit, men could purchase alcoholic drinks, extra clothing, ski ensembles and equipment, watches, cameras, and other such items–things that helped make their imprisonment more bearable. The internees were permitted individual checking accounts with an American company, and the balances were transferred to the United States when they finally left Switzerland at the end of the war.

This orderliness was not evident when 1st Lt. Alva Geron, the pilot of *Death Dealer,* and his crew arrived. They were the first group of American aviators to be interned, and they found themselves treated as oddities. "To our advantage nobody knew what to do with us; neither the Swiss nor the Americans," Geron recalled of his Friday the thirteenth landing in April 1943.[2] "So we were treated as celebrities. It was a real experience." After the initial shock at seeing the plane crash, the villagers cheered the crew members as they emerged untouched. For the first several weeks Geron's crew made the rounds at various ladies' clubs answering questions about life in America. During the first few months he and his crew enjoyed a measure of congeniality and fellowship with the American legation that would not be experienced by later internees.

Adelboden, a remote five-hundred-year-old village in the Bernese Oberland, became the site of the principal American camp, Camp Maloney, named for the first U.S. flier to die in Switzerland. Before Adelboden became operational in 1944, U.S. fliers were lodged in the Hotels Bellevue at Macolin and Trois Sapins at Evilard. One winding road leads into Adelboden: mountains rise sharply on three sides of the village, and a ravine cuts off the fourth. In the 1940s farmers and one-horse carts traveled the road, which connects the village to Frutigen. Just as visitors who travel to Adelboden must do today, the arriving internees boarded a postal bus at the train station. Except through the valley road there is no way in or out of the four-thousand-foot-high village.

A group of other internees usually met the new crews as they stepped off the bus in Camp Maloney. They were always keen to see friends or familiar faces among the fresh batch of prisoners, but new faces were welcome, too. Most interned airmen were quartered in the Nevada Palace Hotel, a once grand structure overlooking the ravine that in the years before the war received many English tourists.

James Mahaffey, of the 351st Bomb Group, 511th Bomb Squadron, 8th Air Force, who landed on 18 March 1944, described the isolation of the hotel: "One entered from the street level which was the back door, but the main lobby was one floor below. There was no front door. Instead there was a thirty-foot picture window about fifteen feet high that looked out over a valley that seemed about two thousand feet to three thousand feet below us. The valley appeared to end just below the hotel. You could see clouds move up the valley and then they would just stop below the hotel. In fact, one day when I was looking out the window, the sun was shining on us, but looking down the slope, you could see it snowing."[3]

The onset of the war left Switzerland bare of tourists, but the hotels filled up once again when the internees began to arrive. The rooms were sparsely appointed. The Nevada Palace, like other hotels across the country, was kept unheated. In the winter months the water in the washbowls and toilets froze. The airmen often ate breakfast with gloved hands. Every ten days or so, usually in the afternoon, the hot water was turned on in the rooms. On that day everyone headed upstairs for a bath, anticipating a few rare moments of comfort. The tubs in the rooms were filled with hot water, and a flip of a coin determined who got the first soak. On more than one occasion no hot water came forth. "Getting dressed," Mahaffey remembered, "we went downstairs and discovered that the hot water was only on for two hours and since everybody had the water on at once, those above the first floor didn't get any water. Most of us couldn't have a bath."

Infrequent bathing and cold were not the only discomforts. Switzerland produced only about 50 percent of the food required for its population, depending for the rest on imports now largely at a standstill because of the war. To stretch food stores, extensive rationing had been introduced throughout the country on 12 November 1941. Military internees were restricted to about fifteen hundred calories a day, the same as soldiers serving in the Swiss Army. The daily rations were reduced on 22 September 1944: the daily allowance of bread was cut from 375 grams to 350 grams, meat was cut from 150 grams to 50 grams, sugar from 40 grams to 20 grams, and chocolate from 17.1 grams to 3.5 grams.

The Swiss authorities devised rules to prevent citizens from eating more than their share or hoarding basic foodstuffs like bread and sugar. For example, recognizing that stale bread was far less appealing than fresh-baked, they made a rule that bread could be sold only two days after it was baked. No meat could be set on the table on Wednesdays and Fridays. By March 1941 butter was limited to ten ounces per person per month. Chocolate, cheese, tea and coffee, and even dog food were also tightly controlled. Bread rationing began in October 1942. At first, Swiss citizens were allotted three thousand calories a day; in 1941 the number was cut to twenty-four hundred.

For the prisoners, breakfast was little more than ersatz coffee or hot chocolate and a roll. Typical dinner fare consisted of watery soup and potatoes that had been harvested in the town square. Once a week the men were served meat; most remember it being either goat or blood sausage. Accustomed as they were to U.S. Army standards of between twenty-one hundred and twenty-three hundred calories a day, many of the men shed a considerable amount of weight.

Joyce "Jake" Freeman, of the 492d Bomb Group, 857th Bomb Squad, 8th Air Force, left Switzerland in much worse shape than when he arrived, said his son Ron Freeman. "Jake was very healthy and in good physical condition upon arrival in Switzerland. His diet while interned in Switzerland consisted of one egg per week and water also what they could scrape up, mostly weed soup. When he returned to the USA he weighed about ninety pounds and suffered from near starvation."[4]

Although there were areas in which the Swiss authorities might have made life better for the internees if they had chosen to do so, they had little control over the availability of food. Switzerland had to feed its own population in addition to the refugees constantly streaming across its borders, and there was little arable land on which to grow food. Starting in 1940 the landscape began to be altered. The amount of available farmland almost doubled when 90 square kilometers of forest were felled, 480 square kilometers of marshland were drained, and the livestock population was reduced so pastures could yield more crops.[5] The Swiss raised food on any land that would grow it; rose gardens were turned into potato plots, parks into vegetable gardens.

The 26 May 1944 issue of *Marking Time* noted that the internees were taking an active part in the farming: "If you take a walk around Adelboden these days you will see quite different scenes to those witnessed a month or so ago. Then, the streets were filled with Evades, carrying skis on their shoulders, on their way to the ski lift. Now you will see British—and also Americans—busy digging fields and planting potatoes. Here and there you will see groups resting and having a picnic on the grass. They will be eating bread and cheese and drinking coffee. The meal is part payment for their work. The Yanks reckon that their present occupation is rather different from their recent job of handling giant Flying Fortresses!"

The poor diet led to long-term health problems for many interned servicemen. Nearly half the camp population had trouble with their teeth and gums, but few received proper medical or dental treatment. "I was able to see a good many things that were screwy," recalled T.Sgt. Edward L. Pribek, 705th Bomb Squad, 446th Bomb Group, 8th Air Force.[6] "Such as some of the men became ill due to the inadequate diet we were forced to eat, nearly half the men had trouble with their teeth and gums and none received proper medical or dental treatment. Some men who were very ill had to wait months to be sent to hospitals."

The U.S. government was not oblivious to the situation. In the fall of 1944 Dr. Jack E. Torin of the U.S. Army Medical Corps inspected the medical, dental, housing, sanitation, and dietary conditions of Americans in Switzerland. His report, dated 24 October 1944 (with an addendum on 2 November 1944), found the men's living and sleeping conditions to be excellent. But that is where the praise stopped. "Soap was only available to Swiss with coupons," Dr. Torin continued. "Dental treatment is poor. Dentists when and if available refuse to give more than one gum treatment per man. . . . Medical care by civilian or military doctors was with indifference and the fees were exorbitant. Hospitalization varied in quality and efficiency. Men are transferred two or three times and weeks elapse before disposition. Due to confinement and lack of activities, the men are notably restless. A large number are drinking excessively. The Swiss Internment Commission for Americans allows a barely subsistence diet even by continental standards. It's surprising a number of internees state they are receiving a balanced and nutritious diet. However, they suffer from bleeding gums, trench mouth and have other symptoms of vitamin and dietary deficiencies."

Complaints to the Swiss elicited near silence. Documents and post-war interviews indicate that the lack of medical care spread beyond the failure to treat malnutrition. The Swiss withheld care on many occasions for injuries sustained during landings and in one case when an internee desperately needed psychiatric care.

In September 1944 S.Sgt. Charles G. Danko sustained a knee injury when he parachuted into Switzerland. The knee steadily worsened, but according to a memo from Capt. Lloyd A. Free of the U.S. legation in Bern, Danko did not receive adequate medical attention, much less the treatment by a specialist that he really needed.[7] And T.Sgt. Vincent V. Hayes, who had broken his foot while participating in athletic activities at the Olympic course in Lausanne earlier in July, still had not had the break set. After repeated requests were made to Swiss authorities, Hayes was finally sent to Bern for treatment. But the doctors there simply removed the cast, wrapped a bandage around his foot without setting the break, and sent Hayes back to Adelboden.

"It is incomprehensible to us how this could possibly have occurred," Captain Free fumed in the legation's memo. "Dr. von Deschwanden at Adelboden fears that by now it will be necessary to have an operation to clear up the difficulty." Calling the treatment of the two men "gross neglect" on the part of the Swiss, Captain Free requested an investigation into the matter to determine who was responsible for the mistreatment of the internees. After that, he said, the authorities should arrange for a "thoroughly competent specialist" to examine Hayes and Danko."[8]

An answer arrived on 5 September 1944. Without ever examining the two men in question, Colonel Girar, the chief of the service for health internment, wrote that Danko's knee was healing and a specialist need not intervene. The Swiss further insinuated that the sergeant had feigned his symptoms solely for the chance to travel out of his internment camp. Colonel Girar acknowledged that Hayes suffered from a bad fracture but denied that an operation was necessary to repair the injury. Girar concluded: "The two cases were taken care of promptly and with the best methods . . . in a general manner, it would be desirable that internees, in their interest, better follow medical discipline."[9]

The internees who did receive medical attention often had to arrange their own transportation between their camp and the hospital. Sometimes that meant a trek on foot or a ride in a horse cart. Such was the situation that led to a lifelong friendship between Jack Dowd and Rolly Colgate. The two met on the road back to camp from a hospital in Cham where Dowd had just been operated on for appendicitis.

"Finally after the pain went on and on and on they let me go to the hospital," Dowd recalled. "It was hard to get medical care. A guard had to be able to take you there and back. There was no transportation and you had to walk each way. I was brought back to prison on a sleigh with two guards after the operation. The platforms were lousy to lie on; there was no sack of straw. I had anger but what good does it do? At the time I hated the U.S. as much as I hated Switzerland. But not now."[10]

Perhaps the worst incident of medical mistreatment concerned James D. Stotts, the left waist gunner on a B-17 that landed in Switzerland on 24 April 1944 while on a mission to bomb Oberpfaffenhofen. According to Hugh Riley, an engineer on the B-24 *Commando,* Stotts's problems started with the trauma of the plane crash and worsened over time. Stotts became obsessed with the desire to write a book. He kept a diary in which he wrote about "the boys on my crew, who collectively understand me at this moment as no other men in the world can possibly do, these men tell me to rest and not think."[11]

His fellow internees grew worried over Stotts's increasingly unstable behavior and were able to get him admitted to a psychiatric hospital in Bern on 4 September 1944. According to testimony from his crew, his behavior grew ever more disturbing after he was returned to Wengen on 29 September. Stotts's crewmates tried once again to get him hospitalized, but the Swiss said there was "no medical available," recalled Robert Hiller.[12] Stotts became suicidal, threatening to jump out a window. One crew member or another constantly stayed by his side in hope of averting a tragedy. But in the early hours of 4 October 1944, as the two crewmen who shared his room were sleeping, Stotts, ranting about the Germans and screaming for his mother and sister, dove headfirst out of the window to his death.[13]

After the war, one of the men who was interned with Stotts reported that he never received proper attention despite his obvious need for it: "Stotz [sic] should never [have] died, he was in need of hospitalization before his tragic end. Stotz was in the next room and Walker had a miserable night, before the tragedy occurred. The last word I heard from Stotz was 'the Germans almost got me again.' It happened about 6:25 and he lay till 11:30 before they took him off the rock. He died, I believe, a day and a half later, on October 4th, I believe."

S.Sgt. Gerald W. Swindell's 12 July 1945 postwar account, later forwarded to the director of the War Crimes Office, offered confirmation of Stotts's mistreatment: "One internee was out of his mind because his crew and plane was shot up badly on their mission over Germany before arriving in Switzerland. He was shortly confined to a hospital at Bern, Switzerland, but was released within a day or two. When he arrived back at our camp, he was still in an insane condition. At night he would stand in his window and call for his Mother and Sister all night. The third night he walked through the window and fell three floors to the ground below. The Swiss Commandant was living in the same hotel and knew the condition of this boy. This boy died two (2) days later from injuries due to the fall. Should have had better medical care."[14]

• • •

The boredom, monotony, and inactivity gnawed at the fliers, who tried almost everything to relieve the tedium.

Joseph Piemonte was born in 1923 in Salem, Massachusetts, and answered to "Giuseppe" throughout his boyhood. He enlisted in the air force soon after Pearl Harbor and became a ball turret gunner with the 384th Bomb Group, 545th Bomb Squadron, 8th Air Force. Piemonte's B-17G, *Frostie*, landed in Dübendorf on 24 April 1944 after completing a mission to Oberpfaffenhofen. "We were concerned about leaking gasoline when [we] landed. We had lost two engines, so we ran out of the plane as soon as it stopped into the arms of Swiss military."[15] The men were taken into a barrack at Dübendorf and interrogated, quarantined for two weeks in Bern, and then sent to Adelboden. "In Adelboden we were encouraged to offer each other courses," Piemonte recalled (much as he does now as part of the Salem State College Institute for Learning in Retirement). Piemonte took math and the violin. "But it didn't last long, there wasn't enough interest among the internees."

George Michel of the *Georgia Peach*, who was quartered in the Regina Hotel in Wengen, said the Red Cross had arranged for a couple of professors to run a school for any internee who cared to attend.[16] He took courses in French, economics, and history. Another diversion was attending the "Bellevue Bivouac," a discussion group with Professor Luigi de Simone, who lived in the Bellevue Hotel. Michel said he read more than thirty books during his time in Switzerland; *The Prisoner of Zenda* by Anthony Hope was a favorite.

Endless card games, rounds of drinking, classes, and photography were some of the other pastimes the men indulged in to relieve the tedium of internee life. "The biggest thing to do was drink and that grew tiresome. So I made a darkroom in my room to have something to do," said Rolly Colgate, an engineer from the 389th Bomb Group, 566th Bomb Squadron, 8th Air Force.[17] His carefully bound photo album is filled with black-and-white photos of different Americans, landscapes, and skyscapes of Adelboden. "I was happy to have been in Switzerland and not Germany. I was there for eleven months. But it got to be a little old." Eventually Colgate tried to escape with the help of a woman he and his buddies knew from the town. She offered to help Colgate reach Basel, her hometown. Colgate had no problem leaving Adelboden, but some miles away he ran into a roadblock at Interlaken. He wore civilian clothes, but his GI shoes were like neon lights flashing "escaping internee." Colgate was caught and shipped to Hünenberg, a penitentiary camp. Every month Colgate's mother sent cigarettes through the Red Cross, which he gave away to other prisoners because he didn't smoke. Colgate finally succeeded in escaping and was honorably discharged from the U.S. Air Force on 11 July 1945.

Boredom also propelled T.Sgt. Edward M. Winkle, a radio operator in the 445th Bomb Group, 702d Bomb Squadron, 8th Air Force, into action. Winkle's plane, *Pistol Packing Mama,* crash-landed near Zürich on 18 March 1944 after losing two engines and hydraulic power. "A large crowd was watching, and as we neared the ground our landing gear went through high tension wires which fell on two small boys on bicycles, killing them," Winkle wrote. "We will never forget them."[18]

Swiss soldiers immediately surrounded the plane and led the crew away to the train station. Winkle was taken to Adelboden and the Hotel Bernerhof. "As the summer went by and we were getting more bored, four softball teams were organized, one from each of the living quarters. We played a schedule, and then had playoffs. Our team was beaten in the championship. Then the boredom set in again," Winkle wrote. "I listened to the news of the invasion and the attempt to assassinate Hitler. I also watched the U.S. 7th Army clear the border between France and Switzerland with interest, and I wanted out. News began to get around that a few of the fellows had gotten out, but the Swiss were getting wise, and if they caught you, you went to the concentration camp at Wauwilermoos. But it was worth a try."

Winkle and his friend T.Sgt. Samuel R. Simms of the 351st Bomb Group, 511th Bomb Squadron, 8th Air Force, notified the officers in charge of the escape committee that they intended to get out. They bought civilian clothing and left on 20 September 1944. Winkle succeeded in escaping and served one more year in the USAAF. He was honorably discharged on 2 November 1945.

• • •

Internment began with a period of quarantine. After interrogation most fliers were sent to Neuchâtel, a town in the western part of the country near the French border, for about two weeks. The men were housed in a chalet perched on a mountain about three thousand feet above the city in an area called Chaumont. Airmen frequently heard the thunder of bombings on the other side of the border.

There were no books or reading materials in quarantine. One internee recalled that one deck of cards circulated among all the crews. Twice a day the guards would escort the airmen for a walk through town. Stepping out of the confines of the hotel gave the men a chance to taste Swiss village life, perhaps have a drink in a café or sample a pastry. They could window shop at the many souvenir shops and jewelry stores; with no tourists coming, the local merchants eagerly eyed the internees as potential customers. Most stores made it a point to display signs in the windows advertising English-speaking clerks.

It was during quarantine that the newly arrived crews first had the occasion to meet Brig. Gen. Barnwell Rhett Legge, the military attaché at the U.S. legation in Bern and the officer nominally in command of the interned American airmen. Legge, a veteran of World War I, had been living in Switzerland prior to the war and was called on to serve in this role. Nearly always costumed in a U.S. Calvary officer's uniform, jodhpurs, and shiny leather leggings, the corpulent general admonished the internees to obey the rules in Switzerland and not to attempt escape. Legge was a stickler for rules and regulations, and he and his subordinates in the military attaché's office inundated the internees with memos concerning everything from proper attire to saluting.

On 15 April 1944, for example, Lt. Col. Alfred R. W. de Jong, Legge's executive officer, wrote: "Since interned military personnel of the United States are in a position analogous to that of prisoners of war (of Article 11, Hague Convention 1907), the rendering of salutes to Swiss officers is mandatory and will be strictly observed. By command of Brigadier General Legge."

A 19 August 1944 memo from the Palace Hotel in Adelboden written by Capt. John J. Stols reiterated the order: "1. In the past the army regulation regarding saluting of our own officers has not been enforced at this camp. This army regulation, also a military courtesy, will be observed by all personnel of this command. 2. All enlisted men will salute all officers and all junior officers will salute senior officers. 3. Even though on detached service, you are still in the U.S. Army. By order of Captain Cardenas."

Unfortunately, the legation personnel largely confined themselves to enforcing discipline and did little to work with the Swiss authorities to improve conditions for the internees. "The treatment by the American legation in Bern was in no way helpful and often antagonistic," recalled 1st Lt. Arthur F. Glasier Jr., pilot of *So What?* which landed on 6 September 1943.[19]

• • •

According to General Guisan's policies concerning internment set forth in his 1940 memo, punishment, if necessary, was to be meted out in the camps. Internees were never to be sent to prison.[20] The Swiss deviated significantly from this policy and from many others as well. Internees were imprisoned in municipal jails for minor offenses such as breaking curfew and were sent to brutal penitentiary camps for months for attempting to escape. They were sometimes denied medical treatment, and their Red Cross packages were often withheld.

"The Swiss authorities and populace were very mercenary and we paid through the nose for whatever we wanted and could get," T.Sgt.

Milton R. Epstein, 446th Bomb Group, 8th Air Force, recalled. "The American Legation either had its eyes closed or its hands tied, for they did nothing for us. It was very difficult to get to a doctor and many boys suffered unnecessarily with improper and insufficient medical attention."[21]

First Lt. Bill H. Rutherford, a B-17 copilot, got into trouble for a curfew violation in Wengen. On 6 November 1944 Rutherford and his band had come from Adelboden to play in Wengen. "We played from 8 o'clock until 9.45, because the men have to be in at 2200 hours. After having finished playing, we went down all together to the Bernerhof to have a drink and sandwiches. Just before 2330 hours Lt. Meyer came down to the Bernerhof . . . [and] told us that we have no right to stay out after 11 o'clock."[22] While Rutherford got off with a minor reprimand, others ended up in jail for their indiscretions.

S.Sgt. Alfred V. Fairall, 68th Bomb Squadron, 44th Bomb Group, 8th Air Force: "Two days later [after flak forced them to land on 18 March 1944] we were taken to the Adelboden Camp, where our stay was not a bad one, but by no means a pleasant one. We received fifteen francs every ten days. We had nice hotel rooms and a movie theater, set up by the Americans, showing two pictures a week. We had a curfew, which we had to be in our hotels at 10:00 hrs. On weekdays and 10:30 hrs. on Sat. nights. Failure to comply with this meant five to fifteen days in Frutigen jail."[23]

From press censorship to mail censorship, evidence of Swiss cooperation with the Germans was apparent in even the smallest aspects of the internees' daily routine. A Swiss journalist and ski instructor, André F. Moillen, was brought before a tribunal in 1945 for questioning the treatment of American internees in Les Diablerets, a penitentiary camp. In *Diableries*, a local paper, he had written: "Here, in our little station, we have seen the internees treated in a scandalous manner, none of whom I know are criminals, frauds, or other. . . . What are the reasons our high authorities are doing this?"[24] In addition Moillen had written about the unevenness of punishment for internees caught trying to escape: a German officer was sentenced to ten days, an Italian officer to fifteen days, and a U.S. officer to between forty-five and seventy-five days. When the tribunal asked Moillen the goal of his article, he responded that he hoped to make things better.

Keeping in touch with family or friends was possible for internees, but their families were reminded that mail and packages addressed to Switzerland were subject to censorship by both American and German censors.[25]

• • •

Although the internees traded gossip with one another and the villagers, there was a dearth of information regarding world events. In an effort to remedy this, British evadees Lt. Col. Desmond Young and Capt. Peter Lewis started an internee newspaper, *Marking Time*, which was published by Vogt & Schild in Solothurn. The twelve-page weekly featured news of the war and of Allied internees in other camps as well as many illustrations and photos and a running comic strip called *Eric the Evade*. The paper also reveled in the rivalry between British and American internees. Although originally intended for British readers, it had a considerable readership among USAAF internees. Civilians were not permitted to buy the paper, which was published between 26 May 1944 and 16 September 1944, when repatriation for the British internees seemed imminent.

Always interested in news from home, the internees closely followed the 1944 presidential elections. While in Davos, 2d Lt. Robert Reno, 467th Bomb Group, 798th Bomb Squadron, 8th Air Force, and Mark Fortune and William Etheridge decided to send a telegram to President Franklin D. Roosevelt. Much to their surprise Roosevelt replied by letter. The original letter now hangs in Reno's home.

Music offered another escape from the monotony. Some internees received musical instruments from the YMCA and formed bands. The nine-piece "Melody Men" and the "Rhythm Stylists" were among the bands that introduced Switzerland to swing. "It was so new for the people of Adelboden to have this kind of music. Swing. Modern. The 'Lucky Strike' cigarettes. It was another world," said Margrit Thüller, a lifelong Adelboden resident.[26]

The bands received rave reviews in *Marking Time,* and articles chronicled their frequent performances. For example: "Adelboden has just enjoyed a spot of dancing. The 'Wil' Band played for four nights in succession at the Grand Hotel. On the last night there were cabaret turns. All four nights were well attended, particularly the last which was a great success. The hall was packed and Adelboden girls turned out in full force. Prize and spot dances helped to make the evening more enjoyable."[27]

The 14 July 1944 edition of the paper reported that "'the Rhythm Stylists,' a hot swing band composed of fourteen Interned American Airmen have just opened their season to the public in the public dance hall of the Palace Hotel in Davos-Platz. The hall was filled to capacity, which goes to show that the public appreciated the talents of the band. Several numbers were encored and special requests were granted. A swell time was had by all. S/Sgt. P. Merletti, who is the leader of the band, also goes to town on the trumpet. He organized the Rhythm Stylists two months ago in Adelboden and through hard work and much patience has whipped them into the music makers they are. We expect to hear more about these Rhythm Stylists."

The newspaper, the band, and sports all helped foster a sense of community among the internees, a community sometimes bawdy and boisterous and sometimes gentle and generous. The Americans showed Mickey Mouse cartoons to the Swiss, and at Christmas they gave the children sacks brimming with nuts and oranges, depriving themselves of food. To the exasperation of the village schoolmaster they also gave the children chewing gum.

George Michel remembered these contacts with the villagers as bright spots in otherwise uncertain circumstances: "On Christmas Eve some of us from the Bellevue Bivouac bunch made a Christmas gift basket and delivered it to a needy family in the village. Going into that family's chalet that evening was almost like going into what we see depicted as the manger scene on so many Christmas cards . . . it was a very dimly lit room and there in a cradle was what must have been a very new baby, or so it seemed to us at the time. It was quite an experience for each of us."

Caught in Switzerland like the Lotos-Eaters of Tennyson's poem, the men looked to holidays to bridge the real and figurative distances between home and the front. The 14 July 1944 issue of *Marking Time* addressed American Independence Day. The Americans made the most of the occasion, somehow getting the requisite supplies to ensure a memorable time: "The American Day of Independence was celebrated here [Camp Maloney/Adelboden] on Tuesday July 4 in the traditional style as far as possible. Unfortunately, a day of steady rain ruined–to a large extent–the open-air barbecue, which had been planned. Evidently this is also quite often the case back in the U.S.A.! However, despite the elements, a crowd of diehards gathered around the blazing fire while whole pigs crackled merrily on the spit."

An extra bumper lunch was served at the various hotels, and the Fliers' Community Fund furnished cases of beer. "Long before dark, Adelboden was startled from its usual tranquility by exploding fireworks and screaming rockets. Subsequent developments tended to put the British in mind of displays at home seen usually on the 5th of November. Cautious as always, members of the local Fire Brigade [were] seen dogging the footsteps of the merry makers."

The 11 August 1944 issue of *Marking Time*, which came out as the Americans were advancing on Chartres and after Le Mans had been taken, took note of Swiss National Day, 1 August: "The Swiss national day was celebrated here in great style. With fireworks flying in all directions, you had to watch out for stray rockets and bombs and there were amusing scenes as people tried to dodge whizzbangs. One British officer was seen giving fire orders to a crowd of Americans armed with rockets. The results were not satisfactory."

Thanksgiving Day was celebrated with a feast of sorts. The Swiss in Wengen did their best to help the American airmen celebrate, even if the meal was not quite the traditional turkey and trimmings the fliers were used to:

THE THANKSGIVING MENU

As the day of Thanksgiving approaches there are those of you who are wondering just how far from the regular American diet for Thanksgiving our menu will deviate. Excepting for a few minor points, we internees shall enjoy a Thanksgiving dinner such as we have always been used to. The age-old problem of where to find a centipede turkey (one with a thousand legs so that we can all be satisfied) has not been solved, but I'm sure there will be enough for all. Here's wishing you good appetite![28]

Instead of the longed-for turkey, dressing, giblet gravy, Brussels sprouts, or ice cream, the internees dined on goose, potatoes, salad, wine, and pudding with cookies. These celebrations gave the American airmen an outlet for their pent-up emotions.

• • •

The villagers were fascinated by the Americans. "We were interested to see these men," said Jürg Aellig, who was eight years old during the time the Americans were interned in Adelboden. "They were heroes. They were pilots [in the eyes of the children]. Most of them were strong, good-looking, healthy young men. They were gentle. We'd run after them and try to learn English. My first knowledge of English was from them. They were so kind to children."[29]

Aellig's father, who ran a bar called the Alpenrose, was called the "Coffee King" because he was the first person in Adelboden to own a coffee machine. During the war, coffee was difficult to come by and had to be stretched with herbs and other ingredients such as chicory. Coffee in Switzerland was no exception. It was often bitter and seldom tasted like the rich black brew to which they were accustomed. But Aellig's father had a friend in Bern who was a coffee merchant, and the Americans loved to frequent the Alpenrose because they could get a decent cup of coffee. This worked to young Jürg's advantage. "Once, when I was asking the pilots for chewing gum, one said 'No, not this time. Sorry.' But the other said, 'Yes, give him some, that's the Coffee King's son.'"

Ernst Oester, proprietor of a sporting goods shop, sold skis to the Americans. He remembered that they "were nice boys. They gave us very little trouble."[30] And generally the internees did cause very little trouble. Except for the times they drank too much. Each night around closing time, the Military Police (MPs) made the rounds at the bars and cafés to tell the men to head back to the hotels. If an internee was drunk or missed curfew–sometimes one might fall asleep at a table in a nightspot–he would have MP duty for two weeks. Naturally no one wanted that because one couldn't go out drinking while on MP duty.

The recollections of villagers like Oester portray a group of men who delighted in teasing their hosts and coaxing them to let down their guard. "They played a lot of music," said Oester. "The English were quieter." Many Swiss citizens, particularly the women, found the behavior of the American servicemen a refreshing departure from that of the Swiss soldiers. "There was a small grocery store next to our house," recalled Peter von Deschwanden, whose father was a physician in Adelboden. "And before the U.S. pilots would come for a checkup they'd buy fruit. Sometimes cherries. And in the waiting room they'd put their feet up, eat cherries, and spit the pits out the window. They would drive my mother crazy. They'd sit on the fences and yell 'Hi, Doll' to the young Swiss girls. They were like angels from the sky when the planes fell. They were like pieces of Liberty."

The Americans seemed carefree, gregarious, and enthusiastic—even during their imprisonment—while Swiss officers were reserved and more serious. While the Swiss would not dare shed their jackets outside the office, the Americans sat bare-chested on wooden fences in summer. This habit of casting off their uniforms shocked the Swiss women, young and old. Ernst Oester recalled an incident in his store: "One time there were three boys in here who wanted to try on ski pants. But there wasn't any dressing room. So they just took off their pants and were there in the middle of the store in their small underpants. A peasant woman came in and she saw them. She left in shock."

"For Switzerland, it wasn't what you'd expect in a soldier. They were well dressed, tall, and carefree. We had a different conception of military discipline, different traditions. . . . But they were disciplined. We had good relations with them," said Margrit Thüller, whose husband was at the front in Simplon during the war. "Sometimes, to meet an American without his uniform created a shock in young Swiss girls. They saw the uniform first as a romantic thing, impressive. So when they realized they were just men, it was sometimes a bit disappointing. An aviator had more status than an officer even. And it was surprising that one could be an aviator and maybe a farmer back home. In Switzerland aviators and officers always held high-ranking jobs in civilian life."

Women from Bern traveled to the village on weekends to socialize with the U.S. servicemen. "High society women from Bern would come," von Deschwanden said. "Many were married to officers, but they would come to Adelboden alone and have an 'adventure.' They would meet these young pilots who seemed like they were from another world. Also, understand that between 1939 and 1940 Adelboden was mostly farmers. For the women, the world stopped at Frutigen and for the men, perhaps it stopped at Bern. So when the American aviators came . . . [i]t was as if the world had come to us all of a sudden. The borders were broken. Of course we had grown up knowing about the United States. We learned about it in school and saw it on the Atlas. But it was a place so far away and then suddenly it was here."

Without doubt many internees harbored some affection for Switzerland as well. If for no other reason, the time they spent there was a respite from the terrors of combat. For the first time in a long time a feeling of peace descended on the crews cloistered in the Alpine land. "We were in a fairy-tale land of beautiful scenery, spectacular mountains, and valleys capped by glaciers with formations of cumulous clouds marching in the valleys," said Siegvart J. Robertson, pilot of the *Georgia Peach*.[31] "Church bells rang every hour and the background noise of rushing waters in the streams was always there."

The friendliest people of all were the many Swiss mothers who had ambitions to catch an American husband for their daughters. They would host wine and fondue parties for about a dozen internees and visitors. "They were always introducing Americans to Swiss girls of the right age," Robertson said. The Swiss authorities could not quite bring themselves to encourage the matchmaking. In one report, the head of the Internment and Hospitalization Commission questioned the desirability of marriages between military internees and Swiss citizens. The government feared these unions would ruin the reputations of Swiss women and wondered, among other things, if they would be allowed to enter the countries of their husbands when the war was over.[32]

In May 1942, however, Swiss authorities granted military internees authorization to marry if they had permission from their country of origin. The question appears to have first come up on 2 March 1942 in the case of *Slubicki* v. *Bern* (Ro 68173 v. Federal Tribunal), brought after a Polish internee married a Swiss woman without receiving permission.

Americans who wanted to marry Swiss women had to go through the legation in Bern. For example, a 6 November 1944 memo from

Capt. Lloyd A. Free of the American legation to the Adjudance 8e Section, Palais Federal, Bern stated: "Gentlemen: S/Sgt. Elmo C. Simpson, who is stationed in the American internment camp at Adelboden, has requested permission to marry Miss Dora Bertha Hermann of Swiss nationality, who resides at Auswil, Canton of Berne. Miss Hermann's parents, Mr. and Mrs. Hermann, reside at Trimbach near Olten, ct. Solothurn. Brigadier General Legge had given his permission for S/Sgt. Simpson to marry. Such a marriage would be considered valid under American law and Miss Hermann would enjoy all of the marital rights customarily enjoyed by the wife of an American citizen."[33]

Most of the more than four hundred marriages sanctified by 31 May 1945 were between Polish internees and Swiss women. Only two Americans married Swiss women during the war. The other marriages came later, after repatriation. Table 1, based on a report submitted to the Internment and Hospitalization Commission by Colonel Probst, is the most complete list of wartime marriages known.

Jim Hewlett, a navigator on the B-24J *Mary Harriet*, met his wife, Trudy Lange, because of a failed mission to bomb the Dornier aircraft

Table 1. Marriages between Internees and Swiss Women

Nationality	Recognized	Not recognized	Total
Polish	203	127	230
English	1	8	9
USA	1	1	2
Italian	21	25	46
Yugoslavian	3	12	15
French	3	3	6
Greek	4	2	6
Cypriot	1	4	5
German	6	2	8
Nationality unknown	–	6	6

Source: Report submitted to the FCIH by Colonel Probst, 31 May 1945. Probst said in his report that the figures were probably incomplete.

factory in Oberpfaffenhofen. On the flight from England on 21 July 1944, Hewlett's ship, of the 44th Bomb Group, 68th Bomb Squadron, 8th Air Force, sustained damage and lost the number one engine. The decision was made to bail out, and the *Mary Harriet* crashed at Neslau. The left waist gunner's chute failed and he was killed; the surviving crew members were taken to Dübendorf and then separated—officers to Davos and enlisted men to Adelboden.

"It was dull and I was feeling a loneliness," recalled Hewlett.[34] "Ted Surila arranged a date for me with his girlfriend's sister named Trudy. I soon learned she liked me and was interested in the same things as I. I hoped it wasn't mere fascination that led me to be charmed by her. Over the next few months I learned it wasn't. We were together as much as possible, attending sporting events and skiing later. Christmas and New Year's were wonderful times. We [the American internees] left Davos 16 February 1945 and received a tumultuous send-off. The evening before departing Davos, Trudy and I became engaged." Hewlett left Switzerland without his fiancée; it took two years for the U.S. State Department to provide the right paperwork so the two could wed. They were married on 25 January 1947.

Romantic pursuits aside, sports played a central role in alleviating the constant ennui. In Adelboden some Americans took to the village ice hockey rink wearing red, white, and blue shirts emblazoned with the USAAF insignia. The American Fliers never won a game; the Swiss were just better. The most popular sports were skiing in winter and hiking in summer, usually with armed guards present. Many of the airmen had never skied before, and there were many broken legs. "They were crazy how they would ski," recalled Ernst Oester. "They would just go straight down, fall, and do it again. There were lots of broken legs. They wanted to go straight down the mountain and not slalom. That would drive their teacher crazy."

Internees participated in sporting events in various locales throughout the country. A 13 May 1944 letter from the Institute Olympic de Lausanne to the chief of the Federal Commission for Internment and Hospitalization, for example, invited the internees to participate in a sports program that summer that included swimming, games, boxing, and horseback riding. The program of 6 June 1944 had 110 participants: ten Americans, ten British, ten French, ten Greeks, ten Yugoslavians, and fifty Italians. The idea of the games was to lift the spirits of the sequestered troops, but the prevention of escapes always continued to be a priority, as memos regarding other events show: "participants had to be very good alpinists, have good shoes and be equipped with all that was necessary. Security guards also had to be in good condition. Each excursion needed an unalterable itinerary."[35]

In the warm weather internees took up swimming. The 11 August 1944 issue of *Marking Time* lamented the poor showing of the Americans in the Anglo-American swimming gala at Adelboden that took place on 6 August: "The Anglo-American swimming gala was held at Adelboden yesterday afternoon. The usual Adelboden afternoon rain came down but there was nevertheless a large crowd present. . . . The Americans did not win one single event and it must have been disappointing for their supporters to see themselves so poorly represented. For a nation which holds most of the world's swimming records and has produced swimmers of the caliber of Johnny Weismuller, Kiefer, 'Dutch' Smith and a host of others, it is most surprising and disappointing that the 700 Americans at Adelboden could only produce three entrants for the gala."

Other ways to pass the time included lighthearted contests sponsored by *Marking Time*. One contest in the April issue, volume 6, asked internees to create and submit titles and authors for various books: "This aroused considerable interest and well over 200 titles were received," the journal reported. "Most of the titles have to be kept under lock and key; in case they fall into the hands of the 'uninitiated.' (Col. Lee's bright efforts made even the Editor blush—and he is a man of wide experience!) The winner of the ties were: . . . 'Four Years in the Army' by Brown Doff; 'Roughing It in Switzerland' by Anne Evade; 'Homeward Bound' by May B. Sune; and 'Food in Germany' by Herr Satz."

• • •

The imprisoned Americans received their full flight pay, converted to Swiss francs—about seven U.S. dollars, or thirty Swiss francs—from the U.S. legation every ten days. They used the money to supplement their rations as well as for more frivolous purchases such as watches, cameras, and sporting equipment. After a time, however, the stipend was stopped and the internees had a difficult time buying meals and other essentials. Internees in Adelboden who ran out of cash before payday sometimes pawned watches and other valuables at Oester's sports store.

Some enterprising internees sold their clothes to local farmers, knowing the American legation would eventually replace the "lost" clothing–that is, until the American embassy asked the Swiss to help enforce a prohibition against selling military issue clothing to civilians. A few internees circumvented the policy, and there was one in Adelboden who turned his room into a veritable military surplus store. For a people who could no longer easily trade with the outside world, the military clothing was a hot commodity, particularly the sturdy shoes, which had thick rubber soles. Flight jackets with sheepskin linings and paintings on the back were also desired.

The food situation at Adelboden eventually improved, but internees still found it hard to get enough to eat without going into town and buying whatever they could. They also tried to buy clothing because the uniforms they were issued were just not enough. No special uniforms were tailored for internees; no POW letters were sewn on their uniforms to identify them as the prisoners they essentially were. Instead the Americans had to wear their GI clothes all the time so the Swiss authorities could distinguish them from the rest of the population. The four pairs of socks, three underwear sets, and two handkerchiefs they were issued were supposed to last eleven months. There was little to buy, however, and Swiss prices were about 50 percent higher than in the States.[36]

Obligatory labor for military internees was prohibited according to the 1907 Hague Convention, but some worked for the American legation in Bern doing clerical work or traveling between the camps taking care of financial matters such as payroll, settling accounts, and other jobs. One legation memo asked "permission for 2d Lt. Carl F. Altimus to come to Bern to take care of financial matters for the American internment camp at Davos. I would like a two-day pass granted for him to leave Davos early Wednesday, November 8, 1944 and return Thursday evening, November 9, 1944. It would be greatly appreciated if this could be arranged."[37] When permission was approved, the men always had to sign a "parole" form giving their word of honor that according to article 11 of the Hague Convention, they would not try to escape. Brigadier General Legge countersigned the form. Many men nevertheless took the opportunity to escape if it presented itself.

Working with the legation may have provided a diversion for a few of the men, but it did not mitigate the internees' overall situation. Many internees were surprised and disappointed at the legation's perceived inability to help them. "Throughout my stay in Switzerland the American legation proved itself to have a lack of push in all matters pertaining to our betterment," recalled S.Sgt. Bernard Segal, a tail gunner on the *Lazy Baby,* a B-17 in the 305th Bomb Group, 364th Bomb Squadron, 8th Air Force. "The only agency in Switzerland who honestly tried to help us was the YMCA. They did some wonderful work for us and they have much praise coming to them. . . . [I]f our Legation had been as much on the ball as it should have been, our stay in Switzerland would have been a very, very much happier one. The Swiss people were very friendly, the Swiss merchants very mercenary, and the Swiss Internment service very obnoxious and petty."[38]

. . .

In time the Swiss opened additional camps to alleviate the crowding at Adelboden. Wengen, situated two hours from Adelboden and three hours from the officers' camp at Davos, opened in August 1944. A beautiful area for hiking and skiing, Wengen had been a popular tourist destination before the war. The village's fourteen hotels were transformed into lodgings for the fliers and a quarantine center.

The front page of *Marking Time* on 25 August 1945 related news from the fronts: "U.S. Troops on Swiss Frontier"; "Grenoble Falls: Tanks Push on to Lyons"; "Patton Takes the High Road to Germany"; and, of course, news from the camps. For example: "Americans Go to New Camp at Wengen": "Adelboden these days seems like a graveyard owing to the departure of three hundred odd Americans for Wengen. A week ago, one could go 'up town' at any time of the day and find Americans sitting on benches in front of the post office or in front of the

Baren restaurant. The town looks very strange without them and many of us have lost good friends. We sincerely hope their new camp is as good as Adelboden."

Wengen sits on a shelf above a valley that leads from the Jungfrau to Interlaken. The best route to the village is via the cog railway that goes from Lauterbrunnen in the valley up to the Jungfrau. "I could look out and see the Jungfrau from the hotel," recalled Joseph Piemonte. "We had freedom within the village and we could go gamboling around in the hills and throw pinecones at each other. I remember seeing the little chalets and I remember seeing a schoolmaster skiing and picking up the kids from each chalet—what a picture, him with all those kids trailing behind."

"At Wengen we had guards at the entrance to our quarters and two who patrolled every twenty minutes or so. I can still hear their hobnailed boots tramping around. We had to 'fall-out' twice daily and listen to the 'poop' from our Commanding Officer and the Swiss Kommandant. Bed check at 9:00 P.M. by our armed guards shining lights in our faces was very distasteful. This made me feel like a criminal of sorts," wrote Louis Joseph, 447th Bomb Group, 710th Bomb Squadron, 8th Air Force, in the June 1987 newsletter of the Swiss Internees Association. "There I was a 20-year-old and surrounded by armed guards. What wrong had I committed? I was not maltreated but I was going crazy because of absolute boredom. I considered escape from boredom."

Arthur Cooper, a waist gunner on Joseph's ship, tried to persuade him to join in an escape. Americans who decided to escape knew that they risked not only arrest and imprisonment but also injury or even death. The Swiss guards did not hesitate to shoot escaping prisoners. Joseph hesitated, and the men left without him. The last time he saw the group, they were hiking up the mountain path looking like Swiss Alpine men. "The only thing they lacked was Lederhosen. Later I did escape. My greatest fear was that I would be shot."

Sentiments such as Louis's led to the establishment of the Society of Pissed Off American Internees, Camp Wengen, Switzerland. Louis found himself a member after his failure to escape.

Upon receipt of this letter you are a member of our "ANCIENT AND HONORABLE SOCIETY OF PISSED OFF AMERICAN INTERNEES."

You have qualified as a bitcher extraordinary and from reports of other members of our Ancient Organization; you are a "Bitcher from WAY BACK."

The aims of our Organization are for the Prevention of Cruelty to AMERICAN INTERNEES.

At our annual meeting we agreed upon the following punches for you:

5—for your stay in Switzerland up to now.

5—for not being able to leave this GOD DAMM COUNTRY.

1—just on general principals.

Yours truly, T/Sgt. W. E. Aeschbacher[39]

• • •

American officers were sent to Davos-Platz in the far eastern region of the country, both to separate them from noncommissioned officers and to alleviate the overcrowding at Adelboden. Davos, a ski town, is divided into four sections: Davos-Platz, Davos-Dorf, Davos-Wolfgang, and Davos-Laret. Davos-Dorf had for some time been a rest and relaxation destination for German officers. Indeed, it teemed with Nazis when the Americans were there. The first American officers arrived in Davos-Platz on 24 June 1944, among them the officers of the *Baby*, who were assigned to stay at the Palace Hotel, since renamed the Hotel Europe.

The officers in Davos seem to have had a slightly better time than the enlisted men in Adelboden and Wengen. Some former internees said the food tasted somewhat better, and they could see more movies and mingle with young women at dances. Yet the hotels were still unheated, the Swiss officers still domineering, and the penalty for attempting to escape just as harsh.

"The first two weeks the four of us played bridge and hearts in our suite," reported Russell K. Sherbourne, the copilot on a B-24 from the 491st Bomb Group, 853d Bomb Squadron, 8th Air Force.[40] "Downstairs in the lobby there were chess players to be challenged. The south side of the hotel had porches on each floor, and the sun worshippers usually populated these. Every few days a couple of earlier arrivals (George Telford was one) came by with their roving PX—cigarettes, candy bars, playing cards, etc. Naturally, anything we bought had to be paid for out of our $10 per week."

Sherbourne described Davos as an interesting and pleasant sort of limbo. One could even golf if one had enough money to purchase a golf ball. "We were only allowed one—if [you] lost it that ended the game for the day." Tennis enthusiasts had to vie for space on one of four courts and buy their own racquet, balls, and sneakers. The cinemas showed good but old pictures with subtitles. Others found distraction in the town's bars, browsed in the bookstore, or took language courses.

Although Swiss regulations forbade confining prisoners in the same towns as their enemies, the fliers in Davos were lodged at the Palace Hotel, just down the street from the German embassy. Further, Davos was a favored German recreation spot. Trouble was bound to occur.

A few days after the first Americans arrived in Davos, a series of pranks began, most of them targeted at the German consulate. On the Fourth of July the American fliers aimed fireworks and rockets at the German consulate, from which hung a three-foot-high German eagle and swastika. Such behavior was illegal in Switzerland. In 1941, to stay in Germany's good graces, the Swiss had outlawed any form of insult to foreigners, national flags, and emblems. The edict was enforced by punishments that could include prison terms.

"A couple of boys decided the German Consulate Nazi sign staring them in the face every morning needed to go," recalled Lewis M. Sarkovich, copilot on the B-24 *Commando,* from the 448th Bomb Group, 713th Bomb Squadron, 8th Air Force.[41] "The sign disappeared and all hell broke. Gen. Legge and our C.O. Mickey McGuire were called upon by Embassy and Swiss officials. Threats, etc. were rampant." "The Swiss reacted swiftly," Sig Robertson agreed. "Armed soldiers surrounded the Palace Hotel the morning after it happened. The Swiss commandant gathered the Americans into the dining hall and berated them."

The German consulate immediately reported the incidents to Berlin and issued a strong protest to the Swiss. The Swiss complained to Washington and came down hard on the internees. The commandant told the internees that under no circumstances could Americans leave the hotel or receive any further meals until the German property was recovered and the perpetrators sent to prison. "The sign reappeared," noted Sarkovich, "but those responsible disappeared. We heard later the OSS (Office of Strategic Services) and Swiss escape network got them out of Switzerland."

The perpetrators, copilot 2d Lt. Oscar Sampson and bombardier 2d Lt. John H. Garcia of the 92d Bomb Group, 407th Bomb Squadron, 8th Air Force, were indeed sent to prison–at the request of General Legge. In an 11 August 1944 letter to Colonel Probst, Legge wrote: "I had a careful investigation made in order that the final result, as far as the U.S. Army is concerned, would be clear. I find the conduct of both of these officers culpable, and request you to transfer them to Wauwiler-moos as soon as possible and that they be left there until I request their return to another camp, which will not be Davos."

Sampson and Garcia were sent to Wauwilermoos on 16 August 1944 and escaped the next day–all the way back to England. They hid in Geneva for a week, then crossed the border to France, where they met up with the Resistance and proceeded on an escape route through occupied France and North Africa before finally returning to their base in Podington, England.

The U.S. camp commander at Davos, Capt. L. F. McGuire, wrote a letter of regret about the incident to the Germans dated 16 August 1944. The letter did not apologize but said: "As Camp Commander of U.S.A.A.F. Internees at Davos-Platz in the name of the officers here I regret the incident. All efforts on my part have been made to prevent such untoward incidents. It must be believed that this was an immature prank on the part of two irresponsible officers."[42]

The American internees were well aware that the Germans in Davos were treated like honored guests. In a 1945 interview with the Department of the Judge Advocate General for the War Crimes Office, Wallace Northfelt, 44th Bomb Group, 506th Bomb Squadron, 8th Air Force, described Davos as "more or less . . . a German rest camp and the Germans seemed to come and go as they pleased. For recreation we were allowed to play ball and stuff like that and we were always being told to shut up and not to make so much noise." Northfelt thought the Swiss, particularly the German-speaking Swiss, seemed very pro-Nazi.[43] He gained the impression through talking with various people that thousands of Swiss were working in German war industries.

S.Sgt. John J. Hughes of the 44th Bomb Group, 66th Bomb Squadron, 8th Air Force, minced no words when describing the Swiss attitude. Hughes successfully escaped from Wengen on 24 September 1944. "My impression of the country and the Swiss people is pretty low," Hughes later wrote.[44] "I thanked god when I landed there, but was damn glad to get out of there. You might think they like the Americans. But underneath they hate us. They should make up their minds whose side they're on. Thank god I was never in one of their supposed jails. But some of the American boys were and they tell me its hell."

S.Sgt. Lavder C. Cameron, who was shot down over Augsburg and interned in Adelboden, agreed: "Swiss authorities to my knowledge never gave an American a break, in my mind they are a very small minded race of people. The fellows that had to do time in Swiss jails were not treated the way they should have been, in regards to cleanliness, food and warmth."[45]

Jack McKinney, copilot on the *Winson Winn II* of the 384th Bomb Group, 547th Bomb Squadron, 8th Air Force, remembered his eleven months in Switzerland as a time of boredom. After landing, McKinney and the rest of the crew were sent to the Chaumont Hotel near Neuchâtel for ten days of quarantine and briefings from people on General Legge's staff. Then it was off to Adelboden for two months. "Endless card games and boredom took up much of our time and we felt more at ease," McKinney wrote in a 1992 article. "Then D-Day. Those of us who were officers who had been in Adelboden the longest were transferred to Davos and offered first choice of rooms in the Palace Hotel. I remember the march from the Bahnhof to the hotel. All doors and windows were closed; no one on the streets. The town of Davos seemed deserted. Later we learned the Germans were in town . . . they told the Swiss the American 'gangsters' were coming. We got even, someone not me, stole the Nazi swastika from the Embassy wall. The early days in Davos consisted of card games, touch football and meeting Davos Swiss."[46] McKinney tried to escape twice but was caught and sent first to Wauwilermoos and then to Les Diablerets, without a military tribunal in either case. He was repatriated in January 1945. "My eleven months of internment was over but the memories, both good and bad, linger today."

On 1 February 1945 the Internment and Hospitalization Commission decided to close Camp Davos "following the high number of escapes lately among American internees." The internees from both Davos and Wengen were transferred to Adelboden. At that time there were 150 internees in Davos and 202 in Wengen. At Adelboden, there were 74 internees in the Nevada Palace, 65 in the National Hotel, and none at the Bellevue.[47]

• • •

Downed Allied fliers found a measure of sanctuary in Switzerland, but the realities of war were never far away. The not infrequent funerals were poignant reminders. Most of the airmen who died when shot down by the Swiss or in crash landings were buried in Münsingen, a small cemetery on the outskirts of Bern; others were buried in Bad Ragaz. Münsingen is a crowded cemetery with narrow dirt paths between rows of headstones. There are no longer Americans buried there. They were all moved in 1946 to a cemetery in Epinal, France, or back to the United States. But during the internment years they were watched over by Sgt. Christy Zullo. A right waist gunner on the *Lazy Baby,* Zullo, of the 305th Bomb Group, 364th Bomb Squadron, 8th Air Force, had arrived in Switzerland on 14 October 1943 after having to bail out on the return trip from Schweinfurt. The Germans captured two of his crew—the copilot, 2d Lt. Brunson W. Bolin, and the engineer, George H. Blalock Jr. Of those who landed in Switzerland, the navigator, 2d Lt. Donald T. Rowley, died the next morning from wounds, and Zullo and the rest of his crew were interned. Zullo married a Swiss girl, lived in a house in Münsingen, and cared for the American cemetery. He also used his caretaker position to help fliers escape.[48]

On 1 March 1943 James Mahaffey attended a burial for the pilot of his crew and a radio operator from another crew. "The Swiss civilians stared at us. You could see that they were really curious about us. Upon arrival at Münsingen, we got off the train, were lined up again for the count (there were still twenty-two of us), and we marched into a very small town. Hardly any people were around. We were brought here for the funeral of the two crew members killed. One was for our crew, and the other was the radio operator from Proctor's crew. He was killed by flak when they were hit.[49]

When an American flier was buried, the enlisted men from his crew were the pallbearers. The men dressed as nearly alike as possible, which required borrowing clothes from other crew members, and wore black armbands. All the other crew members marched behind the coffin. A Protestant missionary usually led the funeral procession, followed by someone carrying a floral wreath. Next, according to Mahaffey's written account, came "the American Ambassador (in formal attire, top hat and all . . .), then about eight officers from the American Embassy, followed by the crew members with the Swiss officer commandant leading them. Sgt. Zeno and two other sergeants (former crew members who had been shot down) were at the rear of the procession. There were a number of Swiss civilians standing around watching us. When we reached the cemetery, a Swiss honor guard came to attention while we put the coffin on boards across the grave opening."

That act of respect from the Swiss offered little consolation to those who knew that Swiss gunfire had killed their friends. An officer from the American embassy delivered a short talk, and then the missionary gave the funeral sermon. A bugler played Taps. Then the leader of the Swiss honor guard barked a command in German and they fired three rifle volleys.

"I didn't know they were going to fire a rifle salute," recalled Mahaffey. "On the first volley, I must have jumped up in the air as it scared the daylights out of me. We then lowered the coffins in the graves, Mr. Tracy gave the prayer (or rather read the prayer) and took a handful of dirt and threw it on the coffins, with the saying ashes to ashes or dust to dust. I have never really understood what they meant by that."

On Memorial Day in 1944 *Marking Time* covered the rededication of the American cemetery at Münsingen.

In attendance were: the American Military Attaché, his Staff, a delegation of American internees and escapees, members of the Legation of Berne, the Consuls General of Zürich and Basel, Americans living in Berne and vicinity, Brigadier Cartwright, the British military Attaché, and Colonel du Pasquier of the Swiss Internment Service, accompanied by Lieutenant Picot of the same service. After invocation by Dr. Strong, the Honorable Leland Harrison, the American Minister, addressed the gathering, including in his talk Lincoln's Gettysburg address. Major Strader, Senior American Air Officer in Switzerland then unveiled a memorial tablet dedicated by the internees and escapees. It is of copper and bears the same inscription as the plaques at the National Cemetery in Arlington: "Enshrined forever in the hearts of their countrymen—Here lie our gallant dead." Brigadier General Legge then called the roll of the dead. At each name, a comrade of the dead man stepped from the ranks of the internees drawn up in formation at the outside edge of the cemetery and responded: "Died for his country." This was repeated thirty-two times since the dead from Ragaz, Baar, and Basel had previously been transferred to the new Münsingen Cemetery. Taps then followed and then the Stars and Stripes, which had been at half mast, was raised to the top.

5

ESCAPE AND ESPIONAGE

We must oppose, even by arms, all escape attempts.
Swiss military communiqué

I regret to inform you that the commanding general European Area reports your son First Lieut. Martin Andrews missing in action since six Sept. If further details or other information of his status are received you will be promptly notified.
Western Union telegram to Capt. Andrew Andrews from
the Adjutant General, Washington, D.C., 14 September 1943

On 6 August 1943, 1st Lt. Martin Andrews of the 306th Bomb Group, 423d Bomb Squadron, 8th Air Force, had been assigned to bomb Bosch Magneto Works in Stuttgart, Germany. The 8th Air Force had alerted its heavy bomber groups in England to prepare for the mission, which meant flying deep into German airspace, the evening before. Group commanders began spreading the word before dinner, alerting flight crews that they would be awakened at 2:00 A.M.

As he always did the night before a bombing mission, Lieutenant Andrews picked up his worn copy of *The Lotos-Eaters,* Alfred, Lord Tennyson's rhythmic work woven with images of death and isolation. Strangely, the surreal images usually spun a sense of calm for the twenty-three-year-old airman, but tonight sleep stayed stubbornly away.[1] Tomorrow's mission weighed on his mind. The fact that he and his crew had already completed eleven of their twenty-five missions coupled with the knowledge that only one in ten crews survived all the required missions jangled his nerves. He tried to distract himself by thinking about the events that had brought him to England.

Andrews had never been inside an airplane before he joined the Army Air Corps. But he had closely followed aviation and devoured the stories about the dogfights of World War I and knew he would someday make a career in flying. When the Japanese bombed Pearl Harbor and the United States entered the war in 1941, Andrews went to the recruiting office with his fellow classmates. He had toyed with the idea of joining the navy, but the thought of taking off and landing on aircraft carriers made him queasy. Instead he joined the U.S. Army Air Corps and was sent to flight school. Upon graduation in April 1942 he was lined up with the other men. The taller ones were sent to fly bombers, the shorter ones to pilot fighters. Andrews had desperately wanted to be a fighter pilot, but at nearly six feet, he was too tall. That August, after a three-month stint training other pilots in Mississippi, he left for Europe.

Getting up in barracks was never a quiet affair; beds creaked, feet slapped on the wooden floor, men groaned and grumbled and then shuffled off to the bathroom to splash cold water on their faces. Donning woolen socks, undershirts, flight suits, and scarves, the flight crews prepared for the cold skies to come, then walked to a wooden building near the mess hall for the preflight briefing.

A mission like this one to Stuttgart, deep inside Germany, would mean the bomb group would run so low on gasoline they would have to cut their outboard engines and power-glide to return to base. Not only that, the bombers would be without protection most of the flight. The American and British fighter planes still lacked the range to go much farther than the coast of France before having to return home. Eventually the fighters would get drop tanks—huge aluminum tanks filled with extra fuel that fit under the wings—that would allow some to fly all the way to Poland and back, but in 1943 the bomber pilots had to go it alone. Alone they might have been, but they were never lonely. The Luftwaffe provided constant companionship.

Before the morning briefing the crews descended on the mess hall for a hearty breakfast; it would be some hours before they ate again. Flying at high altitudes in open, unpressurized, unheated planes seemed to increase their appetites tenfold, so the six hundred men noisily tucked into their meals.

Some of Andrews's crew had bad feelings about the mission that morning. He tried to get them to harness their fear before takeoff, but a near-fatal jeep accident just before the briefing involving Leo Liener, the engineer and top turret gunner, and Kenneth Rood, the ball turret gunner, had made everyone especially jittery. Both men were seriously injured and were replaced with two new arrivals, Sgt. Ralph Biggs and Sgt. Guido Di Pietro. Andrews kept telling himself none of that mattered, that it shouldn't be too difficult a day. In and out.

Glints of gold and rose lit the clear dawn as the bombers taxied out to the runway. The weatherman promised good weather over most of the Continent. Hundreds of B-17 Flying Fortresses lined the runway like geese poised to fly south for the winter. Engines churned grit into the air, and the sun glinted off the propeller blades.

After takeoff that September morning the 306th Bomb Group flew in a high box formation to the right and rear of the leaders. As they neared the French coast, under German occupation since 1940, the Me-109s and Focke-Wulf 190s buzzed up like hornets with their usual predictability. At least the crew could count on the German fliers following a standard pattern. When Allied planes entered Germany, the German fighters would often attack from the right. The theory—or rumor, rather—was that this put the sun at their backs. The planes would usually fly up alongside U.S. aircraft, staying just out of range, but sometimes they flew close enough for the Americans to see their faces. The German fighter pilots were well trained and dauntless. They were faster than the bombers and would pull ahead, wheel over, and hit the Americans head on. Every dragon has its soft underside, and the Luftwaffe pilots quickly learned that one of the most vulnerable parts of the B-17 was its nose. Or they might come straight in, roll over, and fire at the belly of the Flying Fortress. Unfortunately for the crews of 1943, extra teeth would not come until later in the war, in the form of B-17Gs, which carried two extra guns extending from the nose in what was called a chin turret.

The Luftwaffe welcoming committee was right on time. The German fighters mounted several attacks. Bursts of orange and black flak peppered the air as well. The bomber tried to dance through the flak, to no avail. Flak proved to be one of the worst enemies of the 8th Air Force; it was at least partially responsible for downing about half of the

2,622 bombers lost.[2] Suddenly the number two engine, the inboard engine on the left side of the craft, caught fire. The oil pressure was down—the bouquet of bullets had punctured an oil line, causing the oil pressure to plummet to zero. Andrews feathered the propeller to keep it from spinning out of control. The bomber started falling behind the other aircraft in the squadron, making it easy prey for the enemy fighters that were sure to return.

Andrews started to wonder whether they should turn around and return to England, but the target seemed close enough. And if they turned back now the mission would not count, leaving them with fourteen more instead of thirteen. On top of that was the memory of what had happened in July when Andrews had lost two engines over the Ruhr. Andrews had flown the plane back alone, and he and his crew nearly got their heads shot off. At least there was a degree of safety inside a formation, where a plane was just another schooling fish. Alone it was appetizing prey for German fighter pilots salivating at the chance to expand their list of bomber kills.

So onward they flew. Andrews outlined the plan to his copilot, 2d Lt. Keith Rich. As soon as they delivered the bombs they would dive for the deck and skim at treetop level across Germany, France, the Channel, and then on to England. The plan was a good one, but the plane would not cooperate. It kept losing ground. They fell behind their own bombing group, so they joined the next . . . and the next. Before long the crippled B-17 became a straggler struggling to stay up with the stream of bombers. Looking at his watch, the copilot said it would be another hour until they could drop their bombs. Unknown to Andrews and his crew, however, someone in the lead position had made a fateful decision.

A brigadier general sat in the lead plane. When they got near Stuttgart, a cover of clouds hid the target like a smokescreen. Unable to hit the spot on the first pass, the brigadier general decided to make a second try. This triggered a chain-reaction disaster for the bomber groups approaching from behind. The meticulous flight plans decided back in England were upset, and the aircrews could not locate alternate target objectives. Andrews's aircraft began losing fuel, and he soon began to "feel like his plane was a lone cipher in a great mass of orbiting airplanes; sucked into a giant maelstrom flying aimlessly over southern Germany."

As the seconds slipped by, the situation worsened for the plane and the crew. It was now clear that the bomber would not be flying back over the white cliffs of Dover. There was not even enough fuel to reach the coast of France. The plane had gone way over the estimated fuel consumption because its three remaining engines were going at full manifold pressure and high RPMs to keep up with the bomber formation. Andrews considered the only two choices available. They could keep flying until they ran on empty and then bail out; but diving down to treetop level would not be an option because they would be too low to safely parachute to the ground. If they tried this strategy, they might make it as far as France, where they could all parachute out with some chance of evading the Germans. Or they could try to make it to Switzerland, thought to be a half-hour's flight away. That idea did not appeal to Andrews; it seemed like quitting. Instead, he, the copilot, and the navigator decided to fly as far as possible before they were forced to abandon the plane.

Seconds after the decision was made, Henry Hucker, the tail gunner, called over the intercom to announce a fire in the number four engine, the outboard engine on the right side of the craft. Andrews looked past his copilot and out the window. The engine did not seem to be on fire, but from Hucker's vantage point it must have looked that way. The engine had only overheated, causing pre-ignition sparks in the cylinders and black smoke to pour out of the cowl flaps. The only thing left to do was throttle back.

They were alone in the sky now; royal blue fading into denim with the waning of the afternoon light. Only clouds for company. The last of the American bombers were flying fast away. The crew was in dire straits. Only two of the four engines were functional, and it seemed less and less likely that the plane would make it to France. Andrews and Rich changed their minds about their course. They would attempt a landing in Switzerland while time allowed. But there was a problem. No one really knew its exact borders. A little mistake and they would fall into German hands.

Like others before them, the crew used the silk escape maps in their survival kits for orientation. The tiny Alpine nation was marked on the map—encircled by occupied France, Germany, and Italy—but not very precisely. In fact, it looked more like a doodle on a cocktail napkin. But that would have to be enough.

Gordon Bowers, the navigator, gave them a heading and they turned south. Andrews's voice buzzed over the intercom. "Gentlemen," he said, "two engines are out. We have fallen too far behind the fighters. We're going to try for Switzerland." Murmurs sounded through the plane's interior. At that moment four German Focke-Wulfs came at them head on. A spray of bullets hit the plane. The crew braced themselves for more, but it did not come. The enemy planes made only one pass. Andrews never figured out why the Germans did not try to destroy an easy target. Perhaps they didn't want to waste time toying with the lame bomber; or maybe they were saving their bullets for the grouped American bombers ahead, which would be a bigger, more satisfying shoot.

They continued flying south until they approached a German town called Friedrichshafen. Lake Constance, which shared a border with Germany, was just past Friedrichshafen. Andrews knew that Switzerland lay on the south shore of the lake. As the plane flew over Friedrichshafen the Germans pumped up a plume of antiaircraft fire. These bursts were not as worrisome to the crew as a flock of fighters would have been, but still the explosions made them wonder whether the Germans might occupy part of the lake's southern tip. Were they flying straight into German hands?

Andrews kept the plane on a southerly course toward the snow-capped peaks of the Alps. They continued to lose altitude and soon were skimming the summits of the mountains. Robert Huisinga, the bombardier, had rendered the Norden bombsight inoperative, and the two waist gunners, Walter Kozlowski and Elmo Simpson, had tossed their .50-caliber machine guns into the wildest parts of the Alps in an effort to lighten the aircraft. Andrews mused that come spring, hikers would find some interesting items strewn among the wildflowers.

Some of the crew began to worry about flying so close to the high peaks. Venton Scott, the radio operator, called up to ask if the crew should prepare to bail out. "There's no need to jump," Andrews told everyone. "You could kill yourselves trying to parachute into those mountains; but don't worry about this airplane. We've still got two good engines and we should be landing somewhere very soon."

Three minutes later the crippled bomber crossed the Alpine divide that cuts Switzerland along a northeast-southwest axis. As the plane continued to descend, Andrews could discern airfields on the barren Piedmont that lay just ahead. Rather than feeling relief at the sight, the pilot felt only fear. German airplanes marked with black swastikas were parked on the fields.

The B-17 had crossed the Swiss border and was now flying over northern Italy. The plane would be noticed momentarily, and even a potshot would be enough to finish them off. They had no more machine guns, their fuel was almost gone, and the plane was badly damaged. With two engines on fire and the plane shot up, Andrews was flying on the whims of the gods. Again he studied the swatch of silk and felt confident that the northern tip of the lake lay in Switzerland; later they would learn its name, Lake Maggiore. They flew over to the Swiss end of the lake without incident.

Suddenly, a Swiss fighter, an Me-109-E designed for air combat and actually manufactured in Germany, appeared at the B-17's side. The Americans recognized its markings, a white cross on a red field, but were nonetheless surprised. The pilot swung in close to the bomber. He pointed down, directing the pilot's attention to the ground. Capt. Gottfried von Meiss, of the Magadino air command, opened the canopy of his cockpit to guide them to a landing spot on a small grass field just at the edge of the lake.[3]

Von Meiss had been up teaching pilots how to fly Moran aircraft. He had just landed when one of his command jumped on his wing, reporting that the SRS, the Swiss observation system, had been alerted that an American aircraft had been circling the region for the past ten minutes apparently trying to find Switzerland. Von Meiss had enough fuel and ammunition, so he took off again and flew alongside the bomber. He could not talk to the American pilot on the radio owing to different operating frequencies, so he opened his canopy.

Lt. Martin Andrews had never before landed a Flying Fortress on the grass, much less on a field that looked smaller than a driveway basketball court. But he figured that if he approached from very low over the water and used every inch of space it would work. Additionally, since the crew had jettisoned all the bombs and many of the plane's weapons, and the gas tanks were nearly dry, the plane was now quite light. As Andrews swung the plane low across the lake on the final approach, he noticed that Swiss soldiers had ringed the entire field.

Andrews addressed the crew one more time before bringing the plane in for a landing. "We are landing in Switzerland, but go out of the plane with your hands in the air! I see soldiers all around and they all are armed. I don't want anyone hurt. We are landing in Switzerland, but go out of this plane with your hands in the air!" Then the Flying Fortress smacked the ground. The thud of the impact shuddered through Andrews's skull. The plane skidded, slid, and rolled right up to where the Swiss soldiers stood their ground, bayonets fixed and ready.

All Allied aircrews had orders to destroy their airplanes if they were forced to land, even in Switzerland or Sweden. For that purpose four incendiary bombs were a standard part of each plane's equipment. The bombs, filled with thermite, were the size and shape of a soda can; when ignited, after a time delay of a few seconds, the contents would burn quickly. Andrews told one crew member to detonate a bomb in the nose of the plane after landing, another to set one off just behind the bomb bay, and a third to set one off in the cockpit. He intended to ignite the fourth one himself from the pilot's side window. As soon as he stopped the plane, he had planned to crawl out on the fuselage and make his way back to the wing and set the bomb right above one of the empty gas tanks. Once the thermite burned through the wing's aluminum skin and reached the tank, the plane would blow.

As soon as they landed, Andrews's crew attempted to destroy their aircraft. As Rich struck the cap of his incendiary bomb on the control column, Andrews opened the side window of the cockpit, picked up his thermite bomb, and began to work his way out. As he did, one of the Swiss soldiers standing just below him started barking in German. Andrews, who understood neither German nor Swiss German, had no idea what the soldier was trying to say. He did, however, think it would be unwise to set off a bomb on the wing while the soldier was pointing a gun at him from fifteen feet away. He decided it would be better if he too set off his bomb in the cockpit. After doing this, he exited the plane through the bottom escape hatch.

"Halt!" commanded a soldier as the first of Andrews's crew came out of the plane. One by one the crew members were ordered to line up in front of the plane. Seconds passed and the plane remained intact; it turned out that all four incendiaries were duds. When it became clear that their efforts to destroy the plane had failed, the crew took a moment to notice their surroundings. A Swiss flag flew from a low building just to the left of the airfield, a reassuring sight for some of the crew, who still were not sure where they were.

The men were made to surrender their weapons, compasses, and maps when they got off the plane. That should have immediately triggered something in Andrews's mind, but he was preoccupied with trying to figure out where they were. Then he understood. The Swiss had confiscated all means of escape and survival.

While the crew waited to be questioned, Von Meiss approached Andrews. "The phrase on your aircraft, under the woman, 'Est Nulla Via Invia Virtutui.' Why?"

It was not the question Andrews had expected, but he answered that nose art decorated many American planes and there were men at the bases who would paint whatever you wished. "The crew wanted something on the plane. I didn't want a girl. So we all put our ideas in a hat. The radio operator won. We compromised and they painted the Latin phrase right under the window for me. . . . 'No road is closed to the man who is courageous.'" The name of Andrews's plane was actually *Special Delivery,* but there had been no time to have it painted on.

From Magadino airfield the crew was taken under guard to Bellinzona, where they were housed for the night on the third floor of an empty school. The next morning the train took them to Dübendorf, the military airport near Zürich, for further interrogation by Swiss pilots.

During the trip, the door to Andrews's compartment opened. "Excuse me, gentlemen, I am looking for the pilot of the plane that landed at Magadino yesterday. I was told he was sitting in here," Andrews remembered the man saying.

"That would be me," Andrews answered, relieved to hear an American accent. "Come in, have a seat."

"Actually, I would prefer it if you might come with me." His tone was such that Andrews knew he had no choice.

Andrews followed the man to the front of the car and into a separate compartment. The man introduced himself as Allen Dulles and proceeded to question Andrews. "Look, Mr. Dulles, I'm sure you're for real, and I've heard of your brother [John Foster Dulles was a U.S. foreign adviser at the time], but until I meet with a military attaché here in Switzerland I can't tell you anything about what I was doing yesterday," Andrews said. "I'm perfectly willing to talk about my boyhood in Wisconsin or about my days in college, but about what I did yesterday, nothing."

It seemed that Dulles appreciated Andrews's response. The two had a long conversation in the train compartment. Dulles told the lieutenant about his boyhood days in Auburn, New York, and about his student days at Princeton. He also told Andrews a bit about his work. Dulles cut something of a gallant figure, Andrews recalled; "the spy business was patriotism wrapped in romance." He spoke to Andrews of a plan to smuggle certain objects out of Switzerland and asked Andrews about the feasibility of sending an aircraft carrier up the Adriatic and then a seaplane to Lake Maggiore. This chance encounter with Dulles would lead to Andrews's early departure from Switzerland six months later.

When Andrews met him, Allen Welsh Dulles was on his way to Bern after a clandestine meeting in Locarno. He had arrived in Switzerland in 1942, reportedly one of the last Americans to enter Switzerland via an overland route. His journey to the landlocked country had taken him from the Bahamas through the Azores, Lisbon, Madrid, Perpignan, and Marseilles to Annemasse, a small French town on the French-Swiss border. Dulles was the grandson and nephew of former U.S. secretaries of state; his older brother, John Foster, would be the secretary of state from 1953 to 1959. In 1942, Dulles became the chief of the New York office of the Office of the Coordinator of Information, later known as the Office of Strategic Services, or OSS. He had been a successful Wall Street lawyer before William J. Donovan, head of the OSS, sent him to Switzerland. Although his official title was legal assistant to the U.S. ambassador, he was actually chief of the OSS for central Europe. Because Switzerland was landlocked, getting tactical intelligence there bordered on the impossible. Dulles recruited and relied on several highly placed German officials who made regular trips between Berlin and Bern.[4]

Dulles established his headquarters on 23 Herrengasse, in the old quarter of Bern with a view overlooking the winding Aare River. The vineyard next to his lodgings offered the perfect screen for the visitors who came and went unseen at night. His mission was to gather information regarding German shipments of armaments and supplies, the level of Germany's morale, its strategic intentions, troop movements, bombing results, and who in Germany truly opposed Hitler and whether they were working to overthrow the Nazis.[5]

Switzerland was a mecca for spies during the war. As a technically neutral nation it attracted wealthy refugees and dissidents, people with large international holdings. Its banking laws permitted numbered accounts and were therefore an invitation for private and public interests to route clandestine transactions through Swiss banks. And there were thousands of Swiss holding corporations that were ideal for cloaking Axis assets. Agents from all countries and organizations–Germany alone had agents from the Wehrmacht, the Gestapo, and the Nazi Party running around Bern–practiced the craft of spying in Bern's embassies, cafés, legations, and restaurants. Diplomats, embassy employees, consular officials, and agents tapped phones, went through luggage, stole and read mail, and tailed each other. It was the perfect place for Allen Dulles to set up his spy operation. He had many contacts, but two of them proved invaluable when it came to a particular episode in 1944. Mary Bancroft, a psychologist, handled couriers from French Resistance organizations and had many contacts with interned American airmen. Wally Toscanini, an Italian countess and daughter of the conductor Arturo Toscanini, supervised communications pertaining to the payment and supply of partisans in northern Italy. Her diligent work supplied Dulles with precise information regarding financial, commercial, and arms deals concluded between Switzerland and Nazi Germany.

In 1943, wanting to get these firsthand accounts of top secret information to Washington, Dulles formulated a plan to exchange seven German prisoners—three Luftwaffe pilots and four student pilots—for seven American internees: pilots Martin Andrews, William Cantwell, Alva "Jake" Geron, Sam Turner, Donald Oakes, and Stephen Rapport, and navigator Robert Titus. Dulles persuaded the Swiss government to approach the German authorities to sound them out about this man-for-man deal. The Swiss accepted and the Germans agreed to the exchange.

Dulles had Andrews and Geron memorize classified information regarding German troop positions, spy code names, and the amount of war matériel Germany was moving through Switzerland to Italy by rail. In the planning stages of the operation, on 29 November 1943, Lt. Col. Raymond Chauvet of the Swiss Commission for Internment and Hospitalization wrote in a transfer order that the airmen were to take the train from Frutigen to Bern on 2 March 1944 and would be allowed to bring only their personal equipment and coats. He stressed that "the repatriation must be kept secret vis-à-vis the other internees." In short, the Swiss were to conduct the Americans to the Germans, who would then escort them to Madrid. The German prisoners would be released on the Americans' safe arrival in Spain. On 23 February 1944, just before the exchange, Brig. Gen. Barnwell R. Legge warned the Swiss Army in a memo, "May I invite your attention to the fact that failure to complete these arrangements satisfactorily in advance might cause disruption of the proposed exchange, and constitute a serious matter for us."[6]

On 3 March 1944 Andrews and the six other Americans were taken from Bern to Basel's train station, which straddled Switzerland and Germany. The vast waiting hall gaped before them, empty of people. Banners with swastikas hung from the walls. Andrews was extremely uneasy as the two Swiss diplomats handed them over to the waiting Germans. "What heightened our common concern was the fact that the particular officer to whom the Swiss were handing us over wore the black uniform of Himmler's sinister SS. I thought to myself, 'We are at war with these people, especially with evil looking people like him. What if these Germans change their minds about an exchange when they get us in their hands? What then could prevent them from accusing us, in our Swiss civilian clothing, of being spies? What if some of these SS people found out that I had memorized so many things about their armed forces, including information about certain treasonable people in their midst?'"

Andrews noticed that the SS officer was a major. He carried a dagger at his side rather than a sword, which struck Andrews as a rather peculiar affectation. With a stiff-armed salute and a loud "Heil Hitler!" the major greeted the seven Americans. The Swiss walked away and Andrews realized that their only protection now was the seven German airmen still held in Switzerland, who would be released only when the Americans had safely reached Madrid.

The SS ushered the Americans to a German train where a Wehrmacht guard consisting of a captain, a sergeant (the only English speaker), and a corporal took charge of them. Worry was a constant companion on the journey that followed. It was bad enough that they were in the hands of the Germans, but there was a distinct possibility that they might die at American hands. The Americans frequently shot at German trains, and the two antiaircraft guns on the train's roof made it an especially appealing target. "We were worried in the train because the Americans were shooting trains like mad. We were sweating out our own people," Andrews recalled. Indeed, Alva Geron noted that the trip was delayed en route because of a bombing raid by Americans on the railroad yards ahead of them.[7]

As the train snaked past World War I cemeteries in France, Andrews and the other pilots tried to keep to themselves. En route to Paris the train stopped periodically, and word quickly spread about the American prisoners. Several German officers arranged to speak with the men. There was a German lieutenant who had attended Western Reserve in Ohio and a colonel who had commanded troops on the Normandy coast. The latter told Andrews the Germans and Americans ought to join forces against the Soviets. A Luftwaffe fighter pilot displaying a Knight's Cross at his throat informed Andrews that he considered American bomber crews to be terrorists and barbarians. Some German soldiers approached the fliers merely to bum cigarettes, said Andrews.

Finally they arrived at the Gare de l'Est in Paris and were escorted to a station wagon emblazoned with a swastika. The men piled in and were taken on a carefully controlled tour of Paris, whose great monuments had been swathed in enormous Nazi banners. "They took us on a sightseeing trip through the city on a bus with guards with machine guns at each of the entrances to the bus," said Alva Geron. They were shown a few cathedrals and the Louvre, but it was what they did not see that would later interest the officers who would debrief them in Washington. Absent from their Parisian excursion was a view of the Renault plant, thought to have been severely damaged; for that matter, the tour excluded any destruction at all. The Germans took great pains to show the Americans that they were winning the war.

From Paris the Americans were taken south by train through Bordeaux. In Hendaye, on the French-Spanish border, the same spot where Franco and Hitler had met in 1940, their German guards released them. Andrews and the other six airmen walked across a small bridge spanning the Bidassoa River to Irun. At the same time, four members of the Spanish Blue Division, which had fought with the Germans in Russia, were crossing the bridge. They were "extremely anti-American and yelled and screamed at us," Andrews recalled. "But this came only to shouting, for a Swiss diplomatic courier soon joined us and took us by car to San Sebastian."

In San Sebastian the seven boarded yet another train bound for Madrid. Inside the train the Swiss pointed out two Gestapo agents, dressed in civilian clothes, who were closely following the Americans. They never did more than watch, but their presence was unnerving, especially that of the agent who was missing part of his left hand.

In Gibraltar the seven newly liberated Americans were ordered to change into uniforms (they had been outfitted in Swiss civilian clothing) in order to meet with a high-ranking British officer. "We had to borrow enlisted men's clothing; we were all officers, and it was ill fitting. We looked so terrible, didn't get to the reception, and instead just walked around Gibraltar," Andrews said. Once the men reached

Casablanca they again exchanged their uniforms for civilian clothes. This caused quite a stir once they returned to the United States.

From Casablanca the men went to New York City and then to Washington, D.C., where they were debriefed at the Pentagon. "On the train, we were in civilian clothes and middle-aged women yelled at us, thinking we were draft dodgers. We were taken to the Astor Hotel where we had breakfast and I remember all the food," Andrews said. "Afterwards the cabby was complaining there wasn't any white bread and I just couldn't get over all this food."

Maj. William H. Rhoades conducted the debriefing in Washington. The goal was to ascertain the degree to which the Swiss were aiding the Germans. A transcript of the interview remains in the U.S. National Archives. During the course of the meeting the Americans talked about tours they had taken through Swiss watch factories. While it was widely suspected that the Swiss were producing fuse mechanisms for the Germans, none of the Americans could confirm this. They did, however, verify that certain plants in Biel were manufacturing precision instruments for Germany and that numerous industrial plants near Zürich were producing mechanical items.

The seven also relayed firsthand information regarding Switzerland's oil consumption—oil imported from Germany—that allowed the U.S. intelligence service to determine the state of German oil production. At the time of the debriefing, the Third Reich was still exporting oil to Switzerland, although one American officer noted, "The Swiss belly-ache all the time that it is not enough." It also appeared to the Americans that the Swiss were storing about half of all the gasoline that came into the country in reserves in the mountains with enough food, gasoline, and medical supplies for two years.

Another area of concern for the Allies was the amount of war matériel Nazi Germany was shipping through Switzerland. "I came up through St. Bernard Pass last September [1943] and there were long train loads of coal then going through the pass, and perhaps other materials of such nature," answered one of the pilots to a question on this subject (the transcript of 1944 does not identify speakers save for Major Rhoades). "I saw several train loads. They were using Italian cars to carry the coal, with Swiss locomotives."

•••

Unlike Andrews and the six other men involved in the prisoner exchange, most internees who managed to get out of Switzerland had to rely on their own means. They hoarded civilian clothing; they pawned watches and other valuables for money to buy train tickets; and in some cases they just tried to walk out of the country. Some internees were smuggled in coffins out of Münsingen, the American military cemetery; others tried to pass themselves off as civilians or women. And although they risked arrest and imprisonment for doing so, some Swiss citizens helped them. Guido Meyer, the Swiss cook at Adelboden's Nevada Palace Hotel, secured passage for many airmen. He directed his friends in the Jura to secure civilian clothing, bicycles, and money in order to help the Americans cross the border.

Hans Hungerbuhler, a personal aide to the Swiss commandant in Wengen, also helped airmen escape, according to Robert Vail of the *Liberty Run,* 91st Bomb Group, 401st Bomb Squadron, 8th Air Force.[8] Vail and his roommates, Elmer Sutters and Clem Skuka, arrived in Switzerland on 27 May 1944. After learning of the American ground forces' advance in southern France, the trio planned their escape. Hungerbuhler, who had become their friend, offered his help. The three wrote to the owner of a hotel in Lucerne asking to be invited for five days, a legal requirement for an internee to travel from a camp. Hungerbuhler advised the men to follow the rules, so rather than forge a pass from the Swiss commandant, the three applied formally for passes. Each man was required to sign a parole, a promise that he would not try to escape while on pass. This is where Hungerbuhler put himself on the line. He made it possible for the fliers to retrieve their parole statements. Vail, Sutters, and Skuka escaped, but Hungerbuhler was discovered and sent to prison. "He had broken Swiss law and was considered a traitor in his country," Vail noted. Hungerbuhler later wrote to Vail from prison asking him to write to the U.S. State Department and explain what he had done to help American soldiers escape from Switzerland. After his release Hungerbuhler immigrated to the United States.

Norris King, a gunner on the ill-fated *Sugarfoot,* decided to escape in late September 1944, mostly because of an overwhelming desire for adventure.[9] Together with Dale Pratt and three other Americans, King left Adelboden early in the morning on 29 September 1944. The men began their preparations three nights before their planned departure. They rid themselves of surplus equipment, packing only items essential for their escape. The morning of their escape they put on as much civilian clothing as possible underneath their uniforms, wrapped everything else in small bundles, and then simply set out as if they were going for a stroll.

"As we passed through the village we saw many of our friends, Swiss and American and it seemed a shame that we couldn't even say good-bye," recalled Pratt.[10] A mile out, they came upon a small barn filled with hay. Inside they finished putting on civilian clothing and discarded their uniforms, burying them in the hay. Then they started out again. "From this moment we all began to feel like fugitives."

From Adelboden the group made their way through Thun, Münsingen, and Bern. As they neared Lausanne, they passed several convoys of Swiss soldiers. On 6 October 1944 the group went to the Lausanne train station and separated to increase their chances of success. When the train pulled into the station in Geneva, King and another man disembarked, made their way to the frontier, slipped across the border, and met up with French Maquis. "The man in charge reminded me of Captain Easy, Soldier of Fortune, . . . in the comic strips. The Maquis treated us well, gave us a shot of potato schnapps that burns even as I think about it. We spent overnight with the Maquis and the next day the good old U.S. forces took us under their wing. Joe and I were flown back to the 99th bomb group where we met with our ground crew. . . . We were issued uniforms, given the Purple Heart, Air Medal with four oak leaf clusters and unit citation. Then on to Naples and a troop ship back to the States."

Pratt's road home was not quite as smooth as King's. When he boarded the train in Lausanne, he took a seat next to a friendly looking old gentleman reading a Swiss German newspaper. "I was in constant fear that he would start a conversation with me. I kept looking out the window and pretended to doze. He never said a word. When the conductor came through for tickets I pretended to be snobbish and the conductor took my ticket without a word."

Pratt did make it to the border, but that is as far as he got. He and two of the other men literally bumped into a Swiss guard. With rifle ready the guard demanded in both French and German that the trio show their passports. "We told him we were American soldiers and he ordered us to march ahead of him down the road. We knew we would not be leaving Switzerland that night." Pratt and company were taken to a nearby customs house and interrogated. Despite the driving rain the airmen were then marched to a police station an hour's walk away, put on a streetcar, and sent to jail, where they were taken to a large room. The Swiss made the internees pay for their own fares and that of the guard.

"When we entered this room my heart sank. There were about thirty men . . . lying around the wall on straw, sleeping. . . . I saw several boys I knew. These men had all the blankets, so the guard went around and took two or three from the men. I was cold, wet, and very discouraged." After five days in the prison, without a trial, Pratt and the men were put on the train to the penitentiary camp at Wauwilermoos.

• • •

Even today, with full knowledge of the camps and the harsh penalties meted out to those who tried to escape, some in Switzerland still contend that the government winked at American escape attempts. At the time a popular saying in Switzerland was: "For six days a week Switzerland works for Nazi Germany, while on the seventh it prays for an Allied victory."

Nothing could have been further from the truth. The authorities took strong measures to prevent the fliers from breaking out the moment they entered Switzerland.

On arriving at the internment camp, airmen were forbidden to leave their quarters for two weeks save for meals and one hour of exercise a day under armed guard. After the quarantine period ended they could roam the village streets, within limits. But those who ventured past the posted limits risked being shot by the Swiss guards.

Although the guards were supposed to call "Halt" three times before firing, some internees wounded by Swiss gunfire reported that the command and the firing occurred simultaneously. First Lt. George D. Telford of the 44th Bomb Group reported that when he tried to escape, the Swiss soldier shouted "Halt" and fired without waiting to see if he did.[11] The bullet pierced Telford's left leg just above the ankle. Fortunately, it was a clean wound and no bones were broken.

First Lt. Francis L. Coune, who escaped with Telford, witnessed the shooting. "As we were running, a Swiss guard stepped out of the bushes and hollered halt and fired at us. Lt. Telford was hit in the left leg but we were already on the French side of the road and near the wire, so all three of us tried for the wire. We all got tangled in the wire and got scratched up some but the Swiss guard couldn't get us as we were then on the French side. We bandaged Telford's leg and hiked across the fields to a road."[12]

Brigadier General Legge of the U.S. legation in Bern, not generally a favorite among the internees, sent a memo to Colonel Divisionnaire Dollfuss of the Swiss Internment Service trying to put a stop to the practice.[13] Apparently a Colonel Rudolph had issued the order for Swiss guards to fire on American personnel attempting to escape after the first—not third—order to halt. Although Dollfuss indicated to Legge that Rudolph did not have the authority to issue such an order, U.S. camp commanders confirmed that such orders had been issued verbally at each camp. Legge eventually succeeded in having the order to shoot on first "Halt" rescinded.

Airmen apprehended while trying to escape were first imprisoned in city or town jails similar to medieval dungeons in structure and style. After a military tribunal, if one was convened, the escapee then found himself on a train bound for one of three penitentiary camps: Les Diablerets, Hünenberg, or Wauwilermoos. In most of the penitentiary camps the Swiss guards confiscated the shoes of the Americans each night to impede nighttime escapes—even in the middle of the winter.

"I ended up at Les Diablerets which is in a box canyon, one way in and one way out," wrote Albert H. Burns, copilot on the B-17 *Frostie*.[14] "An old three-story building was taken over to house 'incorrigible escaping hard core Americans.' Just before I arrived some Americans had escaped including our navigator. The Swiss were not about to let that happen again. They took our shoes away. With snow, yea deep, it was impossible to escape. The food was nothing to talk about. The place was full of rats and they were jumping on the beds at night. You learned quickly to keep your head covered and to throw the covers [so] as to throw the rats to the floor."

Imprisonment in the penitentiary camps did little to deter the internees from trying again to escape. It was, after all, expected of them. Sig Robertson, a pilot, received a paperback book from the British Women's Club with escape stories from World War I as well as a dozen cans of pepper and several boxes of cigars.[15] Some of the stories described how airmen filled their socks with pepper and then tore holes in them. The men would put these socks on over their shoes; with each step a little cloud of pepper puffed out, throwing the tracking dogs off their scent. Another trick was to eat as many cigars as possible. Within an hour one would feel nauseous, weak, feverish, and clammy. Once one was taken to a hospital, it was usually much easier to escape.

Correspondence from the Swiss Military Archives documents the official and practiced policy on escapes, further buttressing Americans' testimony. One letter notes: "In brief: I want to say: those who attempt to disobey the order to stay on our soil, have the faculty to disobey internment. . . . From now on all escapees caught—and there is a great many—will be sent automatically to the special camp of Witzwil where they will stay under a strict regime until the end of internment. They will be sent before a military tribunal. . . . They don't have the right to food, etc. equal to those of Swiss soldiers."[16]

The exact steps for punishment were clearly laid out by the Swiss Commission for Internment and Hospitalization: For the first attempt, "without aggravating circumstances, a mere disciplinary punishment" would be imposed. For the second attempt, "criminal proceedings" would be instituted if the escape took place in large groups after a previously made arrangement, especially: "a. if it is connected with the use of civilian personnel with compensation, as a result of bribery, or through deceitful means; b. with resistance and use of force towards security and police agencies; c. through theft, robbery, or otherwise criminally obtained means of transportation or civilian clothing; d. in recidivism after disciplinary or criminal action, or in spite of solemn promise to renounce attempts at escape."[17]

The authorities anticipated that escape attempts would escalate once the internees heard about the invasion of Normandy on 6 June

1944. Guards were tripled and the machine-gun emplacements were doubled at some camps. "After Normandy, the closer the Allies got to Paris, the more the American fliers tried to escape," recalled Jürg Aellig, who was an eight-year-old Adelboden resident at the time.[18] "The Swiss Army was supposed to stop them. The pilots would listen to the radio a lot. They would get nervous about the war reports. Nobody knew exactly who helped the pilots escape. But at the end of the war my dad had three gold watches from the U.S. who left them as 'collateral.' They would ask my dad for money and since things were a bit tight, he couldn't. So they would exchange like this. Well when the first pilot didn't come back, my father knew what was going on."

Before the OSS officially intervened in 1944, the American legation also posed obstacles to escape. Brigadier General Legge issued a memo to all USAAF internees on 29 August 1944 explaining the legation's official policy:

> Your attention is called once more to standing orders against attempting to escape without my instructions.
>
> Disobedience of these orders by a small group of officers and men is bringing about reprisals against the mass of those who are carrying out my orders loyally, thereby creating unnecessary difficulties for this office and serving no useful purpose.
>
> Those who attempt to escape under the present circumstances, in addition to subjecting themselves to such disciplinary action as is deemed appropriate by me, will receive no support from me against punitive action by the Swiss Internment authorities, which will be 5–6 months' detention at Camp Wauwilermoos.
>
> The present military situation indicates the probability of early repatriation and the wisdom of exercising patience.[19]

"The American authorities gave us no help in the matter of escaping and even promised us heavy jail sentences if we tried," wrote S.Sgt. Bernard Segal in a postescape report.[20] Many internees recall being told during the first days of quarantine that no one was to attempt to escape from the country, and that those who were caught would be given a court-martial and dishonorable discharge from the army.

S.Sgt. Alfred V. Fairall, for example, recalled: "We were threatened by General Legge with a court-martial . . . for escaping from Switzerland saying that it was an order from the War Department not to escape. Our orders while in combat were if captured to try, and to keep trying till we made it. Fortunately I made it on the first attempt. Failure to make it was a six months' sentence in Wauwilermoos."[21]

Yet even Brigadier General Legge seemed to concede the futility of such orders. "Regardless of any repressive measures taken," he wrote in a 19 October 1944 memo to Colonel Divisionnaire Dollfuss, "our aviators will continue to attempt to escape. The proximity of the frontier, the fact that many of their comrades have already left and the call to return to battle will be too great a temptation in spite of any existing regulations or conventions, and of all the orders which I have published."[22]

At last, in 1944, with repatriation talks between the United States and Switzerland at a standstill, an extensive underground network was organized under the direction of the OSS. Secretary of State Cordell Hull called on his representatives in Bern to assist such efforts.[23] For a period of several months fliers making their way out of camps were hidden at the legation in Bern and then taken in sealed boxcars to the border of liberated France, from where they were flown to England. Others were ferried across Lake Geneva in the night.

. . .

No matter what escape route one used, it was very important to look like a Swiss citizen. To complete the costume, internees had to relinquish their sturdy GI shoes for something civilian that also fit reasonably well. It was a bad trade for those planning on walking out of the country, but a pair of feet shod in GI shoes was an absolute giveaway. And everyone from train conductors to taxi drivers always seemed to be on the lookout for anything out of the ordinary.

"Orders were to try to escape if taken prisoner. Some of us took that seriously and were always looking for a way to do it. It is a bit difficult to explain but with the daily news updates about how the war was going, it was pretty obvious that we didn't have the right to leave it up to someone else. We had been lucky enough not to end up in Germany, we were still alive, and we could do something about it," said George Michel, who had been working on escape plans from the moment he arrived.[24] He was eventually taken out via the underground.

"You can't just bug out," is how many former internees put it, particularly when news of engagements such as the Battle of the Bulge reached the camps. Not realizing that they would not be allowed to rejoin their units and fly missions over Europe again, the internees were desperate to get out and fulfill their responsibility to their fellow Americans, and they used every tactic they could think of to do it.

George Michel and his buddies used an interesting ploy. A representative from the U.S. legation would occasionally make rounds at the camps to see what kind of trouble the Americans had gotten into. "Illness, drunkenness, girl trouble, anything that you can imagine a bored bunch of nineteen- to maybe twenty-two-year-old males could be involved in and needed to be taken care of," said Michel. It quickly dawned on Michel and a few others to ask this representative to bring extra round-trip tickets–Bern/Wengen/Bern–the next time he came and to lend them his ticket. With these in hand, someone went straight to work filing large nails into the shapes of the holes the train conductor had punched in the courier's ticket. The internees used the nails to punch holes in the other tickets to make them look like they had been used for travel between Bern and Wengen. Passes were then "made" with the forged signature of a Swiss officer stating that said serviceman was authorized to go travel to Wengen on a certain date and return to Bern on a certain date. Passes, train tickets, and the like satisfied the appetite of Swiss officials for paperwork. Official-looking papers and appropriate clothing were the rungs of the ladder many internees used to climb out of Switzerland.

Now Michel and his buddies had the means to officially leave Wengen. They had tickets "proving" they had come from Bern and were expected back there, an essential point since they were wearing GI clothing. The group made it to the American embassy on 22 January 1945. After being outfitted with civilian clothes and shoes, they received tickets for train travel from Bern to Lausanne. They were told to spread out in the train, not to bunch up in one car. "We tried to follow instructions and at one point all ended up in the aisle in the same car as we were looking for a place to sit. The situation seemed funny at the time and we darned near blew it by laughing as we passed each other," Michel said.

When the train pulled into the station, a tall man in a leather coat was waiting for them on the platform. He led them to a funicular that whisked them down to lake level, and they walked to Pully in the cold night. "We were huddled along the shore of Lake Geneva, the dense fog had rolled in, and we waited. No one made a sound," Michel said. "All of a sudden we could see this small rowboat approaching the shore and the moment it beached we were motioned to get in. The tall man pushed us off and left."

The group was rowed out into the fog for about two hundred meters and then transferred to an open twenty-foot fishing boat with two outboard motors. As soon as the rowboat was tied to the stern of the fishing boat, the motors were started and they headed full bore for France. "By the time we reached France, the side of each of us that had been facing the bow of the boat was covered with ice from the spray that came over the bow. It seemed to us that night as we raced across Lake Geneva, that the lake was liquid ice," Michel recalled.

Oilskin-clad brothers Jean-Louis and Raymond Servoz captained the boat twelve kilometers across to the opposite shore. The brothers were part of the Forces Françaises Independent (FFI) cell coordinating efforts with American contacts inside Switzerland. As a group the cell helped 118 English, Polish, and American airmen to escape from Switzerland via Lausanne to Lugrin, France, and on to freedom.

The Servoz brothers operated out of a safe house in Lugrin, just on the other side of Lake Geneva. Every precaution had to be taken when arranging an escape because the Swiss could intercept phone calls from Switzerland to France. So an agent within the network walked the message across the border at St. Gingolph from the Swiss side to France to alert them that a new group would be coming through. By the time Michel escaped in January 1945 the FFI had liberated St. Gingolph and the southern shore of Lake Geneva.

At the time of Michel's escape the biggest worry was Swiss patrol boats—and they were a real threat. The two brothers had already been detained at least once in Lausanne. When the shivering group landed on the shores of France they were taken to a house. "We were told to strip and all of us put into one large bed, naked as jay birds, given a large mug of hot red wine, and lights out for all of us. The next morning we were given back our clothing that had been dried around the potbellied stove that was used to warm the room. There was a whole bunch of French kids who wanted to see the Americans. One little girl wanted someone to go sledding with her and I volunteered. We went up what was a cobbled stone road covered with snow and came flying down on this little luge sled, steering with my feet that were out in front."

From the Servoz home in Lugrin, Michel and the other men were taken by truck to Sevrier and billeted in the Beau-Rivage Hotel until 25 January 1945. Then they were taken by truck to Lyon, put on a plane to England, and processed at Stone. Michel took a plane back to the United States via Iceland, Greenland, and Newfoundland, and arrived home in Saginaw, Michigan, on 23 February 1945. He was not allowed to fly combat in Europe anymore, but he instructed radio operators for French crews flying the B-26. More than forty years later Michel finally found the Frenchmen who had taken him across the lake. He also met the little girl with the sled—now a woman with her own family.

● ● ●

Sam Woods, the U.S. consul general in Zürich and a former Marine Corps aviator, was instrumental in running the underground escape organization. He personally helped two hundred Americans cross the Swiss border into France. The consul general had actually begun his work long before the OSS entered the scene, starting in midsummer 1943 when the Allied bombers began landing in Switzerland.

An operation of this complexity needed money to run properly. Woods was fortunate to get financial help from the president and founder of IBM, Thomas J. Watson. Early in 1943 Watson had concerned himself with the situation of American internees and had given ten thousand dollars toward the purchase of recreational equipment for them. In August 1944 the acting head of the European office of IBM, Werner C. Lier, suggested the money would be better spent if it were given to Woods to help fund the underground.[25]

Various means were used to move internees along the underground route to freedom. One method called for the American airman to feign illness so he would be taken to a hospital in Zürich. At the hospital the internee telephoned Sam Woods, affectionately known as General

Sam, identified himself as a "friend in Lucerne," and arranged a meeting. At the prearranged time and place the internee would find Woods's black Opel waiting to drive him to the train station and was given specific instructions on what to do when he crossed the border.

Another scenario called for the airman to meet Woods inside the Hofkirche church in Lucerne, whose double spires could be seen from any vantage point in the city. The internee entered the church and sat in the left rear pew. Woods and one of his associates, wearing green ties, would be waiting in the pews. After a moment one of them would go down on bended knees as if to pray, cough, and drop a handkerchief. At this signal the flier would come forward. According to some who took this route, Woods would say, "I am an alumnus of Washington University."[26] The internee would then follow Woods and his associate outside and climb into the black Opel for the drive to the frontier.

If the escape occurred at night, the internee knew to call the consulate and say, "There's a friend in Lucerne." The internee then had to make his way to the cemetery in the churchyard, where someone, usually Woods, would be waiting to drive the airman or airmen to the French border in the black sedan.

The American military cemetery in Münsingen was also a stop on the underground. Norman Gibbard, a tail gunner with the 464th Bomb Group, 778th Bomb Squadron, 15th Air Force, found himself in front of the Münsingen depot at midnight. Gibbard and his group were on their way to the Hotel Löwen, where they would stay until contact could be made with Bern. "One of our group went ahead to the hotel to make sure it was safe for us to proceed and the rest of us waited in what we considered to be the safest place—the cemetery," Gibbard recounted.[27] "It was very cold and we waited in shivering silence, sitting on various tombstones until our scout returned. Finally we trouped singly down to the hotel and entered a back room through a window."

Inside were five other escapees who had spent four days there, taking turns sleeping on the two beds. With the additional six, things got a bit crowded. There was hardly enough floor space for the whole group. Together the two groups of airmen made it to Vevey, a quaint town on Lake Geneva, where a husband and wife team working in the employ of the FFI met them. The couple led the internees inside what Gibbard described as the filthiest, most thoroughly rundown house he had ever seen: "Twenty-two of us were crowded into six unheated barn-like rooms. I shared a single-place bed and a single blanket with Rudolph, who was fortunately of small stature. By this time I was so hungry that sleep was out of the question, and so I waited for the morning, when I would at least break the enforced hunger strike. The bread and jam we had that morning still remains the meal to top all meals for me."

Once Sam Woods got internees to the border he would go into a tavern that was connected to the French side by an underground sewer tunnel. A telephone line ran through the passageway, and Woods used it to alert his contact at the French pub on the other side that the Americans were coming. Of course, the internees were not always home free once they crossed the frontier. Second Lt. Peter Zarafonatis of the 338th Bomb Squad, 93d Bomb Group, 8th Air Force, made it across the border only to find himself looking into the barrel of a gun. Zarafonatis raised his hands. The man jabbered something at him. Zarafonatis kept repeating that he was an American looking for help. Thinking the Frenchman understood and had said, "*Avancez*," he moved forward. But the guard had said, "*Attendez*." He fired four shots at Zarafonatis. The bullets whizzed around the American's head. The fourth one hit the fourth finger of his right hand. He yelled. The shots stopped. People poured into the streets. One of them spoke English. Zarafonatis was taken to a nearby pharmacy where his wound was dressed. The French still did not believe he was an American, for although he had dog tags he was dressed in civilian clothes. Somehow Zarafonatis finally made himself understood and the FFI man apologized for mistaking him for a Nazi.[28]

In October 1945 the 7th Army reached the Swiss border. It was a time of feverish escape attempts. The internees divided themselves into those who wanted to escape and those who wanted to stay for the duration of the war. Those who wanted to leave began escape preparations. They called themselves members of the OHIO Club, for "Over the Hill In October."

Escaping took ingenuity, guts, and connections. But it also took sheer will, as the case of Lewis Sarkovich shows. He tried five times before succeeding. "I had a map on the wall and followed the progress of the Southern France Front," Sarkovich later wrote in his memoirs.[29] "When I knew the Allies were at the Geneva border thoughts of escape rose among many. The Swiss authorities sought to stem the flow of escapers. Some Americans were caught and sent to the Swiss concentration camp, Wauwilermoos, a bad news joint I was to learn about first hand." Sarkovich spoke Serbo-Croatian and was friendly with some Yugoslavs, and they helped him arrange his first escape. "I consulted my Yugoslav friends. I was given a Yugoslav uniform, briefed how to hold a cigarette, use a knife and fork, and a Yugoslav name. I had a fresh travel pass and papers, which were all forgeries. I was to speak only Serbian with my escort. We went to Zürich."

Once in Zürich Sarkovich's escort went directly to Sam Woods's office and informed the consul general that Sarkovich awaited on Limmat Quai 76 on the river, upstairs over a beauty parlor. Woods sent word to Sarkovich to prepare to leave. Soon afterward, the Opel pulled up with Sam Woods sitting in the back. He asked if Sarkovich had proper identification to show the FFI once in France and then took him to the border. Woods dropped Sarkovich off just near the border from Geneva, where an Englishman carrying a million French francs in a fat money belt met him. Sarkovich dismissed his waves of suspicion as nerves and followed the man to a deserted house where other internees started arriving one by one. They were fed. Around midnight the internees were led out to a wooded area in small clusters. They regrouped and began walking in silence.

"Suddenly we heard the sound of a round being rammed home in a rifle. The guide yelled, 'Run for the fence.' Someone hollered, 'Halt.' I grabbed the fence and started to climb. Something grabbed my calf. It was an Alsatian guard dog sinking his teeth into my leg. I fell back and someone barked commands to the dog. He let go but put his paws on my chest and snarled in my face. I was silent and froze. The Swiss guard leashed the dog and told me to stand up. The guards rounded up the others but our smuggler was nowhere to be found." The group was taken to a jail. "Blood was seeping into my shoe as we were taken to prison and told to sleep on the hay or the ground. I was given a bandage and told not to worry; the dog had had his rabies shot. That was good to hear, but one thing I'll never forget, the dog had bad breath. I can still smell it."

Sarkovich was returned to Davos and spent ten days in the dungeon. On his release he was taken before Captain Kramer, the camp commandant, who laughed at Sarkovich and warned him not to try to escape again. "I was back in business that very day." Caught a second time, the American was transferred to Camp Greppen on Lake Lucerne. But Greppen could not hold Sarkovich either. He stole a boat and rowed across Lake Lucerne to a chapel, hailed a cab, and asked to be taken to Zürich where he telephoned Sam Woods.

This time Woods drove Sarkovich as far as Lausanne to get a cab to Geneva. He was instructed to meet a woman at a trolley stop precisely at 2:00 P.M. He didn't make it and spent a cold night hiding under a fire escape. At 2:00 P.M. the next day Sarkovich went to the stop. This time a woman appeared and signaled. He countered with a signal, followed her to her apartment, and was given something to eat. After that he went to sleep. The next morning she told him a truck would appear and he was to go with the driver. Sarkovich recognized two of the other five passengers. Then there was a roadblock. "We got out and scattered. I did not get far. We were taken to the police station. I asked to go to the rest room. The window was not locked so I crawled out and took off toward a park. A Swiss officer on a bike passed. I almost fainted. He was the one at the roadblock. He stopped, pulled his pistol. Yes, caught twice in the same day by the same person."

This time Sarkovich found himself imprisoned in a civilian jail in solitary confinement. He spent days there and began talking to himself just to hear a voice. One morning a guard opened the door and told him he was being transferred. "I was trucked with the guard to the train station and boarded the train. We stopped at Wauwil and I was trucked to a camp that looked like a Nazi concentration camp. Wauwilermoos was the worst lock-up ever. Filth, no toilets, cold barracks, food was mere slop. The Commandant rifled packages and Red Cross boxes and sold goodies on the black market. After the war he was tried, sentenced, fined, etc. They should have shot the bastard."

After some weeks Sarkovich was returned to Davos. Never wavering in his commitment to escape, he tried again. This time Woods picked him up in Zürich and dropped him off in Vevey, which is now the international headquarters of Nestlé. "That night I stole a rowboat and followed a compass course determined from the map I set out. During the night patrol boats could be heard and searchlights seen. The waves increased and the ups and downs into troughs were rough. My feet were soaked and I was chilled, with numb legs and feet. I noted a sandy beach and a wooded area behind it. I'd made it my way—Sinatra and I. After searching the beach, I was rubbing my feet as a man with rifle and flashlight approached. He had a red armband, FFI. I said, 'American pilot.'"

The Frenchman took Sarkovich to a military compound of sorts where the commandant spoke English. Sarkovich presented his identification, and the officer called Sam Woods in Bern to confirm his identity. An FFI soldier then drove him to Annecy, France. From there he was trucked to Lyon, where a C-47 flew him to England and then back to the United States. Sarkovich still bears the scars from the dog bite and was one of the few Swiss internees classified as a POW.

• • •

If perseverance did not get one out, there was always creativity, as Stuart Goldsmith, who escaped from Davos, knows firsthand. In Davos Goldsmith became quite friendly with a young Swiss Army officer who was in the village getting treatment for tuberculosis. He taught Goldsmith some French, and in return the airman taught the patient English. Through the Swiss officer, Goldsmith, wearing civilian clothing, went to many parties attended by Nazi dignitaries. The Germans, never in uniform, traveled freely between the Reich and Switzerland, some even living as tourists in the town.

Yet even with such diversions Goldsmith became ever more restless. Finally, he and 2d Lt. Ralph T. Ritter decided they were ready to get out of the Alpine prison and back to their base in England to finish out the twenty-five missions required to complete their tour of duty. "We decided that we could escape past the Swiss guards in Davos dressed as a peasant man and a peasant woman. I tied up my guard in Davos and walked by the very guards and other Swiss people that I had gotten to know during my period of internment, but no one recognized me."

Ritter and Goldsmith traveled to Geneva, crossed the border, and were met by the French underground on the other side.

• • •

Russell K. Sherbourne was also interned at Davos. "Everything considered it could be a very pleasant existence but without anything real to look forward to beyond day-to-day existence," Sherbourne reported.[30] "It's true that an end to the war was somewhat foreseeable. Maybe it would be next year or the year after that or within a few years anyway. Prison might have been different but the prospect of several years of a supported, safe existence constrained to the boundaries of Davos was not very palatable. I began to think about getting out." He decided to escape from Davos after hearing that American forces had landed at Marseilles. He and his roommate, Stanley Scott, resolved to go together. They decided against asking anyone else to come along, thinking they had a better chance of succeeding with only two. "I had no special knowledge of Switzerland and absolutely no experience in attempting to escape and moving as a fugitive," Sherbourne wrote. He and Scott planned to leave at night: "If we left about seven, leaving dummies in our beds, . . . it would be at least 11:00 P.M. the following night before it was discovered that we were missing."

Sherbourne and Scott figured they could succeed with a little ingenuity and a lot of luck. They planned to head for France, following the railroad tracks out of Davos to avoid the roadblocks. "I hoped to be in France in about two weeks. It was rather nebulous but certainly better than waiting in Davos for the end of the war." The two men used a map of Switzerland that Sherbourne had bought in a bookstore. For rations they had some chocolate bars. They wore GI oxfords, flying clothes that had been modified by a tailor to have a civilian look, and lightweight ski jackets. As evening fell they started toward the train station. The tracks led east toward Austria and west through most of Switzerland to Italy and France. "Anyone who has ever walked the tracks knows that there is no good way to do it. In daylight it is not too bad staying to the outside or between the tracks. The alternatives are to balance along a rail, OK for a short distance, or walk on the ties, which are always too close together for a step at a time and too far apart to use every other one. On a dark night like this one the last two methods are impossible and the first difficult but the only choice. Leaving Davos the tracks followed the banks of a small stream. Stumbling along the tracks we occasionally dropped a few feet into the water. This compounded our problems but kept us on course."

Progress was slow. The two men had reservations about traveling in daylight, but the difficulties of night travel convinced them it was a risk worth taking. Furthermore, they were now in the mountains where there were no roads, just railroad tracks. A train whistle of any approaching train would give plenty of warning to duck out of sight. The tracks forked and they had to decide whether to go left and south over a long, high trestle, or right and west. Their map did not have enough detail to help. "However, in my mind the choice was easy. The trestle supported a single track for about 100 yards over a valley, which dropped precipitously below us. Just walking across the trestle peering down between the ties was uninviting enough. Even less appetizing was the thought of a train coming along when we were somewhere near the middle. The only place to go was down between the ties with a subsequent climb up after the train had passed. This would be a good scene for a Harold Lloyd movie but we were not ready for it yet. We struck out along the west branch."

Sherbourne and Scott moved at a steady pace through the cool morning hours. Occasionally the tracks passed through a tunnel; these were usually short enough that the exit could be seen from the entrance. The tunnel walls were smooth and close to the rails. Every fifty or sixty meters there were niches large enough to shelter one or two people. There was no going around the tunnels because of the steep mountainsides. The two were treated to spectacular views of valleys dotted with farms. "We had barely started but with such a beautiful day and magnificent scenery how could we feel anything but optimistic."

About noon the pair entered another tunnel. This time the entrance disappeared behind them with no sign of an exit ahead. Then the unmistakable sound of a train filled the tunnel. There were two sets of tracks, but they had no idea which track the train was on. "Did the railroads use a right hand rule? Anyway we should be able to find a niche to get into. We moved along the wall feeling for a place to get back from the tracks. Behind us the tracks curved around a bend and out of sight.

After the headlight appeared we would have practically no time to do anything. Also, suddenly staring into a blinding headlight, we would not be able to decide which track it was coming on." Unable to find a niche, Sherbourne and Scott lay down on the ground as close as possible to the wall. The train roared past on the track next to them, and they got up and continued to the end of the tunnel. They followed the rails for some time, past houses and a road. The country had become very rural, so they started walking on a dirt road, encountering a few people along the way.

They passed some small villages and checked the names against their map, only to discover that they were heading south toward St. Moritz—the wrong direction. Refusing to be discouraged, they retraced their steps to a point where they could go west. The men arrived at Disentis by early evening and continued on their way toward Andermatt. "Our luck continued through the town. By dark we were out of town, tired and needing a place to rest," Sherbourne wrote in his recollections. "The countryside was dotted with small haylofts, some of them close to the road. We chose a convenient one, slipped inside, climbed to the second deck, and burrowed down into the soft warmth of the hay."

Dawn roused the two fliers from sleep. They shook the hayseeds from their clothing and started west again. Gradually the road climbed, and by late morning they had reached Oberalp, a seven-thousand-foot pass where Swiss soldiers were repairing the road. Hungry, Sherbourne and Scott went into a bakery to buy a loaf of bread. "The road was hot and dusty. The bread helped for nourishment and we had plenty of water from small streams. The mountains in the distance, our next goal, looked far away but each step got us closer."

The road began rising sharply. They used the steep footpaths that cut across the switchbacks, and in the late afternoon, when the sun began casting long shadows, they crossed the timberline. They reached the Furka Pass, about nine thousand feet high, around seven o'clock. A small lodge, nearly empty, sat just off the road. The opportunity to get something to eat was too tempting to pass up. The proprietor slapped some cheese between two slices of bread for two francs and asked no questions. Sherbourne and Scott walked on through the night, not willing to take a chance in the lodge.

Descending now, they finally reached the timberline at Gletsch, the foot of the Rhône glacier where the first melting of ice feeds the Rhône River. They moved into a grove of trees and made a bed on pine needles. It was too cold to stay there. Sherbourne could barely rouse Scott, whose feet were in excruciating pain. Sherbourne carried him down on his back to a small hay barn where they settled in for the night.

Voices outside the barn startled them awake the next morning. With relief Sherbourne saw through a hole in the loft door that it was two bicyclists stopping off for breakfast. After they left, he and Scott set out again toward Lake Geneva. Now they were on a paved road, and traffic started picking up. A car stopped and the driver offered the two a lift. Hikers in the area were common, so they aroused no suspicion. They got to Martigny and from there to Montreux and Vevey.

"Down by the shore some boats were moving about," Sherbourne recounted. "The possibility of 'borrowing' one to cross the lake to the French side was tempting, but the ones we checked were pretty secure—we also saw what appeared to be patrol boats passing periodically. Perhaps we could make it by swimming—perhaps, but the cold water made it appear unlikely that we could make it all the way."

The two headed back to town. Overcome with fatigue, Sherbourne and Scott lay down on the floor of a concrete bandstand. A few hours later they were on their way toward Lausanne. Their shoes were now completely worn through; Scott could barely walk. They decided to risk hitchhiking. While they were waiting for a car or truck to come along, a little boy approached and said his parents would like them to come in for some lunch. They went and supped on potato soup. They asked about conditions along the border and learned that control was tight. The family would not help them but would not turn them in either. And so they continued walking.

"We were both pretty miserable but knew that the night would pass eventually and that in the morning we would be close to our first major goal," Sherbourne wrote. "It was pitch dark so we moved slowly along the road. Suddenly, we were surprised by a flashlight straight into the eyes. Swiss soldiers were protecting a barricade across the road." The two surrendered without a fight. The soldiers checked their dog tags and asked where they were going. During the questioning Sherbourne realized that the soldiers had no sympathy for the Allied cause and were not going to let them continue. They spent the night in an abandoned building with the soldiers.

In the morning they woke up with feet so swollen they could not put on their shoes. After they had a breakfast of coffee and bread, the police came and took them to the train station. One police officer guarded them during the ride. It appeared that they were going to be returned to Davos. "When the train stopped in the late afternoon I was still relaxed in my seat until, looking out the window, I saw a Swiss officer with a police dog," Sherbourne wrote. "I didn't have to be told that this was our destination. When our guard stood up I knew that my protest that this was not Davos was futile. We were turned over to the officer. . . . We started walking again, this time through easy, rolling countryside. Within an hour we came to the gate, with barbed wire."

And so Sherbourne and Scott were imprisoned in Wauwilermoos without ever facing a tribunal. They spent several weeks there before devising a new escape plan with another prisoner. This time they were successful. The three essentially walked out of Switzerland into France and freedom.

• • •

Apprehended American fliers were loyal to their fellow soldiers, no matter the consequences. S.Sgt. Howard Melson, who was a ball turret gunner on the same B-24 as Lieutenants Telford and Coune, was caught during his first escape attempt from Adelboden. He was appre- hended on the Italian border after going six days without food. "For this escape I was taken to Wauwilermoos," Melson said. "All my money and my dog tags were taken from me. After being in this camp with not very much to eat I decided to leave. One night I went over the fence with the intention of going to France."

Melson was caught and brought back. "I was very ill, but was told that I looked well so I must feel well." Three days later, however, he was taken to a hospital and operated on for hemorrhoids. A few days after the surgery Swiss military police came and took Melson to Bern for questioning. "I wouldn't tell the name of the person who helped me escape from Adelboden. I was then sent to a dark cell with one small slice of bread and two cups of soup a day. At the end of ten days I was called before a captain," Melson said. "But I still wouldn't talk. I went back for ten more days. After twenty-four days I was free and went to my camp at Adelboden. They never found the names of the persons who helped me escape."

Once the airmen returned to Allied hands in Annecy they still had to get back to England. Usually a liaison in the Maquis would coordinate with Supreme Headquarters, Allied Expeditionary Forces (SHAEF), to get a C-47 to transport the men back to their base in England. They were debriefed there and then returned to the United States, never to see combat again in the European theater. No matter how an internee escaped, on reaching American lines he had to sign a form stating that he would discuss nothing concerning the circumstances of escape except with approved people.[31]

6

THE WAUWILERMOOS
PENITENTIARY CAMP

*Even death, though unknown, would have been more welcome than
what I was about to face.*

DANIEL CULLER, 66th Bomb Squadron, 8th Air Force

*There isn't any abuse here, but on the contrary strict control on the
part of the commandant of the Camp.*

INSPECTION REPORT from the International
Committee of the Red Cross, 18 August 1944

On 16 March 1944, 2d Lt. Larry Lawler, a pilot with the 381st Bomb
Group, bailed out over Swiss territory.[1] His crew had completed their
mission that morning, but there was no chance they would make it
back to England. The plane was riddled with flak and gliding on one
engine. The bombardier and navigator had already jumped—over
Germany—following the agreement among Lawler's crew that if the
plane had no chance to return to England, the crew could parachute to
safety.

As the bomber approached Switzerland, the eight other airmen decided to bail out. With the Swiss Air Force firing on his damaged plane,
Lawler grabbed his chest chute, which he had stored under his seat.
The bomb bay doors opened and out went the young copilot. Oscillat-
ing in his parachute, Lawler hit the top of a tree and then slammed into
the ground, breaking his leg. Fortunately, all of Lawler's crew survived
the unprovoked attack and perilous descent.

After his broken leg was treated at a hospital near Davos, Lawler, a
North Carolinian who had joined the Army Air Corps immediately after Pearl Harbor, was sent to Adelboden. Impatient with his confinement and desperate to return to the lines, he tried to escape. He had
married his childhood sweetheart just two months before he left for

the war, and thoughts of finishing the war and returning to her were always in his mind.

While he was in Davos, Lawler had met Lewis Sarkovich, the Serbo-Croatian-speaking American airman mentioned earlier. The two befriended some Yugoslavian partisans who were in Davos at the same time; some weeks later, Lawler called on these men to help him flee Switzerland. The partisan fighters gave Lawler Swiss civilian clothing to wear during his flight across the frontier as well as the names of contacts in Geneva who would help him reach the French Resistance on the other side of the Swiss border. The contacts informed him that a certain doctor would meet him near the border and guide him to the rendezvous.

The restlessness in Lawler's gut blossomed after three weeks of waiting in Geneva for this plan to materialize. He wanted to return to his unit. The people sheltering Lawler told him they had their own connections and would make the necessary introductions. A new plan was devised. There was a definite danger in this new plan since it was known that some Swiss with a taste for deceit and profit played both sides. They took money from the Americans and promised safe passage across the border to the French Resistance, and they took money from the Germans on the other side of the border and promised the delivery of U.S. airmen. These Swiss would not think twice about selling out an American if the Germans offered a higher price.

"It was a rainy night and we were at the border and someone came up behind me and put a gun to my head and said, 'You're under arrest.' I think I was sold down the river. I was put in jail for two weeks. They were saying I wasn't American but they knew exactly who I was. The jail was dark, straw covered the ground, and I was with a group of men who were unshaven and stunk. Finally we were transferred to Wauwilermoos. I stayed in Wauwilermoos for nearly three months. It was so bad."

After May 1944, most of the Americans apprehended while trying to escape were sent to Wauwilermoos, a penitentiary camp where disease and violence were rampant. Some were sent because of violent behavior or drunkenness, but most of the men in Wauwilermoos had been caught trying to escape. In May 1944 there were 278 Americans imprisoned in the camp; by February 1945 there were 376.

Wauwilermoos was built in 1940 on the swampland of Lucerne. Double rows of barbed wire and guard towers surrounded the prison compound. Convicted Swiss murderers, robbers, and rapists populated the camp along with the servicemen. The prisoners slept on filthy straw inside wooden barracks that offered little protection from the elements. They suffered from inadequate nutrition, were denied mail, and received little or no medical attention. Rifle-toting guards with attack dogs patrolled the perimeter. Guards sometimes set their dogs on prisoners just to watch the terror on their faces.

"The angriest I got while in Wauwil was one night as I left the latrine a guard set one of the dogs on me just to train him," wrote Dale Pratt in his wartime memoirs.[2] "I was walking back to the barrack when suddenly a dog came silently from behind and leaped at my left arm. He missed and landed about four feet in front of me, he turned with a growl and started for me again when the guard called him off."

The snow fell heavily the night that 1st Lt. Siegvart J. Robertson arrived at the camp. As he approached the enclosure, Robertson glanced to his right toward a snow-covered field and saw several guards training attack dogs. A guard would release a dog, either a Doberman or a German shepherd, about a hundred yards from a trainer swaddled in thickly padded coveralls. On command, the dog raced through the snow and pounced on the trainer's shoulders. "Man and dog disappeared in a flurry of powdered snow," recalled Robertson.[3] "The scuffle ended, the snow settled and the dog was straddling the trainer, gripping his heavily padded neck. The vicious growling and barking of the dogs echoed through the valley, sending chills down my spine. The guards would give us a grin and say, 'See what happens when you try to leave?'"

Flimsy wooden barracks surrounded by barbed wire provided the only shelter against the elements. Inside, at either end of the building, a single light bulb dangled from the ceiling. On his first night there, Lawler curled into himself to find warmth on his damp straw pallet on one of the twenty-five double-decked wooden bins that served for beds. He faced at least two months, and perhaps as many as seven, in the prison.

Lawler's sentence directly violated the 1929 Geneva Accords, which dictated a thirty-day maximum sentence for escape attempts; further, the accords called for the sentence to be served in a facility within the internment camp. It also violated article 186 of the Swiss Military Code, which said that sentences could not exceed twenty days. Nevertheless, airmen were sent to the camps of Wauwilermoos, Hünenberg, and Les Diablerets without a military tribunal and with no set limits to the time of their confinement—both clear breaches of the law. The international law also stipulated that disciplinary punishments exceeding thirty days required a trial and legal representation.[4] If convicted, the serviceman was to serve out his sentence in a dedicated military facility. The Swiss blatantly broke the law here, too, by sending American men to Swiss federal prisons populated by an assortment of the worst criminals in the country.

Throughout the war—and since—the Swiss maintained that the Geneva Accords did not bind them because Switzerland had never signed them. The Swiss defended their policies by arguing the need for strict discipline and punishment. Internees' parole "must be guaranteed and compelled not only by the use of force (which would consist in long term imprisonment) but also by criminal sanctions. . . . If we were to apply merely disciplinary punishment, . . . this would surely not be the case. We must keep to our criminal and procedural regulations, even towards American internees, if we do not wish to run the risk of being forced out of our neutral position."[5]

It seems obvious that the Swiss were aware that their conduct in this regard was questionable, for representatives of the Swiss Military Department, determined to make their case, called a meeting on 29 June 1944 at which Brigadier General Legge and other staffers from the U.S. legation were present. It was one of the few times Legge asserted himself on behalf of the American fliers. Records from the meeting indicate that "the American Delegates did not wish to recognize the legal view of the Swiss, and insisted upon the interpretation, that the internee, after attempts at escape, should be punished only according to the treatment of prisoners of war as set out on 27 July 1929, that is by a maximum of 30 days in jail."[6]

For the most part, however, the American legation overlooked the appalling conditions inside the town jails and penitentiary camps across the country. Brigadier General Legge almost never objected to the conditions at Wauwilermoos, and he never personally visited the prison camp. He did make a few isolated attempts to intervene. On 19 October 1944, for instance, Legge wrote to Colonel Divisionnaire Dollfuss demanding the removal of Americans imprisoned in Camp Wauwilermoos for having attempted to escape: "Their trial drags on; charges are never preferred promptly and they remain indefinitely in this camp mingled with soldiers of other nationalities who are being punished for misdemeanors, drunkenness, insubordination, and kindred offenses." Legge continued, "I am informed by British officers who have been prisoners of war that the punishment meted out in Switzerland for attempting to escape is more severe than that in German prisoner of war camps."[7]

The U.S. authorities in Bern did intervene a bit more often for servicemen imprisoned in other camps. For example, on 18 July 1944, 1st Lt. Dean R. Rexford, the assistant military attaché, addressed "the unauthorized imprisonment" of Lt. Donald Toye and Lt. Robert Tucker for ten days, from 5 July 1944 to 15 July 1944. The lieutenants had been taken under armed guard to the prison at Morges, a town near Lausanne, for allegedly violating Swiss regulations during their authorized visit to Bern. Lieutenant Toye, however, could not read the charges as they were written in French.

On the day of their arrest the pair was told that there was no possibility of a trial and that they would be taken to prison before being allowed to request one. Military personnel from several countries, including Switzerland, and civilians were also incarcerated in the prison at Morges. It was hardly a place to punish an officer for a minor infraction. Toye and Tucker were not distinguished from soldiers and noncommissioned personnel in any way. Their food rations included only one small serving of meat per week.

No one in a Swiss prison ate well, of course. In the municipal prisons and the penitentiary camps rations were cut to bare subsistence levels and could hardly be classified even as nutrition. Prisoners were fed watery potato or cabbage soup and stale bread, and had small cupfuls of water to drink. "Our daily meals were cabbage soup," Larry Lawler reported. "We got our protein from worms that were in the cabbage."

The men at Wauwilermoos usually received a quarter loaf of bread that had to last all day. They fought over that bread, vying for the larger pieces from the middle of the loaf. "They had it in a dirty, filthy sack and they would give us a piece of bread and sometimes it was green and moldy. It was equivalent to a slice of ours. . . . The way it was served, they'd open a door and shove in a kettle. . . . It was just like feeding a bunch of hogs. Everybody grabbed like mad to get it. We did have some tin plates, knives and forks," noted Wallace Northfelt.[8]

Internees in Wauwilermoos were assigned to wooden barracks built on fetid swampland. Their boots sank deep into the muck, and their feet were always wet and cold. A single wooden stove provided the heat for each building. Inmates were allowed outside the prison gate only to get mail or to chop wood for their barracks. The Swiss sergeant watched them closely to see that they did not get too much, recounted Pratt. Prisoners were permitted to be outside the building in the morning for exercise.

Although the barracks had been built to hold a maximum of twenty men, close to ninety were packed into most. Prisoners were given two coarse blankets and told to find a space on the filthy straw to sleep. Straw also served as toilet paper, and a large ditch running the length of the barracks functioned as the latrine. Once a week the guards doled out water to the prisoners so that they could clean the pit. The appalling "sanitary" conditions led inevitably to disease. The camp accounted for 5 percent of the local population of Wauwil during the war, but accounted for nearly 20 percent of the patients in the town's hospital.[9]

"On the fifth day [after a failed escape attempt], October twelfth, we were taken to the station and put on the train to go to the Concentration Camp at Wauwil," wrote Dale Pratt in his wartime log. "When we arrived at the Concentration Camp we were again searched and everything taken except cigarettes and matches. Then we were taken to the barracks." The first two nights Pratt slept in a building with only Polish soldiers as company. Then he was moved into a barrack with

forty-three other Americans. Pratt knew he could expect to be imprisoned there for at least three months. He found the prospect extremely
discouraging.

Periodically the prisoners received care packages from the Red
Cross—or rather what was left after the guards had picked over the
contents. Although they tried to write home, the Americans were never
certain that their letters were mailed. Indeed, a folder in the Swiss Federal Archives holds many letters from Americans and other prisoners
that were never sent. Pratt was one of the few prisoners who did receive a care package. It contained much-needed underwear and socks.
He also got a Red Cross package containing blankets, clothing, cigarettes, candy, and cards.[10]

"On our arrival at Wauwil the Swiss had given us a pair of ragged
trousers, and jacket. A small piece of soap, and a small towel. That was
the limit of what they gave us. I had always defended the Swiss, but
here I almost began to hate them," Pratt wrote. "We were caught doing
what is considered by every power as an honorable thing, and here we
were treated more like criminals. Wauwil . . . is a dirty, filthy prison
with miserably small barracks with many men in each. Double barbed
wire fences around it, with an armed guard every few feet."

The single latrine for each barrack "was a long, low brick affair. The
washroom in the back was fixed with a long pipe with holes in the bottom. The water came from the pipe, ice cold, and fell into a wooden
trough. The trough was exactly like a hog trough and almost as clean.
The latrine was used French style and one had to watch his step or he
might come up missing."

No former inmate of Wauwilermoos has good memories of wash-
ing—Larry Lawler included: "Once a week they'd take us out of the barracks we were in and take us to the guard house and let us shower. We
would strip. The water would come on for 10 seconds and then go off.
We would soap. Then the water would come back on for 10 seconds so
we could rinse. In this guard house there was a potbelly stove which
was warm and there was a line by it with clothes hanging on to dry. I
was badly in need of a pair of socks. On that line was the most beautiful pair of Swiss wool socks and I took them. This is what we stooped
down to."

Showers were infrequent and meals were scanty, but head counts were a daily occurrence. Prisoners were required to muster inside the barracks and await the guard. The barracks were partitioned into stalls. When the guard started the count, some Americans might decide to test his tolerance—or perhaps to cover for anyone who had tried to escape—by jumping back and forth over the barrier to prevent an accurate count. This behavior usually resulted in the guard having to summon other armed guards to keep order, and in some cases the perpetrators got solitary confinement.

Fliers did escape from Wauwilermoos. James Misuraca, a bombardier on a B-24 from the 44th Bomb Group, 8th Air Force, escaped with the help of everyone in his barrack, including the Russians. Misuraca and two others timed their departure to take place between guard and dog rounds. They exited through a window in the middle of the wooden barracks to avoid the corner spotlights. Moving among the shadows, they climbed over the two barbed-wire fences. "We headed west as fast as we could," Misuraca wrote in his wartime memoirs.[11]

"We ran all night and were wet, cold and hungry as well as exhausted. We found a stack of firewood and since it was foggy we started a fire and dried out and were warmed and slept some." When the fog lifted, a building, an inn perhaps, appeared about a half mile down the road. Misuraca, the only one of the three who could speak passable French, ventured inside. He ordered a beer from the waitress and asked her to telephone the American legation. Once in Bern the three bathed and were given clean clothes and a good lunch. They slept until noon the following day. On 12 November 1944 they were taken to the border.

"We waded an icy stream, climbed the Swiss fence, then the French fence," Misuraca wrote. "Shortly I encountered a French guard and I asked if we were in France. 'Oui' was his reply, grinning widely. The guard got on the phone. 'The Americans will be here to pick you up in a couple of hours.' After several cognacs, we saw the American truck approach. A great moment. We were back with friendly forces."

• • •

In addition to the frequent head counts, Capt. Andre Béguin, the commandant of Wauwilermoos, decreed that Sundays were parade days. He ordered each of the prisoners to file before him each Sunday "to

146 SHOT FROM THE SKY

study his soul, study his character . . . so each man could confess to me."[12]

Physical descriptions of Béguin are never flattering: "He was a big fat Captain who was in the foreign legion for thirteen years," wrote S.Sgt. Morris Seifert in a questionnaire for the War Crimes Office dated 5 September 1945. "I think he was about fifty years old and was about six feet tall. I think he weighed between two hundred and fifty and three hundred pounds. They had a little PX there and he wouldn't let any of us Americans buy cigarettes or any of those privileges. He said we didn't want to work and we were all non-coms and we weren't supposed to. He told the guards not to give us any wood for the fire. He didn't like us."[13]

Forced labor compounded the arduous conditions in Wauwilermoos. Some inmates were forced to work at draining the surrounding swampland, at nearby farms, or in the prison garden. Punishment in the prison camp, one to several days of solitary confinement, was meted out for minor infractions—indeed, one witness reported that an internee received five days in isolation because of a missing button.

First Lt. Wallace Northfelt was put in solitary confinement for trying to escape: "It was a little bit of a room about 10' x 10'. There were no blankets and nothing to sleep on but a cement floor. They just served water and bread. One guy was in there for twenty-five days or so. I can't remember his name, but he was an American S/Sgt. There were no lights in there either. When I came out I was in awful shape. I'd say if a man stayed in there for a month, there was a possibility of him coming out dead in my opinion."[14]

The prison guards were quite willing to shoot. Jack Dowd, a sergeant, recalled that "two people tried to get out at night. They were shot at by the guards and sent to solitary."[15] Conditions in the hole were abhorrent. There were no sanitary facilities to speak of—only a trench running along one side of the enclosure that prisoners hosed down weekly. Guards served the prisoners' food in a trough.

As a result of the overcrowding and poor nutrition and dental care, the men imprisoned at Wauwilermoos suffered from pyorrhea, dysentery, boils, and a multitude of other health problems. The commandant sometimes denied medical attention, another violation of international law.

In 1945 the U.S. War Crimes Office began interviewing the thousands of American soldiers who were imprisoned in German and Japanese prison camps as well as those imprisoned in neutral countries. What is striking about the questionnaires filled in by the internees in Switzerland–a country never at war with the United States–is the number of men who attest to imprisonment under unlawful conditions: the failure to provide proper medical care, food, or quarters and unlawful sentencing.

"When I was in prison I was full of sores all over my body and I needed medical attention, but you were foolish to even ask for it. The one doctor that was assigned to take care of us internees was a sixty-five-year-old woman's doctor. He specialized in women's cases and that's all he did. He was assigned to us and he knew about as much about medicine as I did," Northfelt reported in a 28 June 1945 questionnaire for the War Department. According to Northfelt many of the men had chronic stomach disorders. Lt. Cass Smith underwent surgery three times within a week for stomach disorders, and died.

• • •

There were also some Royal Air Force airmen imprisoned in Wauwilermoos. Murray Bartle, an Australian radio operator who flew with the RAF, was there because he had made an unsuccessful attempt to escape from Adelboden. His memoirs record his experiences there. "We alighted from the train and were escorted to our next place of residence–Wauwilermoos–my diary says concentration camp." In the several months that he was imprisoned there Bartle saw only the inmates housed in the same barrack. His barrack had some Russians and Americans, and more Americans arrived on 9 October, coinciding with OHIO (Over the Hill In October), a time when many U.S. fliers tried to escape. Bartle's memoirs also discuss the food: coffee and bread for breakfast, soup for lunch and dinner. The daily bread ration was 4.5 grams; "this meager fare was at times supplemented with a sausage–frankly it presented a revolting sight, about four inches in length, width about two inches. The skin a light grey colour, inside was a grey mixture–the sight was enough to make one vomit. I ate it–such was the hunger."

Like the Americans imprisoned at Wauwilermoos, Bartle did not face a military tribunal until several weeks after he was imprisoned. On 30 October 1944 he and four other prisoners attended one in Bern. About five senior military personnel sat on the bench. No questions were asked other than names and ranks. "After some considerable time of listening to their Germanic prattle, they sentenced us to a further 30 days, which meant we would be at Wauwilermoos until the 16th of December."

Bartle also reported that the actions of one prisoner affected all the others. When Americans were caught trying to escape, for example, all the inmates suffered. "They [the Americans] engineered two escapes–on both occasions we all paid a penalty for these attempts. Guards yelling and screaming raced through the hut, ordering everyone outside. They forced us to stand in rain and snow. They were armed with machine guns and had us remain so, sometimes up to one hour. These attempts also brought on a shortening of our rations." Bartle nevertheless admired the Americans' determination: "Even though the escapees were invariably caught, the Yanks kept trying."

• • •

The guards did not hesitate to put down incipient violence by any means necessary.[16] After an unsuccessful attempt to break out of Wauwilermoos, James Mahaffey returned to rumors of a riot in his absence: "I had heard that while I was away the Russian barracks had been raising hell, shouting, etc. To quiet them down, the Swiss lined up outside the barracks and shot a few volleys into it. Reputedly several Russians were killed. The Swiss had no great love for the Russians."[17]

Testimony from R. K. Sherbourne supports Mahaffey's account: "One night we heard about a riot in the main camp . . . ten to twenty people were killed when guards fired into a building to halt the brawl."

Additional testimony from Wallace Northfelt fleshes out the details: "My pilot, 2nd Lt. Winston Irwin, came back from their first escape attempt. He was thrown in on March 28, 1944 and came back a prisoner and he stated something about two Russians getting killed and afterwards when I got there the same story came up again and I heard it from prisoners that had been around there for months. The story as I heard it was that the Russians were having a little trouble between themselves and were talking loud and making a lot of noise. They were arguing [about] Communist Russia and some other kind of Russia and the guards came in and told them to shut up. And the Russians told them to shut up and the guards sicced a dog on them. One of the Russians took a board and hit the dog over the head and killed it and then the guards immediately turned their guns on them and shot them."

Violence was rife in the other prison camps as well. While imprisoned in Les Diablerets, Sgt. Jacob L. Alpert, 457th Bomb Group, 749th Bomb Squadron, 8th Air Force, witnessed the beating of Sgt. Thomas McGee. In a postwar interview with Capt. Robert A. Crone on 13 August 1945, Alpert related: "While I was at Les Diablerets, the guards were very sullen if you didn't do everything they told you to, or if they wanted you to do something. I saw them jab fellows in the back with the butt of their rifle. Quite frequently, someone would escape from the prison and then at frequent intervals during the night of the escape, the guards would come in and wake us up by prodding us with their bayonets."[18]

Occasionally, small groups of Americans were allowed to take walks in the village near Les Diablerets under armed guard. On one of these outings, Alpert, McGee, and a couple of other airmen went to buy some rolls and coffee. When they returned to the hotel, one of the guards "either tripped or knocked Sgt. McGee down. He just hit the floor when I got downstairs. One of the guards kicked him three or four times and pushed him down with the butt of his rifle or knocked him down with his shoe when he tried to get up." The beating left McGee bruised all over and with a "big lump on his head."

Peter Lysek, who had been interned in Wengen after parachuting to safety on 20 July 1944, found himself in Hünenberg after a failed attempt to escape in early January 1945. He had walked down the mountain from Wengen to Lauterbrunnen, where he boarded a train for Bern. A Swiss guard on the train began questioning Lysek, who was nattily dressed in civilian clothing. "Since my German wasn't that good, he soon realized I was an American. Then he notified the military up ahead and I was taken from the train at the next stop," Lysek reported.[19] In Interlaken, Swiss police locked him in a prison cell that "looked like it must have been built during the Middle Ages. A sort of dungeon looking strong hold. I knew what a caged animal must feel like after about a week in that hell hole," Lysek said. After a week in the dismal cell he was sent back to Wengen, where a Swiss military court-martial tried him for attempting to escape. As punishment Lysek was sent to Camp Hünenberg.

"While I was at Hünenberg there was an escape attempt from that barbed wire hellhole," Lysek said. "With all watches hacked in to the second, at precisely the pre-set time, a dozen men with blankets rushed the barbed wire fence, threw blankets on the barbed wire and bolted over the fence. The Swiss guards began shouting 'Halt! Halt!' and firing." Some men made it to the preplanned rendezvous point, but their contacts were late due to the dense fog. Police dogs tracked down the escaping Americans and in a few hours the men were thrown into solitary confinement.

. . .

Capt. Andre Béguin, an ardent Nazi, ruled Wauwilermoos with intense brutality. He was born in 1897 into a middle-class family in the French-speaking canton of Neuchâtel. The Béguins were farmers, architects, and military men. His father, Jean, was an architect. Raised in an atmosphere of rigorous Protestantism, Béguin worked as an apprentice in his father's firm until 1918 when his father succumbed to influenza and his oldest brother, Jacques, became head of the architectural firm and family. After Jacques took charge of the family firm, Andre Béguin left Switzerland. In his unpublished autobiography, which he wrote in prison after the war, Béguin explained his early infatuation with, and subsequent rejection of, Marxism as the result of his experiences living abroad in Tunisia, where he "was in contact with the worker and the masses. I had been surprised by the hate that existed here against the Marxists. The only remedy was to ameliorate the social situation of workers. . . . In North Africa I encountered the heinous mentality of the indigent worker. . . . I fear for our country if ever this communist doctrine arrives and penetrates the masses of not only workers, but the peasants. *It's thus that I became a member of the National Front,* it was the only party to actively fight against communism."[20]

Béguin's autobiography portrays a man who constructed a world in which he was the sole victim. He blamed his failures on his father's favoritism toward his elder brother and the perceived inadequacies of the Swiss military system. This view of the world helped fashion the manner in which he would control Wauwilermoos.

The Swiss assigned Béguin to the post of commandant despite his professional and personal record–he had been dismissed from the army in 1937 for financial fraud and various confrontations with the local police–and with full knowledge of his open endorsement of the Nazi Party. He frequently paraded through the streets of his hometown dressed in a gray shirt, black tie, and black boots, and signed much of his correspondence with "Heil Hitler." As commandant, Béguin showed a penchant for cavalry boots and riding pants. A horse whip hung from his belt that he cracked for emphasis. He signed nearly every document during the war years with a thick red grease pencil. These documents ranged from missives about supplies to musings about his role as camp commander. "The commandant of the camp is the soul of the camp," he wrote in a particularly striking passage, "the animator of these disoriented beings . . . who only ask one thing: to be commanded and to obey. He represents the country . . . he is the agent of propaganda, the ambassador, he represents the Swiss."[21]

Béguin considered the Americans to be immature and undisciplined and took a protective stance toward the Germans under his care. A letter dated 22 June 1945 describes several threats to internees by civilians of the neighboring towns of Schotz, Egolzwil, Wauwil, and Nebikon: "We have complained many times about the lack of courtesy extended by the civilian population toward the German internees; (a) Sunday evening young people stopped the internees in the street between the train station of Nebikon or of Wauwil and demanded the internees present their permissions [papers]. This type of control is the sole responsibility of the canton police, the military police or military patrols in service. (b) June 10, 1945 Sunday; some civilians threatened a German internee, Pohlmann. (c) June 17, 1945 Sunday; civilians injured a German internee Wartenberg. (d) June 17, 1945 Sunday, civilians hit a German internee Steinmann. . . . [O]ur foreigners have the right to asylum and . . . civilians don't have the right to act as the police."[22]

Béguin showed no such compassion for his Allied charges, who were often targets of verbal and physical abuse from the commandant and his cohorts. Daniel Culler was one such American.

Born to Quaker parents on 22 March 1924, Daniel Culler grew up in Syracuse, Indiana. A fierce sense of duty compelled him, at age seventeen, to join the army. It was a decision quite at odds with his mother's beliefs. When she signed his permission form (because he was underage) she told him she felt that she was signing his death warrant. He attended gunnery school in Utah and flight training in Clovis, New Mexico, before flying to England in *Hell's Kitten,* a B-24H, to join the 66th Bomb Squadron of the 8th Air Force.[23]

The night before Culler's twenty-fifth and final mission, he pondered his recent decision to sign up for more. He had just returned unscathed from a raid to Munich, one of the longest and toughest he and his crew had ever flown, and he was not at all sure that it was wise to test fate and sign up for another tour. In any case, he never got the chance to fly the missions. Just four days before his twentieth birthday, on 18 March 1944, he left to bomb a large ball-bearing plant in Friedrichshafen, a city bordering Lake Constance. Fuel reserves would be scant, and there was a great likelihood of encountering heavy German opposition. The fact that the southern half of Lake Constance lay in Switzerland posed an additional problem—the Swiss fighters and anti-aircraft guns were always ready to shoot at Allied planes.

As expected, the squadron faced flak and fighters on the way to Friedrichshafen. Well into the mission something exploded under the left wing of Culler's aircraft. The plane began pulling left. Gas started to leak. The oil pressure dropped and the temperature rose in both of the left-side engines. With absolutely no chance of flying back to England, the pilot decided to head toward Switzerland. Suddenly four Me-109s appeared. At first the U.S. pilot thought they were German, but they turned out to be Swiss. The Swiss fighter pilots came alongside *Hell's Kitten* so their markings were visible, and the lead pilot signaled the Americans to land or be shot down.

First Lt. George D. Telford, the pilot of *Hell's Kitten,* worried that any unusual movement on his part would provoke an attack. That the Swiss flew in German fighters led Culler and some of his crewmates to believe that Switzerland had allied itself with Germany. As a result, 1st Lt. William E. Carroll destroyed the Norden bombsight. The radio operator smashed any radio parts that could be used to transmit and receive messages. He also destroyed the codebook and flung it out the waist window.

After landing, Culler and his crew tried without success to demolish their aircraft. Swiss soldiers had already ringed the plane and proceeded to march them under armed guard to a large theater with folding chairs and desks. After being interrogated the men were placed on trains and sent to Adelboden.

Thoughts of escaping weighed heavily on Culler's mind. Finally, on 12 May 1944, Culler decided to escape along with his crewmate Howard Edmond Melson of Delaware and Matthew Thirlaway of England (Thirlaway had previously escaped from an Italian POW camp). News of the U.S. 7th Army's advance in Italy hastened their decision. The men planned to reach Ticino, Switzerland's Italian-speaking canton, cross into Italy, and with the help of partisans try and connect with the U.S. Army. They left Adelboden dressed in civilian clothing and boarded the 6:35 A.M. bus to Frutigen, where they purchased three round-trip tickets to Zürich. They hoped the purchase of return tickets would quell any suspicions about their intentions. From Frutigen they traveled to Zürich via Bern, arriving between 3:00 and 4:00 P.M. They purchased three tickets for Bellinzona, the capital of Ticino. They arrived in Bellinzona at 8:00 P.M. and set out on foot for Locarno. For three days the men slept outside. They foraged for berries in the woods and wandered, unsure of where the frontier lay.

Soon Culler began feeling ill. Choosing to return to Adelboden rather than jeopardize his friends' chances of reaching the border, he trekked back to Bellinzona on Monday, May 15. The young sergeant boarded a train to Frutigen and the bus to Adelboden, where he reported back at 8:00 P.M. The camp commandant immediately sentenced Culler to ten days' close arrest, or solitary confinement, in the Frutigen jail. Meanwhile, Melson and Thirlaway continued toward the Italian border. They would not reach it. On 17 May a Swiss guard near the frontier captured the two men. Thirlaway was given twenty days' strict disciplinary imprisonment before being transferred to Wauwilermoos on 17 June. Melson was sentenced to serve time in prison in Bern and Wauwilermoos. He tried to escape again, this time on foot, but Swiss soldiers captured him on 19 June.

What started out as a straightforward story of escape and capture quickly spiraled into a nightmare for Culler. Although he had turned himself in, he would be treated in a most inhumane manner. Shortly after Culler was arrested on 17 May, Captain Kramer, the commandant of Adelboden, sent a memo to the Committee for Internment and Hospitalization regarding Culler's escape attempt: "Culler is very young and weak in character. He was led into the escape attempt by an English escapee Thirlaway. Culler reentered his camp voluntarily. He was never punished for poor discipline. Culler is very depressed and sincerely repents his act. I propose that you accept this 10 days of close arrest in Frutigen as sufficient punishment."[24]

The young sergeant was taken under guard to jail in Frutigen and locked into a cell behind an iron door. There were no windows in the cell; a small, square opening in the door allowed broken beams of light to enter. Culler slept on dirty straw. A hole in the corner of the cell was the toilet. Bugs crawled in and out of the hole and all over Culler. Every few days guards shoved a bucket of water through the door so he could wash. He nourished his sick body with hard black bread and mouthfuls of stale water. Twelve days later, two days longer than his official sentence, Swiss guards returned Culler to Adelboden. He thought he had served his punishment. He was wrong.

During the night several armed Swiss soldiers entered Culler's room, ordered him to dress, and took him before the Swiss commandant. Kramer told Culler he had been ordered to send Culler to another prison to serve three additional months as punishment for his escape attempt. Further, he was to be classified as a civilian prisoner, not a military prisoner. This change in classification meant that neither the Hague Convention nor the Geneva Accords could protect him—not that the Swiss abided by the latter in any case. The consequences of this change would prove disastrous for Culler.

The first sign that he would no longer be treated according to the rules governing internees or prisoners of war came when Culler asked Kramer to allow him to see a doctor about his feet. The frostbite acquired from high-altitude flying had become infected. He was also ill from having unknowingly eaten poisonous berries during his time wandering in Ticino. Kramer assured Culler he would receive medical treatment, but told him that he would have to take up the matter with his new commandant. The guards escorted Culler from the room, forbidding him to retrieve any personal effects, and put him on a train to Wauwil. When the train pulled into the station the next morning, three guards and two German police dogs waited on the platform.

Almost immediately Culler became a special target of Andre Béguin. When he was first brought before Béguin, Culler was defiant. "I only take my orders from the American Army Air Force," he said, "and those orders are: when an airman falls into unfriendly forces, it is his duty to try and rejoin his own command." After that, Béguin's Swiss guards took Culler to another building and forced him, at bayonet point, to remove his clothing and dress in a tattered, waste-covered suit and shirt several sizes too large for him. He was not issued any underwear. Culler felt dirtier than he had ever felt in his life. The guards handed him boxlike shoes with laces fashioned from twine for his injured feet. At this point Culler asked for a doctor to examine his feet. His request was denied.

Next Culler's guards led him down a path between the barracks through a gauntlet of gaping prisoners. Feeling vulnerable, he wrapped himself in his blanket. The guards stopped in front of a ten-by-thirty-foot building, Barrack Nine. A latrine ran the full length of the outside wall. Inside, straw covered the concrete floor, unfinished wood formed the sides, the roof rafters were exposed, and grime obscured the windows.

"As I entered the barrack, the stench was mind boggling," Culler recalled. "Every barn I had been in as a child, even in the cattle stalls sections, smelled 100 per cent better than this hellhole did. One look at the inside and I knew this was a place designed to break prisoners down to nothing more than the lowest type of earthly creature. The Swiss treated their animals better than this."

Soon after that, Béguin contacted the Federal Commission for Internment and Hospitalization regarding the young sergeant. Culler had attempted to contact the American authorities to complain that he was unaware of the consequences of an escape attempt; he had thought a first attempt would be punished only by a reprimand. In his memo, Béguin said he had made it quite clear to Culler that the American legation could do nothing for him, "that he is under Swiss laws and international laws related to war on neutral territory."

The boxlike shoes made Culler's feet bleed; to protect them, he stuffed his shoes with clean grass every day. But failure to contact the U.S. legation, hurt feet, and a filthy, overlarge suit would soon prove to be minor troubles. A few days later, at least four Russian internees grabbed hold of Culler. They forced his mouth open and crammed it full of straw, then held him down and sodomized him, finally leaving him battered and bleeding from every part of his body. The twenty-year-old crawled into a corner, pulled his blanket around his shoulders, and prayed for death. "What happened to me that night, and many more to follow, was the worst hell any person ever had to endure. Even death, though unknown, would have been more welcome than what I was about to face," Culler later said.

In the morning the men started on him again. They forced two large sticks into his mouth and nearly knocked him unconscious. They held his hands behind him and repeated the brutality of the previous night. Afterward they dumped Culler into the latrine. A few hours later, the young sergeant crawled to Béguin. "As I busted in screaming, they all stared at me as though I were some kind of freak, and a sort of nasty grin came across their faces," Culler recalled.

That night Culler tried to stay outside the barrack, but guards forced him inside for the head count. As soon as it was completed, Culler again tried to run outdoors. A Swiss guard saw him and forced him back inside. The four men pounced. The torture would endure for many more nights.

By now infected sores had spread over Culler's entire body. He was throwing up blood and had continuous diarrhea. What little energy he had was slowly ebbing away. Finally Culler mustered enough strength to once more seek an appointment with the Swiss commandant. When he finally found himself before Béguin, Culler lost control and began swearing. The guards threw him into solitary confinement, a punishment Culler welcomed because it released him from the grip of the other prisoners. An occasional tin cup of watery soup complemented his sustenance of bread and water. Bugs infested the cell. Culler had nightmares of them feasting on his open sores.

On 21 June 1944 Culler endeavored to send a letter to Pvt. Hugh McWhinnie, a British internee in Adelboden. It is not known whether the letter ever reached McWhinnie because it was forwarded to the Swiss authorities and now sits in a folder in the Swiss Federal Archives. The tone of the letter is despondent: "Here is behind me barbed wire and just enough to cut my throat. I detest being here so and this is the first time that I have been treated like a dog. I would prefer to be shot or in a German concentration camp more than here, because at least I would know why I was being punished, but here they never tell you anything. Can you imagine, me the son of a minister, in prison? My father would turn over in his grave if he knew. This weighs on me the most, that the Africans in the South who were caught trying to escape were let free.[25] And me, who came back, I receive all possible punishment. Melson and other Americans escaped the day before I was locked up. I hope they succeeded."

In spite of his ordeal, an ember of hope remained alive inside Culler. On 27 June 1944 a Dr. König interviewed Culler: "The British Legation came here yesterday to talk with the men in the English Army who are here; when he approached those who escaped with me he didn't know why we were here the moment we had been punished and he couldn't figure out why the Swiss used such harsh punishment here. As soon as he comes back, he is going to . . . see if he can do something for us because I am under the same inculpation as the English. I can't blame the Swiss because if our Legation knew what [the] Swiss were doing, it would get me out of here. I suppose that if anyone will help me, it will be the English."[26]

On one occasion, in the presence of Béguin, Culler met with a visiting British sergeant. Culler asked the British sergeant why the Red Cross had not come to inspect the prison and check on his condition. He also wanted to know why the American attaché had not been informed of his imprisonment and why he had not been able to communicate his complaints to the legation. A Swiss officer told Culler that the American attaché failed to officially recognize Wauwilermoos, and that Brigadier General Legge was adamant: if an airman broke Swiss rules, he was subject to Swiss law.

After serving his time in solitary Culler again sought an appointment with Béguin, only to be dragged back into isolation. This went on for weeks. Béguin constantly denied Culler the chance to go outside for medical treatment, and Culler was repeatedly told that the commandant did not want the prison to spend the money to bring one in. One Swiss sergeant told him that Béguin looked at Culler just as he would an animal. In addition, Culler was informed—falsely—that since he was no longer classified as a military internee and Wauwilermoos was a federal prison, the Red Cross had no authority there.

Finally Culler was presented with what seemed to be an opportunity to leave Wauwilermoos. The legal division of the Swiss Military had at long last granted him a trial. Present at the trial were Howard Melson and Matthew Thirlaway, the men with whom Culler had attempted to escape. Melson and Thirlaway had been imprisoned in a jail near Bern and in Wauwilermoos, but Culler had not seen them because they were in another part of the camp. It quickly became apparent to Culler that this was going to be a mock trial. The entire court proceedings were conducted in German. Only at the end of the trial did anyone address the men in English. Adding further humiliation, the judge charged Culler eighteen Swiss francs and seventy-five cents to pay for the proceedings.[27]

Before Culler was sent back to Wauwilermoos, the court clerk handed him a copy of the testimony translated into English. It recounted only the three men's attempt to escape, Culler's sickness and subsequent return to Adelboden, and Culler's ten-day sentence served in the Frutigen village jail. The document made no mention of Culler's transfer to Wauwilermoos. The transcript also excluded Culler's account of his treatment and rape, despite the fact that he had testified to these things. Furthermore, the transcript omitted a release date or any indication that he ever would get medical treatment.

Since the men who had raped Culler had been transferred shortly before his trial, the sergeant now had only illness to contend with on his return to the prison camp. A respiratory infection had set in, he still had diarrhea and sores, and he was tormented by incessant buzzing and ringing in his ears from being hit in the head so frequently. Daniel Culler feared he was losing his mind.

Once more he stood before the commandant in the company of the British sergeant. The British sergeant told Béguin that if Culler should die in Wauwilermoos because medical treatment had been withheld, the British government would hold the commandant responsible. Culler and the sergeant left the room and headed back to Barrack Nine. Just before they parted in front of the entrance, the British sergeant warned Culler to be wary of treachery from Béguin, who feared that Culler, if released, would tell of his treatment and the camp's conditions.

Culler's respiratory infection worsened. Some guards and prisoners thought he might have contracted tuberculosis. Once, in the middle of the night, guards took him to "the hole" to isolate him from the other prisoners. On the second day of this third round of isolation, a guard came and presented Culler with a pass to the village of Nebikon and the equivalent of five U.S. dollars, supposedly because Béguin wanted to do something nice for the young airman. This unforeseen and peculiar turn of events raised some misgivings, but they were offset by Culler's happiness to be outside the prison compound.

He set out with pass and money in hand to enjoy four hours of liberty. Halfway to the village Culler removed his shoes and tried to find some soft grass with which to line them. On entering Nebikon, he heard a voice. Partly hidden behind a tree stood a beautiful girl. Although he could not understand why she would want to talk with him, he moved toward her. As he approached she moved farther behind the tree, then she pulled Culler to her. In English she asked if he was the American from Wauwilermoos. At first, suspicion didn't arise. But while he and the fifteen-year-old girl talked, it became clear that Béguin was using her and other girls to entrap prisoners with contrived sentences of rape. She pitied Culler and said she would tell Béguin that Culler was too dirty; she feared she would get a disease from him and pass it on to Béguin. Culler finally walked back to the prison. Guards escorted him to the commandant's office, where he passed out; he awoke hours later in solitary.

Culler began acting like a madman then, even trying to commit suicide by suffocating himself with straw. The events of the past few weeks were simply too overwhelming; he wanted to die. As he felt himself floating away, he saw guards standing over him. They were digging straw out of his mouth, pushing on his belly to force it out. Culler's failed suicide attempt, respiratory infection, and body covered with sores finally persuaded Béguin to let the young airman receive medical treatment. He was immediately transported to a Swiss military hospital in Lucerne and then to a tuberculosis sanitarium in Davos, near the Austrian border. From there, in company with another man, he made his final and successful escape from Switzerland. Even when they had crossed the border, the Swiss continued to shoot at them, grazing Culler and hitting the other person. When Culler met with the French underground he was reunited with Melson, who had escaped with several other Americans and British. The men were flown back to London in a C-47.

· · ·

Successful escapes vexed Béguin. So obsessed was he that on more than one occasion he reenacted attempts in an effort to thwart future ones. The commandant had several informants in the area whom he used to monitor the Americans, men he relished outsmarting. He incorporated information from one such source into a 1944 report relating how some sick Americans sent to the hospital managed to escape. "A very discrete investigation into this has proven that a U.S. sergeant evacuated to the hospital in Sursee at 4 P.M. called Zürich at 5:25 P.M. At 7:30 P.M. an auto driven by M. S. Woods [Sam Woods, the general consul in Zürich] arrived at the hospital at Sursee but one of my guards was already in place and the escape didn't happen. This amuses us because in a conversation with M. S. Woods, he said it wasn't possible."[28]

In addition to mistreating the camp's prisoners Béguin also embezzled camp funds and extorted money from his own staff. In an affidavit used at Béguin's court-martial in 1946, Dr. Georges Troesch, the prison physician, recounted several instances when Béguin took money from him: "I arrived to the Camp of Wauwilermoos on 18 December 1944 in the evening and I lived there and worked there from that date without interruption. . . . The first incident of money that I had with Capt. B was the following: Having received a check for 1500 [francs] to be deposited in Bern, Capt. B said he was going to Bern that same day and could do it for me. I endorsed the check to his name. Two days later, when he came back from Bern, I asked for the money and he gave me 10 bills of 100 [francs], or 1000 [francs], and told me the other 500 [francs] would come to me in a few days."[29] Troesch never received the balance.

• • •

Neither the Swiss Army nor the International Red Cross took note of the heinous conditions of the penitentiary camps or of Béguin's brutality. In fact, most reports from these two institutions lauded Béguin for keeping order and described him in the most favorable terms.[30] A letter written in 1942 by a Major Imer demonstrates the extent to which Swiss authorities overlooked the inhumane treatment internees suffered in the camp: "The complaints concerning the treatment of internees at Wauwilermoos aren't justified and are exaggerated for the most part. It's true that the regime of the camp of Wauwilermoos is stricter than an ordinary camp, but this is necessary all the same as this is a penitentiary and disciplinary camp. The general methods there left me with an excellent impression of this camp. Captain Béguin is a man made to direct a camp of this type. The registers [documents] are also kept in perfect order."[31]

In another report written before the war ended, Major Imer again took the position that any unhappiness on the part of the prisoners had nothing to do with Captain Béguin, the "dream man" to command the camp, or the camp's rules and regulations. "There effectively exists in the camp a state of excellent morale that has a good effect on the internees. If they were severely treated, and if the rule at Wauwilermoos was that of iron discipline, then one also finds a spirit of justice and understanding that facilitates reeducation and a bettering of the difficult elements that are sent here. At Wauwilermoos, despite the barbed wire and the police dogs, the men who complain often are the same ones who engaged in chicanery in the other camps. The grievances formulated against Wauwilermoos camp are not founded."[32]

These reports and others reveal that the Swiss authorities chose to allow Andre Béguin's reign of terror over Americans at Wauwilermoos. The Red Cross likewise failed to report the severe conditions at Wauwilermoos. An International Red Cross inspection report regarding Wauwilermoos noted: "There isn't any abuse here, but on the contrary strict control on the part of the commandant of the Camp."[33]

After the war, Raymond C. Baus, a ball turret gunner on a B-24, seemed mystified that the Red Cross allowed the prison to operate as it did, "under conditions that can only be compared with German and Japanese concentration camps." The aid organization, through the American legation, informed prisoners that they were not considered sufficiently in need to warrant food parcels. To Baus's knowledge the Red Cross never came to inspect the prison while he was there. "The International Headquarters of the Red Cross being within 100 miles of the prison and in the same country, it certainly would appear then that an inspection was in order, particularly when complaints were registered with the international Headquarters," Baus said. "All those spending the average time in this prison suffered loss of weight, malnutrition and dental deterioration (from which I am still suffering) due to improper diet and extremely low quantity of food."

George Telford had occasion to go to Wauwilermoos when he was trying to help Howard Melson: "I also saw the living conditions at Wauwilermoos," he wrote at the time, "and the beds are just straw with one blanket, in addition to which the sanitary conditions are about the most deplorable that I have ever seen. From what I have heard, the Americans were treated about the worst of any of the others who were interned."

The Swiss perpetuated a myth of neutrality and hospitality toward internees that endured for decades after the hostilities in Europe ceased. Many of them believed their own myth, or claimed to do so. But many Americans saw the dark reality that lay just beyond the illusion.

The B-24 *Death Dealer*, piloted by Alva "Jake" Geron, crash-landed in Switzerland on 13 August 1943. Geron's crew was the first to be interned in Switzerland. Memorandum of William Donovan to Joint Chiefs of Staff, 26 September 1944, folder 82, box 120B, Donovan Papers, USAWC.

Swiss guards, by Frank Hensley.

Entrance to "Camp Moloney" at Adelboden. The camp was named for Sgt. Joe Maloney, the first American airman to die in Switzerland.

Adelboden, one of three internment camps for American airmen, was chosen for its remote location.

The Nevada Palace Hotel, Adelboden.

Roll call in Adelboden.

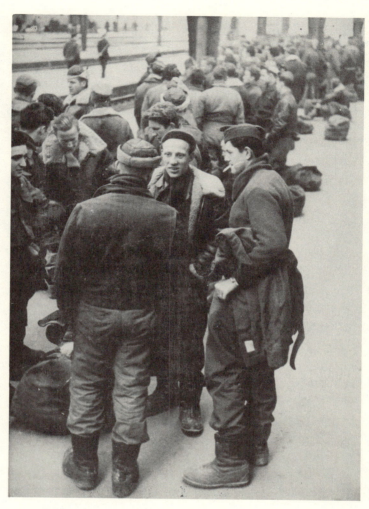

American internees at Zürich train station. Hans-Heiri Stapfer

Crew of the *Georgia Peach*, 15 July 1944. *First row (seated), left to right:* Chester Drake, John Gates, Sig Robertson, Vincent Willis. *Second row:* George Michel, Gerry Landry. *Third row:* Frank Kintana, J. T. Preston Moore, Joe Burdette.

George Michel in California before shipping overseas. George Michel

Swiss military "intimidation parade" in Davos. Siegvart Robertson

The Melody Men, one of two swing bands that entertained internees.

Funeral at Münsingen, 1944.

Brig. Gen. Barnwell Rhett Legge, *left*, and Lt. Col. Alfred R. W. de Jonge attending a funeral service in Bad Ragaz, 1944.

The B-17G *Cahepit* (Can't help it), the one hundredth plane to land in Switzerland, crashed and burned after hitting a high-tension wire near Emmen.

Robert A. Long, 459th Bomb Group, 756th Bomb Squadron, 15th Air Force, was copilot of a B-24J that landed in Switzerland on 24 March 1945.

Dübendorf, where USAAF aircraft were impounded throughout the internment period.

The U.S. Military Cemetery at Münsingen.

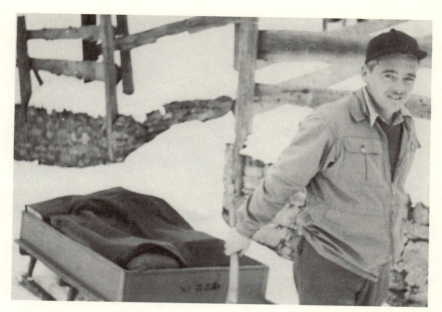

Work detail. Robert Johnson

Swiss soldier securing the B-17F *Lazy Baby*, 305th Bomb Group, 364th Bomb Squadron, 8th Air Force, which crash-landed on 14 October 1943.

This B-17F piloted by Martin Andrews landed at Magadino on 6 September 1943. Andrews was one of seven American men involved in a prisoner exchange orchestrated by Allen Welsh Dulles.

Marion "Dale" Pratt (with bandaged nose), pilot of the *Sugarfoot*, and Joseph Carroll, *far right*, with Swiss guards.

The U.S. Military Cemetery at Bad Ragaz.

American fliers wait to board buses in Adelboden—the first step on the road to repatriation.

7

DIPLOMACY AND BOMBS

The SHAEF people are convinced that the Swiss General Staff is full of German sympathizers.

LT. GEN. THOMAS T. HANDY, Deputy Chief of Army Staff

Finally, in April 1945, the Swiss surrendered—only a month before General Jodl did. DEAN ACHESON

The Swiss policy of internment angered the Americans. Secretary of State Cordell Hull had made formal, but unsuccessful, protests to the Swiss government about the policy, which was troublesome on several levels. U.S. bomber pilots were forced out of action, valuable equipment was taken out of commission, and there was an overriding concern that the Swiss were leaking information to the Germans. But the manner in which the United States, at the highest official levels, responded to the Swiss internment policy begs scrutiny.

Certainly the situation was not pressing when considered alongside the other urgent issues of the war. And although the United States had a diplomatic and military presence in Bern and satellite offices in Basel, Geneva, and Zürich, it could not affect Swiss law. Nevertheless, there was a general feeling among many internees that Brig. Gen. Barnwell Rhett Legge, the head of the U.S. military legation in Bern, could have done a great deal more to improve their lot. Many internees, particularly those imprisoned in Wauwilermoos, recalled Legge as a man bent on pleasing the Swiss government. There was also a sense that except for a few people in the diplomatic corps, such as Sam Woods, the U.S. government representatives in Bern simply did not care about the circumstances the internees faced. The situation became even more difficult and complicated after U.S. planes bombed three principal Swiss cities between 1943 and 1944, embroiling the United States in delicate negotiations that affected the internees.

• • •

The skies were clear over the city of Schaffhausen on the morning of 1 April 1944. Although its citizens as yet had no inkling, today the war would come to this city of twenty-two thousand located north of the Rhine River. Factories in Schaffhausen manufactured antiaircraft shells, ball bearings, and Me-109 parts for Germany—at least until thirty-eight U.S. heavy bombers with no opposition attacked the small cluster of plants. Several hundred people were hurt, and at least thirty-five people were killed in the raid, which had actually been aimed at another city.[1]

The mistake was the culmination of several missteps that had begun that morning back in Great Britain. The radar ships were malfunctioning as the bombers left the English coast on a mission to bomb Ludwigshafen in central Germany. En route to the target the division lost its radar bombing capability. Nevertheless, the command pilot decided to continue the mission to bomb Ludwigshafen and its twin, Mannheim, which straddles the Rhine and Neckar Rivers west of Heidelberg.

Once over the Continent, the 392d Bomb Group slammed into a storm front with cloud tops at least four miles high. Clouds completely obscured the ground below, forcing 165 B-24s of the 2d Bomb Division, 8th Air Force, to fly over, and pass, the primary target. The radar crew simply could not locate Ludwigshafen and the chemical plant that was their target.[2] As no secondary target had been mandated that morning, the division leader had to blindly locate a target of opportunity as close as possible to the primary target. Nine aircraft hit Grafenhausen, fourteen miles from Ludwigshafen; 17 B-24s bombed Strasbourg, thirty-two miles away; and 101 bombers struck Pforzheim, thirty-three miles to the south.[3]

Finally a hole in the clouds appeared, revealing a city below. Group consensus identified the city as Freiburg, Germany. And so thirty-eight planes of the 44th and 392d Bomb Groups opened their bomb bay doors and unloaded 1,184 100-pound bombs on Schaffhausen, Switzerland. They were roughly 130 miles off course at the time.[4]

• • •

When Leland Harrison, the U.S. ambassador to Switzerland, first heard about the bombing he visited President Marcel Pilet-Golaz to express sympathy and regret. Also present at the meeting were Brigadier General Legge, the military attaché, and Jerome K. Huddle, counselor to the legation. During the meeting Harrison learned that fifty planes had violated Swiss airspace and had killed and wounded a combined total of more than one hundred people. Fires caused by the bombs ravaged homes, factories, city buildings, and railway yards. After the conference Pilet-Golaz, who privately viewed the attack as deliberate retaliation for Switzerland's ties to Germany, publicly proclaimed it an error. The commander of the Army Air Force, Gen. Henry H. "Hap" Arnold, decided the prime responsibility for handling the matter lay with the U.S. State Department.

In his usual display of leadership, Carl A. "Tooey" Spaatz, commanding general of the U.S. Strategic Air Forces in the European Theater of Operations, took control of the situation. Before Harrison even met with Pilet-Golaz, Spaatz reported that two bomber groups had admitted bombing in the northern area of Switzerland on that Saturday but claimed they had missed the town. Spaatz and the American ambassador to the United Kingdom went to the Swiss legation in London to formally apologize.

Additionally, Brigadier General Legge relayed a message of extreme regret to Division Colonel Fox Ruhner of the Swiss Air Force and passed on assurances of future precautions against a recurrence. Legge also apologized to Gen. Henri Guisan. And finally, Secretary of State Cordell Hull released a formal statement the Monday after the bombing assuming full responsibility and announcing the U.S. government's intention to make appropriate reparations for the damages incurred. Hull and U.S. Army Chief of Staff George C. Marshall, who was also concerned about the incident, ordered Harrison to ask the Swiss the full amount of personal and property damage. The United States placed one million dollars at the immediate disposal of the Swiss government to put the matter to rest, with assurances that more funds would be forthcoming if the total cost of the damages exceeded that amount. That October another three million dollars in relief funds were released to the Swiss.

These actions did little to mollify the Swiss, who were thoroughly piqued by a statement issued from Spaatz's London headquarters saying that navigational difficulties and bad weather had caused the bombs to fall in error on Switzerland. That afternoon Ambassador Harrison sent a telegram to the State Department: "There is natural popular feeling throughout Switzerland of resentment and indignation on material, moral and theoretical grounds but it is as yet too early to gauge its depth or estimate its effect." This was followed by another telegram: "Terrestrial weather conditions Schaffhausen area were reported exceptionally clear with excellent visibility. If conditions in higher atmosphere were bad, details thereof are essential if statement in communiqué to carry any conviction and not be regarded as inept attempt at evasion."[5]

The reaction of the Swiss press to the incident was decidedly mixed. In Basel the *National Zeitung* expressed outrage over the weather comment, considering it a rather weak alibi, and conjectured that Schaffhausen had been deliberately attacked: "We do not exaggerate in characterizing [this] act as [a] 'war crime' with its destruction of irreplaceable lives, unique cultural objects, and much valuable property." In Bern the *Bund* took a more moderate stance. Accepting that the bombing was an accident, the paper counseled the government to demand that there be no repeat.

Hoping to placate the Swiss and quash budding conspiracy theories, the State Department conducted an independent investigation into the matter. Weather did prove to have been a factor, but more so over France than Switzerland. Clouds and unsuspected winds blowing from the northwest had the navigators confused by the time the planes reached Strasbourg. The bomber formation ultimately scattered and flew off course. Air speed also played a role in the misdirection. The group averaged an air speed of 160 miles per hour. The ground speed was nearly 100 miles per hour faster. So once the clouds had broken over Schaffhausen, the bombardier had just enough time to spot a large city on the east bank of the Rhine, but not enough time to double check for signs that they were over the wrong city. The crews did not search out the intended targets—a butadiene factory, benzyl storage plant, or compressor house—markers that would have confirmed that they were over the correct target.

In spite of stepped-up precautions after the Schaffhausen raid, violations of Swiss airspace continued. The number of incidents actually escalated in conjunction with the increased intensity of the air war over Europe. Pilots who could not make it back across the English Channel had to jettison their bombs before attempting to land, and many of those exploded in Switzerland. There also remained the problem of identification error despite a standing 8th Air Force directive prohibiting target bombing within fifty miles of Germany's borders or in enemy-occupied countries without positive identification. But since the involved crews had been unaware that they were within fifty miles of Switzerland, they would have had no way of knowing they needed to follow this directive.

Cordell Hull concerned himself personally with the repeated violations. He wrote to Secretary of War Henry L. Stimson that while he understood that such incidents would likely increase as more fighting occurred in the region near Switzerland's border, he wanted to be certain that officials and pilots knew about the fifty-mile prohibition. Hull involved himself because he believed the Swiss were instrumental in providing services on behalf of American prisoners of war in Germany. He did not want to close that conduit. Stimson agreed.

Although the Swiss had publicly taken the stance that the bombing was accidental, they expressed an entirely different viewpoint in private spheres. They were frustrated about what they interpreted as the aggressiveness of individual pilots who failed to observe Switzerland's neutrality. This attitude opened the way for the Swiss Air Force to increase its actions against single American planes that violated Swiss airspace. The Swiss Air Force could not do much against misdirected formations numbering one hundred bombers. But they could, and did, act against single planes. The fact that these were often disabled aircraft seeking sanctuary was irrelevant. The next time bombers sought refuge in Switzerland, Swiss antiaircraft units deliberately shot up some aircraft. On 13 April 1944, less than two weeks after the Schaffhausen bombing, six American officers and crewmen were killed when the Swiss attacked their bomber even though they had answered Swiss rockets with signal flares and lowered their landing gear in the international sign of distress. At the end of May, after the War Department pushed him to do so, Hull condemned this attack.

To this day U.S. airmen who flew with the 392d Bomb Group and historians disagree over whether the bombing of Schaffhausen was deliberate, and also about whether subsequent Swiss attacks on damaged Allied bombers were acts of retaliation.[6] On the one hand, Gen. Robert Cardenas, then Captain Cardenas, an evadee attached to the American consulate in Zürich who was ordered to Schaffhausen to evaluate the strike and take pictures, concluded that the bombing was no accident.[7] Roger Freeman, on the other hand, a noted air force historian and author of *The Mighty Eighth War Diary*, concluded that operational records show that pathfinder radar failure resulted in bad navigational errors that sent the aircraft one hundred miles south of their intended course. The result: Strasbourg and Schaffhausen were bombed "in error."

• • •

Several issues complicated the diplomatic situation after the bombing, but in the end the problems were all tied to Switzerland's continued relationship with Nazi Germany. In some respects Switzerland held the upper hand. First, the United States needed Switzerland as a base for its spy operations. Second, Switzerland was holding American internees. Some Allied diplomats feared that chastising Switzerland over its economic aid to Germany would not only affect the treatment and speed at which the interned American fliers were repatriated but might have unseen ramifications regarding the treatment of U.S. and British fliers in German POW camps.[8]

Switzerland was designated the protecting power under the Geneva Accords of 1929, and both the Axis nations and the Allies valued Swiss mediation in matters regarding prisoners of war.[9] In addition, the Swiss-based International Committee of the Red Cross was supposed to oversee POW treatment (despite its utter lack of regard for those in Wauwilermoos, Les Diablerets, and Hünenberg). In many cases the Red Cross brought mail from home and food packages to internees as well as other amenities and necessities that hostile powers were unwilling or unable to provide.

And so Maj. Gen. J. E. Hull of Operations Division of the General Staff told Stimson to pay reparations even if there was lingering doubt over American guilt in the bombing. They too were aware of the ever increasing number of grounded U.S. airmen interned in Switzerland. But America's attention was soon diverted elsewhere once again, and the matter was viewed with less urgency. "We had a war to fight, and we had to get on with it," said General Spaatz's chief of staff.[10]

In June, Col. Harold R. Maddux, chief of the Liaison Section, Theater Group, Operations Division, in the General Staff of the War Department, told the State Department that unless an incident was particularly grave the department was not to bother the commanding general with requests for information. Paul T. Culbertson of State's Division of West European Affairs agreed. Once, when General Eisenhower failed to reply to a violation inquiry, Culbertson said he believed Eisenhower could not respond to an incident that was likely to be repeated.[11]

There were many more violations of Swiss airspace during the period between 1 April 1944 and the near simultaneous bombings of Basel and Zürich on 4 March 1945.[12] The next serious violation occurred when two American fighters downed two Swiss fighters escorting a Flying Fortress in to land at Dübendorf.[13] One of the Swiss pilots was killed; the other was seriously wounded. The Swiss pilots were flying Messerschmitts, and the encounter took place not far from the frontier, so it was thought that the U.S. pilots failed to see the Swiss markings and mistook the aircraft for German planes. After all, German aircraft were known to sneak into neutral airspace.

According to eyewitness accounts, the Fortress made a wide sweep before coming in to land at Dübendorf. The Swiss fighters, which had already taken charge of it, were flying in close attendance. Suddenly two Allied fighters appeared. Combat ensued and the antiaircraft batteries immediately went into action. Flames erupted in the fuselage of one of the two Swiss fighters, which plunged into a steep dive amid thick pillars of smoke. The plane struck a fir tree and then dove into the ground just fifty yards from a house. The crash completely obliterated the aircraft and left the body of the pilot unrecognizable. Above, the fight continued.[14]

The second Swiss fighter also put its nose down and went into a vertical dive, sending out clouds of smoke, but the pilot managed to pull out and land at Dübendorf. Large crowds watched the action, during which a cannon shell struck and ignited the roof of a carpenter's shop. A machine-gun shell from one of the aircraft punched through the roof of a house in Embrach.

The seemingly continuous cycle of violation, apology, reparation, and new violation took its toll on Swiss-American relations. Thus, when in September 1944 General Guisan requested that Swiss military observers be attached to the Supreme Headquarters, Allied Expeditionary Forces, there were some in the War Department who thought it wise to agree. General Legge pushed for approval of the request as well, arguing that having one or two Swiss officers assigned to the Allied staffs in Western Europe would smooth his contacts with the general. Ambassador Harrison and a few others also believed that allowing the observers would vastly improve Swiss-American relations.

Outside that small circle, however, most diplomats and military planners disagreed. Hosting even two extra officers during these crucial days of the war was an inconvenience those on the front lines of strategy could do without—particularly two extra officers who might pass along what they saw to the Germans. It was a risk SHAEF was not willing to tolerate. Maj. Gen. Kenneth W. D. Strong, SHAEF chief of intelligence, and Deputy Chief of Army Staff Lt. Gen. Thomas T. Handy were among those who opposed the idea. Indeed, Major General Strong wrote from the forward headquarters of the Allied forces: "Because of violations of Swiss neutrality by Army Air Forces, the United States War Department has recommended approval of the Swiss request that Swiss observers be attached to the Allied Expeditionary Force with the object of counter balancing the effect of these unfortunate incidents and to establish friendly liaison between the United States and the Swiss. It is my opinion that the proposed action will create a serious security hazard to future operations and should not be permitted. The reason is that the SHAEF people are convinced that the Swiss General Staff is full of German sympathizers. As a matter of fact,

Bedell W. Smith [*sic*] says that they believe about half the Staff has a close tie-in with the German General Staff."[15]

There was some justification for Strong's trepidation. Among those in the highest reaches of Swiss power with known ties to Nazi Germany were Eduard von Steiger, a friend of Himmler, who headed the Justice and Police Ministry Department, and who, later in 1945, served as president of Switzerland; Minister of the Interior Philipp Etter, yet another influential representative of the frontist mentality, who served as president of the country in 1939 and again in 1941; Col. Karl Kobelt, the head of the Ministry of Military Affairs, 1941–54; Walther Stampfli, an admirer of the Wehrmacht who as minister of economic affairs coordinated Swiss industrial production to accommodate the needs of the Third Reich; Dr. Ernst Wetter, finance and customs minister; and Dr. Ernst Weber, president of the Swiss National Bank.[16]

But the diplomats persisted. Finally, after repeated requests, Strong consented, but he insisted that certain conditions had to be met. Only two officers of field grade would be allowed to observe, and the British and American attachés in Bern had to clear their names. All official mail between the officers and Switzerland would be sent through U.S. ciphers. All their personal mail would be censored. Strong also required the officers to stay at least four months, during which time they would not be permitted to travel outside the Allied Expeditionary Force zone or move to the front. In addition, they were to be given no information regarding secret equipment. An Allied officer would escort the Swiss everywhere they went.

Strong hoped that the strict restrictions would make the assignment so unappealing that the Swiss would decide not to send observers. A direct *no* would have been far easier, but diplomatic niceties did not permit that. Furthermore, Legge did not want to offend Guisan. So anxious was Legge to please that on 9 November he tried once more to get Walter Bedell Smith, General Eisenhower's chief of staff, to fulfill the request: "Our situation here is extremely tenuous. Repeated violations of the frontier are bringing about a feeling of bitterness on the part of the Swiss, especially in Army circles. Today, two Swiss bridges and a dam on the Rhine were bombed. In view of my recent approach on the subject of the Rhine control, this puts me in a rather difficult situation.

. . . I feel that with the Swiss it is more a question of loss of face, which is hurting them than anything else. They feel that we are friendly towards them but still we do not trust them on a mission with our Army."[17] Legge argued that he would be better equipped to help the air force internees if Smith would reconsider and allow the Swiss observers.

On 10 November 1944 Gen. Omar N. Bradley, commander of the 12th Army Group, intervened. Bradley, who wanted to guarantee that Allen Dulles would face no obstacles to his intelligence-gathering activities, telegraphed Smith requesting that he accept the Swiss military observers. The intelligence community was concerned because the Swiss continued to harbor resentment over the bombings—enough so that Bill Donovan, chief of the Office of Strategic Services, had apparently sent a message to General Arnold relaying the fears of the Bern spy network that the Swiss might move to impede their work. According to a message from Dulles, General Guisan remained seriously disturbed by the repetition of low-level attacks. Dulles suspected his job of penetrating German intelligence was being compromised because the Swiss were under instructions not to cooperate.

Thus diplomatic and intelligence interests prevailed over military interests. Four Swiss officers were granted a ten-day visit to the 6th Army Group. The British agreed to it as long as the Swiss saw no secret equipment and, even more important, understood this was a one-time deal only. There would be no future visits. With these conditions in place, the tour went smoothly, and by the middle of January 1945 Gen. Henri Guisan had written a thank-you note to the Allied forces.

Despite U.S. efforts to lessen the tensions caused by the violations, the Swiss were relentless in their attempts to manipulate the situation, going so far as to criticize U.S. raids on enemy territory. The Swiss once complained to the American legation about an attack on the French power station at Kembs, a complaint that Colonel Maddux said was "tantamount to the assertion of a right to have the Allies refrain from attacking targets in enemy-occupied territory because Swiss citizens have a financial or other interest therein."[18]

•••

America's misgivings regarding the intentions of the Swiss had roots in Switzerland's behavior during World War I. The current knowledge of Swiss support for the Axis, primarily economic, only deepened the distrust. "If the Swedes were stubborn, the Swiss were the cube of stubbornness," wrote Dean Acheson in his memoir, *Present at the Creation.*

Legally, neutral Switzerland had every right to trade with Hitler's Germany and Mussolini's Italy. Switzerland had traditionally traded with them and was now surrounded by German-occupied territory. Morally, Swiss trade with Germany stepped far outside the laws of both civility and neutrality; it actually sustained the Reich. Switzerland advanced money to Germany so it could import Swiss goods. The Swiss took in gold harvested from the teeth of Jews massacred in the death camps and art lifted from the homes of Jews all over Nazi-occupied Europe. In 1941 Switzerland forbade the export of goods through the mails, ending shipments of small but valuable arms components to the Allies.[19]

Restrictions regarding trade under the Hague Convention, to which Switzerland was a party, required that any limitations on sales be impartially applied so as not to discriminate between the belligerents. According to articles 7 and 9 of the Hague Convention: "A neutral Power is not called upon to prevent the export or transport, on behalf of one or other of the belligerents, of arms, munitions of war, or in general, of anything which can be of use to an army or a fleet." And, "every measure of restriction or prohibition taken by a neutral Power in regard to the matters referred to in Articles 7 and 8 must be impartially applied by it to both belligerents."[20]

The Hague Convention forbade a neutral power to supply, directly or indirectly, warships, ammunition, or war matériel of any kind to belligerent nations.[21] The geographic position of Switzerland might have made absolute balance impossible, and indeed, Germany was not always the favored nation—the Swiss sale of Oerlikon antiaircraft guns in 1939 favored France and Britain. However, once France fell, Germany had the advantage in purchasing weapons and other war-making materials.

The terms of trade changed with the war's progress. In 1943 the

Nazis suffered two severe blows: their defeat at Kursk in Russia and the Allied landing in Sicily. The Allies, sensing that they now had the upper hand, began to increase pressure on Switzerland to curb its trade with Germany. The Swiss avoided meeting these demands, however, and continued to favor Germany until it was starkly clear that the Nazis would be defeated.[22]

Switzerland, being landlocked, depended on foreign ports for its imports, which amounted to about 1.2 million tons per year. Importing foreign goods became difficult during the Allied blockade in the early part of the war and increasingly so as the war continued.[23] So as not to be completely cut off, the neutral countries hammered out a series of war trade agreements with the Allies. These agreements were formulas governing imports and exports to which each country subscribed. If they did not, they risked a total blockade. The point of the agreements was to ensure that the neutrals imported only the amount of goods needed for their own consumption and not an ounce more than they could sell, at a profit, to the Axis.[24]

The Swiss circumvented the regulations and supplied Germany with items crucial for its war effort, including its entire stock of jeweled bearings and large quantities of precision machine tools. Swiss Oerlikon cannons were standard on some German aircraft. Switzerland opened itself to transit traffic that fed Germany's war machine. Oil imported from Romania was shipped by boat to Italy and transshipped by rail through Switzerland. Nickel, chrome, and copper imported from Greece, Turkey, and the Balkans traveled via ship to Italy and then through Switzerland on trains. Pharmaceuticals imported from Turkey were shipped via Italy and transshipped through Switzerland. Sulfur, bauxite, mercury, and silk were imported from Italy and shipped to Germany through Switzerland. And industrial diamonds were imported directly from Switzerland.[25] Switzerland's rail system, and thus Switzerland itself, effectively belonged to the German Reich.

It is now well established that Germany and Switzerland collaborated in trafficking looted artwork. For example, the Lucerne art dealer Theodor Fischer, who held two auctions in 1939 of modern art, had many contacts with Martin Bormann, Joseph Goebbels, and Joachim von Ribbentrop. An OSS report dated 15 September 1945 noted that "Swiss import taxes for works of art were almost non-existent and the prospect of payment in Swiss francs, one of the most stable currencies, made this a most attractive proposition."[26]

Switzerland today sometimes explains its wartime actions by saying it had no choice; the Germans not only surrounded the country, but for a time it looked as if the Reich would be victorious. The first point is indisputable, but the second is debatable, especially after the Allies' 1943 victory in North Africa seemed to turn the tide of the war. And even as the remaining days of the Third Reich were diminishing, Switzerland stubbornly continued to trade with Germany. In December 1943 the course of the war allowed the Allies to insist that Switzerland further reduce the transit traffic between Germany and Italy. Switzerland, however, took its time in the negotiations, worried that Germany would reduce needed coal shipments if Switzerland hindered Germany's coal shipments to Italy.

At the close of 1944 Cordell Hull found the Swiss position disturbing enough to warrant action. Hull favored demanding that Switzerland cease all exports to Germany and stop all German transit through Switzerland. "The delaying tactics the Swiss have employed in this matter are deplored particularly and we are most dissatisfied with Swiss handling of the matter," he noted. "The Swiss should be warned in strong terms that we will be forced to consider measures at our disposal to prevent the enemy from continuing to receive undue assistance from Swiss railway facilities."[27]

The trade negotiations between Switzerland and the Allies were almost a moot point by the end of 1944 because Germany had great difficulty filling coal orders to its trading partners. As well, Swiss exports of armaments and components for arms for the third quarter of 1944 amounted to only 10 percent of the quantity shipped in 1942. Arms and ammunition exports, as well as airplane components and other military supplies, ceased altogether on 1 October 1944 when Allied troops reached the border. By the end of October they had closed the Simplon Tunnel, but not the St. Gotthard, to transit traffic.[28] At this time Switzerland also agreed to forbid the use of its territory to conceal ill-gotten German goods, including money—an agreement the world now knows was not honored.[29]

The transit traffic continued, and the Allies were upset by the amount of valuable material Germany was still getting through Switzerland: railroad switching engines, industrial supplies, machine tools, two billion kilowatt-hours per year of electric power, and more. "Thus painfully we inched along through 1944," wrote Acheson. "Finally, in April 1945, the Swiss surrendered—only a month before General Jodl did."[30]

• • •

The fierce battles over trade rights and the various sentiments expressed by those involved in the negotiations have contributed to the idea that the United States deliberately bombed Schaffhausen, Basel, and Zürich. Like any conspiracy theory there are nuggets of truth embedded in the whole. Certainly when the American ambassador in Britain suggested discussing various options with the British Ministry of Economic Warfare to stop Swiss trade with Germany those options included air attacks on key points in the approaches of Germany and Italy to the two main Swiss railways. But there are just too many holes in the theory for it to be true. Great Britain was not keen to mount such air strikes, fearing they might destroy Switzerland's ability, or willingness, to intercede on behalf of British POWs. Instead, Britain supported pushing Switzerland to prohibit the export of high-priority goods and to cease transit traffic while allowing it to trade in lower-priority items. The U.S. undersecretary of war, Robert P. Patterson, recommended that Switzerland should not be allowed to import goods across France until it stopped sending war aid to Germany.

Not satisfied with Switzerland's response to that, Patterson suggested that SHAEF do something to stop the imports. But doing that would be tantamount to directing General Eisenhower to use the military to shut off the traffic. Rather than put Eisenhower in that position, Hull decided the matter should be handled by the U.S. Department of State. This squabbling left Switzerland with the impression that the State Department did not unequivocally support prohibiting Swiss traffic in France. In reality the State Department was probably reluctant to interfere with SHAEF operational actions until the matter of Axis transits through Switzerland had been settled. As a result, German and Italian transit traffic continued. In January 1945 more than seven thousand tons of clothing, textile materials, and foodstuffs went from Italy to Germany, and the Italians imported valuable products such as chemicals, ore, iron, and fifty-three thousand tons of coal.[31]

• • •

The 1944 trade negotiations hung as a backdrop to continued incidents, albeit minor ones, of U.S. Army Air Force bombings of Swiss border towns. On Christmas Day 1944, flying through cloudy skies that obscured the ground below, bombers from the 1st Tactical Air Force bombed Thayngen, a small Swiss town near Germany, instead of the Singen railroad bridge in Germany.[32]

The New Year heralded a softening in the State Department's strategy regarding Switzerland, partly at the urging of the American legation in Switzerland and partly because of the influence of the British government. Now certain the Allies would triumph, the United States began to consider Switzerland's potential economic role in restructuring postwar Europe. The Swiss had temporarily suspended all exports to Germany until Germany made up its arrears in shipments to the Swiss, and some leniency regarding Swiss-German trade seemed to be in order, according to Acting Secretary of State Joseph C. Grew. Hoping to ease the strain between Switzerland and the United States, President Franklin D. Roosevelt sent his special assistant Laughlin Currie on a mission to Switzerland on 10 February 1945.

The United States made further overtures. On 22 February Currie traveled to Schaffhausen to lay a wreath on the graves of those killed in the April 1944 raid. Unfortunately, another bombing gone wrong marred the somber ceremony. Just minutes before Currie arrived in Schaffhausen, bombers hit Taegerwilen and Stein am Rhein, a town just twelve miles away from the planned service. Seven people were killed and sixteen were injured. Currie's profuse apology did little to placate the Swiss.

Not willing to give up, General Marshall sent a personal cable to General Eisenhower on 25 February 1944 outlining the growing concern in Washington about the apparent increase in attacks on Swiss soil. Marshall reiterated the need for American pilots to be certain they had positive identification of targets before dropping their bombs: "Will you please have someone look into this and let me know what can be done toward preventing recurrence of these incidents?"

Responding to the cable, Eisenhower ordered tactical air forces not to attack within ten miles of the Swiss border—even with good visibility. If instruments were required, then crews could not attack sites within fifty miles of the border. The fifty-mile limit for strategic air forces, save for positively identified targets, would stay in effect. Yet Eisenhower recognized that even the fifty-mile rule was no guarantee against unintentional bombings. As he wrote to General Marshall on 28 February 1945: "Under existing conditions, however, there can be no positive guarantee that such incidents will not occur. Weather conditions [in that part of Europe] are such that air navigation is largely dependent upon dead reckoning except in areas contiguous to our front lines where navigational aids can be utilized. Our Air Forces are performing thousands of successful missions daily in weather conditions that would normally prevent all flying."[33]

• • •

None of the previous incidents prepared the United States for the furor that accompanied the nearly simultaneous bombings of Basel and Zürich on 4 March 1945. Records attribute both incidents variously to inclement weather, faulty equipment, incompetence, or overzealous pilots.[34]

Basel lies in northwestern Switzerland, tucked into a corner between Germany and France. The Swiss had long been concerned that the city's location might confuse Allied bomber crews. Compounding the obvious worry about its inopportune location, Basel had a marshaling yard similar to such yards in France and Germany. The fears were realized on the morning of 4 March when nine B-24s, including the lead ship from the 466th Bomb Group and one B-24 from the 392d Bomb Group, dropped sixteen and a half tons of heavy explosives and five tons of incendiaries on Basel's main freight station. The damage was extensive, and seven people were injured.[35]

Just three minutes later bombs showered down on Zürich, Switzerland's financial capital. Six B-24Hs from the 392d Bomb Group, 14th Combat Wing, 2d Air Division, 8th Air Force, based in Wendling, England, dropped twelve and a half tons of heavy explosives and twelve tons of incendiaries. Five people were killed and another twelve were hospitalized. But that was not all. Twenty-three bombs exploded in an open field. In the Milchbuck quarter of the city, which sustained the most damage, two houses took direct hits. Others were severely damaged. Bombs blasted one residence to smithereens save for a solitary white bathtub, while the sides of another building blew out, leaving the furniture standing in place.[36]

Once again, the train of events that led to the mistaken bombing began in England, before the bombers left Allied airspace. Poor weather obscured the early-morning skies when twenty B-24s taxied down the runway at Wendling and took off under the command of Maj. Myron Keilman, the command pilot in the lead squadron of the 579th Bomb Squadron.[37] The air command decided to assemble the strike force over France, north of Paris, where weather conditions were slightly better. Bombers joined up with the formation of the first group they found and headed for the target of the day, a tank factory at Aschaffenburg, southeast of Frankfurt am Main.

Heading east, Major Keilman and part of his group soon hit solid clouds rising as high as thirty thousand feet. Although it was difficult to hold formation Keilman pressed ahead. Because of the inclement weather, however, it had been decided that Pforzheim, a city on the Enz River between Stuttgart and Karlsruhe, would be the new target. Just as Keilman's group passed Stuttgart, the crew received a recall message from division. The flight engineer fired the Very pistol loaded with recall colors.[38] Keilman turned his group away, leaving the 392d Bomb Group alone in the clouds over Germany.

With the aid of radar, the lead squadron of the 392d bombed Pforzheim. Ten miles from Stuttgart the 44th Bomb Group took a sharp right turn on learning of the recall, disappeared into the clouds, and turned home to Shipdham. One squadron of the 392d Bomb Group remained missing, still loaded with bombs. It was the lead ship of this missing squadron that would be held accountable for the disastrous mistake that followed. Inside the ship were pilot 1st Lt. William R. Sincock, copilot 1st Lt. Norman F. Johnston, navigator 1st Lt. Theodore Balides, bombardier 1st Lt. Alfred R. Williams, radar operator 2d Lt. Murray Milrod, and pilotage navigator 1st Lt. George W. Barger in the nose turret. There was no command pilot on board.

According to testimony given at the subsequent trial, Sincock flew alone in the cloud tops save for two other bombers from the 392d Bomb Group. Eventually three B-24s from other bomb groups joined the trio.[39] They agreed to bomb Stuttgart as a target of opportunity rather than return to Wendling with a full load. At this time, regulations stipulated a target of opportunity as "any military objective positively identified as being in Germany, east of the current bomb line, and west of the twelve degrees [east longitude, approximately the longitude of Leipzig]."

Finding such a target would prove impossible for Sincock. The Germans had successfully jammed the plane's navigational and targeting equipment, making it nearly impossible for Lieutenant Balides, the dead-reckoning navigator, to attain a fix on their position. Furthermore, since Barger could see nothing but clouds from the nose turret, a visual position fix was out of the question. Sincock needed help with a position fix. He asked copilot Norm Johnston to radio the 491st radar ship. There was no answer. Shortly afterward, Lieutenant Milrod, the radio-set operator, said he thought he saw a city ahead.

At this point Lieutenant Balides's chart showed the bomber to be heading west somewhere in the vicinity of the headwaters of the Danube River in the Black Forest. From up in the nose turret Lieutenant Barger reported a break in the cloud cover. Part of a big city came into view. Barger checked signals with Balides and Milrod and gave his opinion that the city was Freiburg—Germany's largest city in the Black Forest. Down rained the bombs.

The mistake became apparent soon after Sincock's aircraft returned to Wendling. The photo interpreters could not interpret the mission film. Maj. Percy B. Caley, chief intelligence officer of the 392d Bomb Group, answered a call to assist and quickly ascertained that Zürich, not Freiburg, had been bombed.

This time the highest in the chain of command knew that no matter how sincere the apology, no matter how much reparation money was pledged, the Swiss were likely to insist on more. At General Marshall's orders, General Eisenhower sent Tooey Spaatz to Switzerland. Marshall cabled Spaatz directly as well, declaring that the bombing of Swiss territory demanded more than an expression of regret. General

Spaatz was ordered to explain how the incidents occurred, what he planned to do about them, and to formally apologize for the United States.[40] The presence of Spaatz, the commanding general of the Strategic Air Forces, European Theater of Operations, would impress on the Swiss the seriousness with which the Americans took the situation. To ensure a productive visit Ambassador Leland Harrison and Sam E. Woods, the American consul general in Zürich, laid the groundwork for Spaatz's visit to Zürich. Together, the two diplomats toured the city. Woods visited privately with the mayor and attended the funerals of several of the bombing victims. Ever mindful of Switzerland's ability to throw a hitch in American intelligence operations, Allen Dulles helped Harrison work out the details of Spaatz's trip and make certain it went perfectly.

Despite the intensive preparation, the first meeting between the Americans and their Swiss counterparts was anything but smooth. Spaatz and his contingent arrived in the French border town of Annemasse attired in civilian clothing to protect the secrecy of their trip. The Swiss greeted the American delegation in dress uniform, either oblivious to or disrespectful of the desire for secrecy. After the first greetings, the U.S. contingent was taken to Geneva, where Spaatz, Harrison, and Brig. Gen. Edward P. Curtis met with Foreign Minister Max Petitpierre, Minister of War Karl Kobelt, General Guisan, and Lieutenant Colonel Ruhner. Curtis took the floor and in impeccable French apologized for the incident. Now the Swiss took their turn. Kobelt spewed a litany itemizing every U.S. violation of Swiss airspace since 1 April 1944, the day Schaffhausen was bombed. The minister demanded no less than an accounting, something more than full indemnity and reparation.[41]

Expressing his regret, Spaatz patiently explained that navigational problems and bad weather were the principal factors in the mistake. He emphasized that every precaution would be taken to avoid future incidents. However, both Spaatz and Eisenhower understood that the Swiss government was unlikely to accept this latest explanation blaming bad weather and promising precautions, particularly the order to pilots to make positive identification of targets within fifty miles of Switzerland. After all, neither the fifty-mile limit nor the insistence on positive identification had prevented the bombing of Basel or Zürich.

In an effort to show U.S. commitment to averting further mishaps, the positive identification zone was expanded to 150 miles from the Swiss frontier. From now on, targets could not be bombed within 50 miles of Switzerland, even with perfect visibility, without personal approval from Spaatz. Should a target need to be bombed in this zone, only highly experienced crews could carry out the mission. The Swiss apparently agreed to keep the forbidden zones confidential to stop the Germans from moving additional targets, such as antiaircraft batteries, closer to the Swiss border.[42] The new rules applied to all of the 8th Air Force's operations and most of the Fifteenth's. Tactical air forces directly under Eisenhower were forbidden to attack any target within 10 miles of Switzerland and were required to have positive identification of any target in the zone extending 10–50 miles from the frontier. The impending collapse of Germany and the fact that few high-priority targets remained within 150 miles of Switzerland allowed such restrictions without endangering the war effort, no matter how exaggerated some in command felt them to be.

It was further ordered that aircrews operating out of the Mediterranean theater, under the command of Lt. Gen. Joseph T. McNarney, would no longer make strategic air force attacks between the Swiss border and a line from Strasbourg through Reutlingen, Laupheim, and Innsbruck. There would be no strikes within 40 miles of the southern Swiss border, excepting at Milan and Bergamo, without special clearance. Crews abandoning airplanes over Switzerland had to set them on automatic pilot heading toward either Germany or the Mediterranean.[43]

· · ·

Unlike the Schaffhausen bombing, which most Swiss eventually accepted as a terrible mistake, most Swiss remained convinced that the attacks on Zürich and Basel were a deliberate response to their wartime dealings with Germany. Both cities lay in the German-speaking part of the country, Switzerland had continued exporting goods imperative to Germany's war effort, and Switzerland had been sending Jews back to certain death in Nazi concentration camps.

According to Jackson Granholm, a navigator with the 458th Bomb

Group and the defense counsel for the court-martial of the pilot and navigator of the plane that bombed Zürich, when Washington and the higher commands of the U.S. military learned of the attack on Zürich, an immediate in-depth investigation was ordered. General Spaatz acted without delay. Sincock and his crew were relieved of lead crew duties on 5 March 1945, as were the lead crew personnel involved in the damage to Basel.

The reason the two officers were brought to a general court-martial is perhaps best explained by a document dated 21 May 1945 written by Lt. Col. Birney M. Van Benschoten, the acting air force judge advocate. Van Benschoten reviewed the case and wrote that both Sincock's and Balides's previous excellent records pointed to poor judgment rather than culpable negligence. Indeed, Van Benschoten considered conviction unlikely in both cases, yet he recommended a trial because "I am advised . . . that the Commanding General, U.S. Strategic Air Forces in Europe, has expressed a desire that charges be disposed of through trial, presumably in furtherance of relations with nations friendly to the United States and injured by the alleged misconduct of accused."[44] In other words, the court-martial was convened to appease Switzerland.

In fact, it would be difficult to confirm exactly who of the many people involved in the affair were responsible. The crewmen of the bombers made significant navigation errors that led them to misidentify targets of opportunity. The weathermen failed to predict the flying conditions the crews encountered that morning. The division commander, Major Keilman, carried on despite having heard the weather scouts advising him to abort the mission.

The formal investigation was launched on 8 March 1945. Lt. William R. Sincock and Lt. Theodore Balides were charged with violating article 96 of the Articles of War in that they had "wrongfully and negligently caused bombs to be dropped on a friendly territory" and had negligently and incorrectly determined the location of the aircraft. The specific charges for Sincock were as follows:

> In that First Lieutenant William R. Sincock, 576th Bombardment Squadron, 392nd Bombardment Group, while in command of and piloting a B-24 type aircraft flying in the position of a squadron leader on a combat

operational mission, did, at or near Zürich, Switzerland, on or about 4 March 1945, wrongfully, negligently and contrary to the provisions of Field Order Number 618, Second Air Division, APO 558, U.S. Army, dated 3 March 1945, cause the planes of the formation he was then leading to drop bombs upon and near the city of Zürich, Switzerland, which territory belongs to Switzerland, a nation friendly to the United States of America and to the United Nations."[45]

Balides faced similarly severe charges:

In that First Lieutenant Theodore Balides, 579th Bombardment Squadron, 392nd Bombardment Group, while dead reckoning navigator in a B-24 type aircraft flying in the position of squadron leader on a combat operational mission, did, at or near Zürich, on or about 4 March 1945, wrongfully, negligently and contrary to the provisions of 2nd Bombardment Division Instructions no. 55-16, Headquarters 2nd Bombardment Division, APO 558, U.S. Army, dated 3 August 1944, fail to maintain a complete and accurate log and chart and did negligently and incorrectly determine the then existing geographical position of his aircraft to be in the area of Frieburg [sic], Germany and convey such incorrect information to the officer commanding said aircraft, who, in reliance thereon, caused the planes of the formation he was then leading to drop bombs upon and near the city of Zürich, Switzerland, which territory belongs to Switzerland, a nation friendly to the United States of America and to the United Nations.[46]

If convicted, the men's punishment would be dismissal from the U.S. military service, forfeiture of all pay due, and confinement at hard labor for life.

The trial, the biggest general court-martial the 8th Air Force had so far seen, was held at Ketteringham Hall, 2d Division Headquarters. It would be a celebrity trial of sorts; rated pilot Col. James M. Stewart–of *Mr. Smith Goes to Washington* fame–would be the presiding officer. Colonel Stewart, the chief of staff of the 2d Combat Wing, had served in the 2d Air Division since November 1943. Unlike the many Hollywood stars and directors who made movies for the war effort and watched the war from afar, Stewart put his own life on the line. He piloted a Liberator and led twenty daytime bombing missions.

The bedrock of counsel Jackson Granholm's defense was the flight log, which he hoped would allow the defense to re-create the flight path of the lost squadron. Careful scrutiny of Balides's navigation records showed that the crew had encountered quite a few navigation difficulties that morning. The first apparent anomaly in the log started at 9:51 A.M. There were no entries in the navigation log for eighteen and a half minutes while Sincock led his squadron on the full-circle turn through the cloud tops searching for the 44th Bomb Group formation. Weather conditions prevented the navigator from tracking a bomber formation through such a wide, wandering turn.

At 10:09 A.M. Balides logged a fix given to him by Lieutenant Milrod. This radar fix—taken from a bearing and distance on Stuttgart—was logged as 8 degrees, 50 minutes east longitude, 48 degrees, 43 minutes north latitude. But Balides fixed it as 8 degrees, 43 minutes east longitude, 48 degrees 50 minutes north latitude on his chart, inadvertently reversing the longitude and latitude minutes. The chart showed him to be flying about twenty-five miles northwest of his actual position.[47] Oblivious to the error, Balides continued to chart his position from that point. Moreover, the wind Balides used to calculate his position was about 70 degrees in direction off the actual wind at operational altitude. This mistake of high-velocity wind at flight altitude meant Balides was using headings about 30 degrees off the actual. The further the bomber flew, the farther north Balides's computed position was from his actual position. As a consequence, Zürich appeared as Freiburg.

In his statement, Sincock said he had been briefed to lead a squadron of the 392d on a mission to bomb a chemical plant in Schaffenburg. It was decided that if clouds obscured the plant, the bombers would use radar; if the radar malfunctioned, the bombers were to hit railroad yards instead. Sincock testified that he knew the locations of all the briefed targets. The statement also noted that Major Keilman, in the lead ship, ordered Sincock back to base to switch airplanes because of malfunctioning radar equipment. Sincock and his crew did not learn that the radar pulse transmitter in the second ship was faulty until they were near the mainland of Europe, but since the radio navigational system worked, Sincock decided to continue the mission.

Balides outlined his attempt to compute a wind at six thousand feet while climbing out over the English Channel and described his efforts to follow the squadron using dead reckoning alone. Balides also said that it was Lieutenant Barger who first identified the target as Freiburg, citing Barger's statement of 24 March 1945: "We crossed the German Border and the Rhine River at a point south of the city [of] Strasbourg. . . . About forty miles further along course, near the point of our briefed turn to the right I last sighted the ground. From that time on until just prior to bombs away I was unable to see the ground well enough to determine my actual, and even relative, position."[48]

When the court-martial began on 1 June 1945, the defendants' chances of acquittal seemed slender given the standing military orders of the time. Army Air Force training standard number 20-2 required pilots of heavy bomber crews to be skilled in bombing and navigation as well as flying. According to 2d Bomb Division Instructions, number 55016, each navigator was to "maintain an accurate log and chart every operational mission." Second Bomb Division Instructions, number 55-15, of 3 July 1944 stipulated that "each Navigator will notify his crew by means of interphone as all international boundaries are crossed on all operational flights." This last order was initiated just after the April 1944 attack on Schaffhausen.

But Sincock and Balides were fortunate. The court-martial found them not guilty on all charges. Several key points contributed to the final determination: first, the cockpit of a B-24 afforded poor downward visibility, so Sincock did not have an unobstructed view of the city; and, second, not only was no map of Switzerland shown during the morning briefing, the flight crews were not instructed to carry the Bern sector map with them and were not reminded in either the field order or the briefing that the briefed withdrawal route passed within about fifteen miles of Switzerland's border.

The numerous bombings of Switzerland ultimately cost the United States millions of dollars. On 21 October 1949 the State Department and the Swiss government agreed on the sum of 62,176,433.06 Swiss francs, or $14,392,692.82. This amount, which represented the balance due plus interest, was in addition to the $4 million already paid after the Schaffhausen incident.

8

AT WAR'S END

We resent the implication that these men are cowards, are low in morale, or lack the will to fight. Such is a base slander against the most courageous group of fighting men in this war.

GEN. CARL A. "TOOEY" SPAATZ, Commander
U.S. Strategic Air Forces Europe

All the survivors of the war had reached their homes and so put the perils of battle and the sea behind them.

HOMER, *The Odyssey*

The first repatriations of American servicemen began on 17 February 1945, but there were still interned Americans in Switzerland when the war in Europe ended on 8 May 1945. The last internee was not repatriated until 27 May 1945. Robert Long, president of the Swiss Internees Association, remembers perfectly the day he learned repatriation was imminent: "I was just as happy as a lark to be leaving. I was on my way home to see my little girl and wife."

A shipment officer arrived at Adelboden bearing enough uniforms for the fliers and instructed them to take whatever fit best so they would be in some semblance of proper uniform for the journey to England and home. After months of wearing worn uniforms, most servicemen sorely needed a crisp new ensemble, no matter if the size was not quite right. Long rummaged through the lot of clothing and found a pair of "pinks" (trousers by that name) and an Eisenhower jacket to wear with his own khaki shirt and tie.

The sun sparkled on Adelboden on the morning of the seventeenth, and despite the biting cold the men stood outside in the streets for hours exchanging farewells. The internees were eager to resume lives so jarringly interrupted by war four years before and elated to be going home to wives, sweethearts, sons and daughters (some of whom they had not yet met), mothers, fathers, brothers, and sisters.

Yet while the internees were euphoric, many Swiss remember the day as bittersweet. The American fliers had been a link with the world beyond their valley. "The day they left the whole village cried," said Adelboden resident Margrit Thüller, whose view typifies the way many Swiss perceived the internment years.[1] "Our friends were leaving us. Of course they were glad to go home after more than two years. The street was packed. A convoy of buses was waiting. There were lots of emotions, like a roller coaster. When they were here we had personal relations with them. We had good memories. It didn't make us forget the war, but all the cruel, inhuman things happening seemed so far away."

Under constant guard the hundreds of internees boarded postal buses to Frutigen and then a train bound for Geneva, via Bern, retracing the route that had brought them to Adelboden. In Geneva the men were taken across the border into France and then flown to England. Once in England many of the men were put on board the USS *Explorer* bound for Virginia. From Virginia, Long went home to New Jersey.

"When I called home my sister had just come home and when the operator asked if a collect call from Lt. Robert Long would be accepted she screamed, 'Mommy, Daddy, Bobby is home.' It seemed like only a second and my Mom was on the phone," said Long, who had been in Switzerland for nearly five months. "I'd called my wife earlier and talked with her. Our daughter Judy was three and a half months old." Long, who had not yet seen his daughter, spent a few days at Camp Kilmer in New Jersey before getting a sixty-day leave to go home.

On 17 February 1945 Peter Lysek, who had been imprisoned in Hünenberg, boarded a French troop train in Geneva and traveled to Marseilles: "From an airfield that was destroyed except for repaired runways we were flown back to England or Italy to our old outfits. So ended my experience as a Swiss Internee or P.O.W. Take your choice! After seven months I was returned back to Allied control and the Good Ole USA!"[2]

• • •

While the end of the war meant happiness for the internees on their way home, it also ushered in an era of misunderstandings and myths relating to their wartime experiences. There were many who welcomed the chance to insult the fliers, calling them cowards who dodged combat by going to Switzerland. Many questions were left unanswered until the former internees were both willing and permitted to discuss their time in Switzerland.

During the war, many among the hierarchy in the U.S. military had encouraged the idea that the American fliers landed in Switzerland to escape the war. The rumors came to a head during the months of March and April 1944, when fifty-five B-17s and B-24s landed in Switzerland. The number of missions had been raised from twenty-five to thirty as the air war intensified, and fighters increasingly pursued German aircraft rather than providing close support for bombers. These facts combined made a convincing argument for those predisposed to the idea that aircrews were trying to avoid combat. And the fact that the Americans were lodged in hotels and could ski or swim helped feed the idea that internment was all recreation and romance for the young airmen. "We were told—we thought—it was like having a picnic for the rest of the war," said one pilot. Many critics of the internees not only insisted that the airplanes landed in pristine condition with more than enough fuel to carry them home, but that the crews had stowed bags packed with vacation wear. Given the incontrovertible evidence to the contrary, these were ludicrous accusations.

One of the most useful bits of evidence refuting such charges is the inspection of aircraft done at General Spaatz's behest after the war was over. The inspection showed that the planes were indeed shot up, disabled, and unable to make it back across the Channel to England.[3] On 18 September, the first C-87s and C-47s arrived in Switzerland, ferrying in ground crews and equipment. As the first C-87 approached for a landing, Swiss ground crews watched in helpless horror as it crashed into a wooded area, killing four American airmen. There were other accidents involved in flying the aircraft out of Switzerland. The first three B-17s left Dübendorf on 27 August 1945. Just after takeoff, the Plexiglas dome blew off the top turret of a B-17 and fell onto a street. Fortunately no one was injured.[4]

Over the course of the next several months, 290 transports landed at Switzerland's main aerodrome. The American crews worked diligently overhauling the bombers, repairing equipment, and taking an inventory of the bombs that had been stored throughout the war. Swiss mechanics assisted the Americans in their work. Between 27 August and 22 October 1945 seventy-two aircraft were flown to Munich-Erding or Paris-Villacoublay. From there they would fly on to Burtonwood, a large U.S. Air Force depot in England: thirty B-17s, forty-one B-24s, and the only airworthy P-51. Aircraft equipment, including bombs, flight suits, and other items, was shipped out of the country in six large trucks, each carrying twenty tons. Much of the equipment was burned after it reached Munich-Erding. Approximately half a million rounds of .50-caliber machine-gun ammunition was taken to an ammunition plant at Altdorf. U.S. military personnel supervised its destruction.

Not all of the equipment and materials made it out of Switzerland. The Swiss managed to keep a great deal. Private Swiss enterprise got about 345 tons of steel and aluminum aircraft scrap as well as all the rubber items, including tires. The Swiss Army got gunpowder and lead and brass from shells.[5] Even after extensive repairs, not all of the bombers met military standards, and many were scrapped in Switzerland. Even the B-17s and B-24s flown to Burtonwood were eventually scrapped.

The report issued after all the interned aircraft had been inspected concluded that save for perhaps one or two, every Flying Fortress and Liberator that landed in Switzerland had done so because of damage or loss of fuel too severe to enable the craft to make it back to England. The number of men who tried to escape and rejoin their units is also clear evidence of the American fliers' loyalty to their uniform. Of the 1,740 Americans confined in Switzerland during the war, a number that includes both internees and POW evadees, 947 tried to escape; 184 failed and were put into Wauwilermoos.[6]

Yet despite the report of Spaatz's inspection teams, somehow the story danced in the shadows of history. Because so little has been written about these events, misconceptions and ignorance about imprisonment in Switzerland abound. American veterans' groups have largely ignored the former internees, viewing them as little better than deserters. The U.S. government itself did not officially acknowledge the existence of Wauwilermoos until 1996 when the Department of

Veterans Affairs published a white paper on the subject. Yet even this document is laden with misinformation. Given the resources at the U.S. government's disposal, particularly postwar interviews with the internees themselves, the persistence of such attitudes is inexplicable.

One such postwar report, dated 4 October 1945, discusses the mistreatment of S.Sgt. Marconi of the U.S. Army Air Force while he was a prisoner at Wauwilermoos, Switzerland, by the Swiss Army. Marconi, part of a B-17 bomber crew based in England, tried to escape from a Swiss Army prison in August 1944. Swiss military police apprehended the sergeant and transferred him to Wauwilermoos. According to the report: "Marconi was kept in solitary confinement in a damp, dirty dungeon. The place of imprisonment was infested with vermin and the left side of Marconi's body was severely 'chewed up' by lice and other vermin that infested the place of his imprisonment. Marconi's diet consisted of a bowl of thin soup and one potato each day. Marconi was finally liberated and returned to England." This document, dated 31 October 1946, was sent to the War Crimes Branch in the Department of State.

Former internee Jack Dowd was frustrated by the disparity between the reality of Wauwilermoos and the prevailing impression of conditions there: "There wasn't too much food and we'd fight over who got the largest piece of bread. It was dirty and miserable. Once there was a mouse or a rat at my incision. It was swampland. You got off the train and you sank a foot. It was as bad as the toughest camp in Germany, but at least there were bunks in Germany. The U.S. government ignored it. I had three brothers in the service, one in the Marine Corps, and two in the Army, but they thought I was leading the life of Riley."[7]

Leading the life of Riley. An apt characterization of what many outside the internees' circle thought of life in Switzerland during the war. "I think a lot of people had the misconception that Switzerland was safe," said Jim Clemines, 34th Bomb Group, 8th Air Force. "The stories we got about those in Switzerland were that the guys there were having a picnic for the rest of the war. Switzerland would be a rest, or a vacation." Other airmen who flew with the 8th Air Force but were never imprisoned in Switzerland had strange ideas as well. Some said they heard life got so boring that the Swiss allowed crews to repair their airplanes and fly them as long as they did not cross the border.

The disparaging comments resonated through the diplomatic corps as well. And they were not limited to soldiers interned in Switzerland; the fliers interned in Sweden were targets as well. The remarks of William B. Corcoran, the American consul in Göteborg, Sweden, capture the feelings of many. Corcoran believed that the morale of the escaped young fliers with whom he had contact warranted serious consideration and surveillance. "Almost every escaped American airman with whom I have talked has emphatically declared that he has had enough war flying and will not do any more of it. . . . Against this excusable distaste for further air action, however, is something which, to the observer, appears extremely serious. That is a complete lack of patriotism and continued sense of duty which, if transmitted by these escapees to their uninitiated fellows preparing for bombing raids, may prove very detrimental to morale."[8]

Reports like this one combined with the steadily rising number of 8th Air Force crews interned after crashing or landing in neutral countries alarmed General Arnold. The 2d Bombardment Division accounted for a significant number of the forced landings, principally because the B-24s' longer range, compared with that of the B-17s, allowed them to fly on deeper penetration missions.[9] In June 1944 about three-quarters of the imprisoned crews, or twenty-eight of thirty-eight aircraft, were from the 2d Bombardment Division. During the 358th Bomb Group's raid on Politz on 20 June, twenty bombers landed in Sweden; and on 21 June, when the Eighth sent out more than one thousand bombers to bomb Berlin, fourteen bombers, seven from the 2d Division, landed in Sweden. In July about 40 percent of the crews interned, or fifteen of forty-one aircraft, were from the 2d Division.[10]

In mid-July, these numbers plus the rumors swirling around the landings led General Spaatz to send battle-experienced USAAF officers to interview crews imprisoned in both Switzerland and Sweden. Spaatz wanted experts to evaluate the reasons why crews were landing in the neutral countries, hoping to resolve the matter.[11] On 29 July 1944 Spaatz defended his aircrews to Arnold: "We resent the implication that these crews are cowards, are low in morale or lack the will to fight. Such is a base slander against the most courageous group of fighting men in this war." In addition, Spaatz stressed that the internees amounted to a minuscule fraction of the crews sent, and that some groups—many groups—had stuck with it despite at least 60 percent casualties.[12]

...

After the war, the interned American airmen faced problems in addition to the unfounded rumors of their cowardice. The U.S. government refused to grant them prisoner-of-war status. This was partly because their status during the war was not wholly clear. A military person captured by an opposing military force who is held in the interior of the country, under guarded conditions, is a prisoner of war. During World War II the term *internee* was given to those captured in a noncombatant country. Yet the situation these men faced—taken to the interior of the country and kept under guarded conditions—was identical with the one faced by those captured by the enemy. The confusion over terms was eventually cleared up when the Geneva Convention was revised, but not in time to help the internees.

The scope and scale of World War II prompted world leaders to cooperate in revising the Geneva Convention in 1946. Among the most important changes was the inclusion of protection for civilians. In addition, combatants imprisoned in neutral countries were henceforth accorded the same status as those held by belligerent powers. The Geneva Conventions of 1949, article 4, paragraph 61, provides that: "The following shall likewise be treated as prisoners of war under the present Conventions: (2) The persons belonging to one of the categories enumerated in the present Article, who have been received by neutral or non-belligerent Powers on their territory and whom these Powers are required to intern under international law, without prejudice to any more favorable treatment which these Powers may choose to give." But that change came too late for the Americans interned in Switzerland.

During the past several years many former internees have labored to gain recognition from the U.S. government for their wartime internment; few have succeeded. Those who have are now classified as former prisoners of war. As such they are eligible for medical and financial benefits such as complete medical coverage including medical and dental exams, treatments, prescriptions, glasses, and hearing aids. POW status also entitles veterans to disability compensation for injuries and diseases caused by internment as well as medical care in Veterans Administration hospitals. These benefits are in addition to the regular veterans' benefits and services to which they are entitled as veterans. The additional compensation is given because studies have shown that the physical hardships and psychological stress endured by POWs have lifelong effects on health and on social and vocational adjustment.[13]

There is also the issue of unfair treatment of the internees regarding injuries. The airman who injured himself on bailing out or crash-landing and was interned in Switzerland receives different treatment than the soldier who suffered injuries and was imprisoned in Germany. Because the latter is recognized as a prisoner of war, he receives benefits to help cover his wartime injuries. The former, because he is considered to be an internee, does not generally enjoy the same treatment. New York State is one state that does accept Swiss internees as POWs.

But for the most part, as of this writing, the Department of Veterans Affairs continues to rebuff former internees on the basis of the U.S. Code, Title 38, section 101 (32). A change in the code instituted in 1988 requires the approval of the secretary of the army to confer POW status on those once interned in neutral countries. Basically the conditions of their internment must have been equal to those endured by POWs of belligerent powers such as Germany, Italy, or Japan. Generally the VA has found that internees fail to meet 38 C.F.R. 3.1 (y) (2) (i), which holds that "each individual member of a particular group of detainees or internees shall, in the absence of evidence to the contrary, be considered to have experienced the same circumstances as those experienced by the group." Scores of fliers imprisoned in Wauwilermoos, Greppen, Hünenberg, and Les Diablerets have been denied POW status as a result.

To buttress its position, the VA has relied on a December 1944 memorandum prepared for the U.S. War Department by Brigadier General Legge reviewing the internment situation of American soldiers in Switzerland, even though Legge himself, in his postwar accounting, said that conditions at Camp Wauwilermoos "were noted to be disgracefully bad, worse than those reported to be normal in German prison camps, and unreasonably severe."[14] The VA also cites *Young* v. *Brown,* 4 Vet. App. 106, 109 (1993), in which the court held that 38 C.F.R. 3.1 (y) (2) (i) provides "objective criteria" for determining POW status; that the VA "must, when comparing the hardships suffered by a veteran while interned in a neutral country with the hardships suffered by veterans interned by enemy Governments and forces, consider 'the kinds of hardship suffered, not the degree of hardships suffered.'"

U.S.C.A. 101 (32) provides that the term *former POW* refers to a "person who, while serving in the active military, naval, or air service, was forcibly detained in the line of duty (A) by an enemy government or its agents, or a hostile force, during a period of war; or (B) by a foreign government or its agents, or a hostile force, under circumstances which the secretary finds to have been comparable to the circumstances under which persons have generally been forcibly detained or interned by enemy governments during periods of war." In other words, to be considered a former POW, a serviceman must have been forcibly detained or interned by enemy governments during a period of war. Such circumstances include, but are not limited to, physical hardships or abuse, psychological hardships or abuse, malnutrition, and unsanitary conditions. In a May 1980 study of former prisoners of war the VA concluded that World War II POWs had endured an extremely harsh and brutal experience characterized by a starvation diet, poor or nonexistent medical care, torture, "death marches," and executions. The average prisoner of war in Germany or Japan lived with the "constant apprehension of impending death, seeing others shot or expecting to be killed at war's end."

The VA has also supported its treatment of former internees by claiming that "Swiss control was limited, apart from attempting to prevent escape, to seeing that the internees were in their hotels at the proper hour each night and to preserving the peace."[15] True, the men could walk freely in the tiny villages where they were held, under tight Swiss control, but many internees held in the camps were in need of medical, dental, and psychological care, and many were undernourished. The conditions of the penitentiary camps were nothing less than abhorrent. And while the general conditions under which the internees lived in Switzerland may pale in comparison with those endured by POWs in Germany and Japan, all were held against their will and in some cases were seriously mistreated.

Too often the VA has tried to trivialize the conditions experienced by the internees. "In a statement of August 1990 in support of claims for entitlement to recognition as a former POW and for service connection for PTSD, the veteran stated that he was forcibly detained by Swiss Armed Forces, but was not physically abused. He described his living conditions as 'livable,' and a food ration consisting mainly of potatoes three times a day, which he considered an unsuitable diet. He stated that he could not come and go as he pleased, and on the basis of such forcible detention in the line of duty, felt he was entitled to recognition as a former POW."[16]

When former internees began filing suits to gain recognition as former POWs, the VA could no longer pretend to be ignorant of the conditions in which they were held, and yet it still routinely denied POW status. In February 1996, the director of the VA Compensation and Pension Service issued a white paper regarding the Americans who had been interned in Switzerland. The white paper describes the conditions of the camps and mentions Wauwilermoos, Les Diablerets, and an officers' camp at Greppen.[17] The paper acknowledges the odious conditions of Wauwilermoos, where men were "thrown into filthy jails where the food was almost inedible and were held incommunicado. They were housed in overcrowded barracks. Enlisted men had to sleep on loose straw strewn on planking, and officers slept on straw mattresses. Food was at the lowest subsistence level." The report even notes the conditions at the camp: the barracks in the small yards surrounded by barbed wire, constantly patrolled by dogs and guards with submachine guns, the ankle-deep mud, and, most important, "that confinement at Wauwilermoos was usually two to three months without trial." The VA acknowledges that conditions in Wauwilermoos "were . . . much worse than those in the other Swiss confinement camps, and were at least comparable in nature to those of the German and Japanese governments," but it has not yet extended POW status to former internees such as Andrew Barber, 94th BG, 332d BS, 8th AF;

Raymond Baus, 305th BG, 364th BS, 8th AF; Peter Boruta, 93d BG, 330th BS, 8th AF; Anthony Bowden, 95th BG, 334th BS, 8th AF; Virgil Broyhill, 384th BG, 545th BS, 8th AF; William Budewitz, 95th BG, 336th BS, 8th AF; Harold Burby, 385th BG, 550th BS, 8th AF; Albert Burns, 384th BG, 545th BS, 8th AF; Robert Carroll, 448th BG, 714th BS, 8th AF; Roland Colgate, 389th BG, 566th BS, 8th AF; Joseph D'Atri, 93d BG, 330th BS, 8th AF; Lorenz Johnson, 448th BG, 713th BS, 8th AF; Oliver Keller, 447th BG, 711th BS, 8th AF; John Kogut, 93d BG, 330th BS, 8th AF; Jarrell Legg, 385th BG, 550th BS, 8th AF; Ferris Martin, 351st BG, 510th BS, 8th AF; Lawrence McGuire, 447th BG, 711th BS, 8th AF; Curtis McCafferty, 385th BG, 550th BS, 8th AF; James Misuraca, 448th BG, 715th BS, 8th AF; Joseph Muscari, 385th BG, 550th BS, 8th AF; Gilbert Nagle, 95th BG, 334th BS, 8th AF; Jay Ossiander, 401st BG, 615th BS, 8th AF; Raleigh Rhodes, 385th BG, 548th BS, 8th AF; and Hobart Peterson, 91st BG, 323d BS, 8th AF.[18]

• • •

After the war ended, the Swiss and U.S. governments began wrangling over exactly how much the United States owed Switzerland for feeding and lodging the internees. Although the legal basis for the payment was rooted in the Hague Convention of 1907, such payments had first been made by France when it paid Switzerland in 1871 for hosting Bourbaki's army.

It took the two nations about four years to reach an accord. On 21 October 1949 the State Department and the Swiss government agreed on $14.4 million as a full and final settlement of the balance and interest due, in addition to the $4 million already paid for the damage to persons and property in the Schaffhausen, Zürich, and Basel bombings. The Swiss wanted Gen. Curtis LeMay, commanding general of the USAAF in Europe, to present the check; instead Brigadier General Schneider represented LeMay when the money was handed over on 26 January 1948.[19]

• • •

Justice came to Andre Béguin, the commandant of Wauwilermoos, in 1946. Switzerland court-martialed him in a trial that lasted 149 days. Among the evidence considered were affidavits from soldiers in the Swiss Army and a camp doctor, the financial records of Wauwilermoos, and testimony from several women claiming to be his mistresses. During the trial, jurors learned much about the vile way Béguin conducted his camp. Béguin constantly tried to portray himself as a man misunderstood and unfairly treated. His affidavit signed in the presence of the Department of Military, Burgunder, stated: "During my four years in Wauwilermoos I had received about 50 companies of troops of guard from all our different Swiss cantons where it was whispered discretely in the ear of each, by the 'Mafia' of Bern, the newspapers, 'You will go to Wauwilermoos poor boys, the commandant, Captain Béguin, is a brute, a monster, a dish breaker.' This is one example of the environment within which I had to work." He affected an air of surprise at the impression he created among the townspeople. "I didn't know the total hate and rancor [directed towards me]. I am by nature happy and of even temper but with a temperament that is full of fire, a man of action to reactions prompt I stay always master of myself."

Some of the most damaging testimony against Béguin came from Georges Troesch, a physician who worked in Wauwil and served the prison from 18 December 1944 until the war ended. Troesch testified to the significant amount of contact between Béguin and Lieutenant von Rintelen, a Nazi, and revealed another very disturbing fact: There appears to have been an American working with Béguin, a man referred to in the documents only as Lieutenant Harvey. According to Troesch's testimony, Harvey would rifle through the contents of packages destined for other American prisoners and give the most desirable items to Béguin. "In Captain Béguin's home where I had numerous invitations, I could see with my own eyes that he smoked American cigarettes, had condensed milk, American fruit. Captain Béguin said these were gifts that Harvey gave him." Béguin awarded Harvey numerous leaves, most likely to buy his silence, said Troesch.

In its decision, the court found Béguin to be a "crook, embezzler, con-man, and inhuman." He was sentenced to a prison term, fined, and stripped of his rights as a Swiss citizen for five years. The trial further found that Béguin had falsified documents of service, abused trust and power, and engaged in fraud and corruption. He was dishonorably discharged.[20]

Béguin was conditionally released from prison on 23 June 1948 with three years' probation and on the condition that should he commit any crime, he would once again stand before a military tribunal. After his release Béguin began to press Swiss authorities to reinstate his civil rights. He pleaded with the authorities, saying, "I could have neglected my service to save my reputation. . . . I could have been what they said I was: A brute and a man without a heart." And he praised himself: "If I didn't have nerves of steel, a need of more than a few hours of sleep to recuperate, a facility to work, the penitentiary camp of Wauwilermoos wouldn't be organized like it was." Although he enlisted several colleagues and friends to intercede on his behalf, his efforts were unsuccessful.

. . .

Shortly after the war ended the Swiss published the "Final Report of the Swiss Commissariat for Internment and Hospitality on the Internment of Foreign Military Personnel from 1940 to 1945," a slick piece of propaganda that portrays the American internment experience as a pleasant sojourn in the Alps. "Since the aircraft crews consisted entirely of officers and non-commissioned officers," the report says,

> they were obliged to perform work only within the framework of the Hague Convention. They refused to perform any voluntary work; all of our attempts at persuasion were in vain. The Americans led, therefore, in their places of accommodation Adelboden, Wengen, and Davos, the life of a visitor at a health resort.
>
> The first Americans landed on 13 August 1943, and from then on with brief temporary interruptions, constantly until the day when the war ended . . . they caused difficulties. . . . Aside from the escapes, the Americans were, notwithstanding occasional excessive drinking and involvements with women, for which the men were not solely responsible, a conflict-free group, who later occupied our attention only in the escape controversy.[21]

Never, in all the years since the war, has the Swiss government apologized. It came close once, to one person. In 1994, after a decade of correspondence with Daniel Culler, the American airman who was raped in Wauwilermoos, the Swiss government officially acknowledged the incident. In 1995 Culler traveled to Switzerland and revisited the site of his internment and imprisonment. He also met with former Swiss president Kaspar Villiger, who told Culler that he "regretted the treatment" Culler received by some of his Swiss countrymen.

Wauwilermoos haunts Culler, who still cannot stand to be in a small room with other men. He wonders why the myth of happy internment in Switzerland has been allowed to stand. "It's amazing to me how only the good things are being published about the Internees of Switzerland, and never any of the bad things."[22]

One reason the story of the Swiss internees has remained in history's shadows is because the internees themselves were ordered not to discuss their internment with anyone once they were repatriated. "*That was an order,*" George Michel said. "My family knew that I had been in Switzerland from the mail that got through. But beyond that, I didn't talk about it for years. In fact the reporter who came to our home to interview me (about thirty minutes after I had gotten in the front door) was not too happy that I wouldn't tell him what had happened."

Michel said no one ever called him a deserter, and he doesn't understand those who might have assumed that the crews who went to Sweden or Switzerland had "quit." "If you take the actual story of each crew, you will find that there was reason for what was done. It also makes the point that those of us who tried or managed to escape did not think that it was right to sit down and let someone else win the war for us. If your choice was Germany or Switzerland after you had just dropped six 1,000-pound bombs on an area that's a no brainer."[23]

Many Swiss treated the interned U.S. airmen with respect. The local Adelboden population had little contact with the world beyond the valley until the Americans arrived. These young men were unlike anything the villagers had ever before encountered. The young airmen brought with them an energy, enthusiasm, and openness quite contrary to Swiss mores. For these Swiss, memories of American internment evoke nostalgia and fond memories.

Today Wauwilermoos Prison has replaced the notorious penitentiary camp. Gone are the double rows of barbed wire and sucking mud. In 1980 the barracks were razed. A low brown brick building with a brightly lit atrium stands in its place. It is the site of a minimal security prison populated mostly by substance abusers.

· · ·

Sixty-one Americans lay buried in Münsingen, Switzerland, at the end of the war: sixty airmen and one embassy employee. An additional American was discovered entombed in his airplane when it was raised from a Swiss lake in 1953. In 1948 the State Department and the Defense Department decided that Münsingen would no longer serve as an American cemetery. The U.S. War Department wanted to keep the number of permanent cemeteries to a minimum, and only large sites were selected. The U.S. fliers were disinterred and removed. Some were reburied at Epinal, France; the rest were returned to the United States at their families' request and laid to rest in the soil of the country they had so gallantly defended.

American Airmen Interned in Switzerland

Abbot, Roy G.

Abbot, Wesley C.

Abernethy, Kyle G.

Abplanalp, Charles R.

Adams, Paul D.

Adams, Robert M.

Adkins, Richard L.

Aeschbacher, William E.

Ahlfors, Harold E.

Aisenbrey, Stephen H.

Alberts, Donald H.

Albin, George L.

Alder, Conrad C.

Aldridge, Charles W.

Alfino, Felice J.

Allen, Garrett F.

Allen, George K.

Alling, Roland F.

Allred, Parlan R.

Alpert, Jacob L.

Altimus, Carl F.

Altman, Herbert S.

Anderson, Ancil L.

Anderson, Donald W.

Anderson, John R.

Andrews, Martin

Annin, Paul

Antl, John J.

Armato, Angelo A.

Armstrong, William E.

Arndt, Jacob H.

Ashcraft, Blaine

Atchison, Robert G.

Aten, Roger W.

Athanassion, Thomas J.

Athearn, Jack M.

Aufderheide, John H.

Aull, Joseph F.

Ayers, Paul F.

Babin, Leslie J.

Backus, Richard H.

Bahr, John W.

Bailey, Everett L.

Baird, James, L.

Baker, Fineous R.

Baker, Floyd

Ball, Murray

Ballard, Allen T.

Ballard, William D.

Ballbach, Michael W.

Ballew, Clarence E.

Baltunas, Anthony P.

Barbar, Jerry V.

Barber, Andrew A.

Barnes, John O.

Barnett, Henry T.

Barnett, Zell G.

Barney, Albert V.

Barone, Anthony

Barrett, Donald A.

Barrett, Francis E.

Bartay, Forrest E.

Bartlett, Edward J.

Bass, John F.

Batchelder, Bruce L.

Batman, Eugene R.

Batts, Stanley C.

Baum, Glenn W.

Baus, Raymond C.

Baxter, William H.

Beach, Clifford P.

Beach, James E.

Beattie, Thomas J.

Beatty, Samuel H.

Beausoleil, Leon J.

Beaver, James F.

Beavers, William D.

Beck, William

Beecham, William P.

Belk, Dewey L.

Bellemare, Harry P.

Bennett, Lloyd G.

Beplat, Raymond F.

Bereschak, William F.

Berlin, Herbert

Berman, Seymour

Bernat, Edward

Berry, Earl E.

Beuoy, James L.

Bielinski, Walter R.

Biggs, Ralph B.

Bigham, James R.

Biglow, Ernest C.

Bilek, Clifford R.

Billiard, Francis E.

Birch, Voral J.

Bird, William E.

Birmley, Dean W.

Bistarkey, John D.

Bjerge, Lloyd A.

Blackburn, William G.

Blair, David R.

Blake, Harry P.

Blakeney, William R.

Blanton, Billie C.

Blaser, Freddie C.

Blalock, George H.

Blaylock, Robert P.

Blood, Kenneth H.

Blumenfeld, Edward

Blumer, Jacob R.

Boardsen, John A.

Boatman, George

Bocchino, Alphonso F.

Bockhahn, Richard J.

Bolick, Sidney R.

Bolin, Brunson W.

Boling, Cyril P.

Bolton, Billy F.

Boltz, Kenneth N.

Bomers, Robert J.

Bond, Thomas W.

Boney, Chester J.

Bonz, Frank J.

Boone, Daniel C.

Boruta, Peter

Boston, Clayton L.

Boswell, Vance R.

Botkin, Stanley L.

Bowden, Anthony V.

Bowers, Bernie P.

Bowers, Charles G.

Bowers, Russel W.

Bowler, John P.

Bowling, Theodore H.

Bowman, Julius R.

Boyd, Grover D.

Boyd, Joseph D.

Boydstun, Marvin R.

Boyle, Donald B.

Boyle, Raymond E.

Bradford, Doyle E.

Bradshaw, Lloyd R.

Brady, Joseph E.

Brandborg, Lloyd L.

Brandt, Malcolm E.

Braund, Cyril J.

Bray, Sheldon H.

Brentar, Joseph C.

Breslin, Walter N.

Brice, Douglas D.

Brick, David J.

Bridges, William C.

Bridges, William W.

Bridson, George L.

Brobst, Russell L.

Brody, Harvey L.

Brooks, Arthur F.

Brooks, Raymond T.

Brooks, William D.

Brovold, Archie J.

Brown, Arlie L.

Brown, Barlow D.

Brown, Charles J.

Brown, Earl F.

Brown, George F.

Brown, James S.

Brown, Jefferson C.

Brown, Robert D.

Brown, Roland A.

Browning, Albert E.

Broyhill, Virgil R.

Bruckman, Robert E.

Bruhns, Lowell

Buchanan, Robert J.

Buck, Donald J.

Buckholz, Roger W.

Budewitz, William P.

Bullock, Gene C.

Bunin, Norman H.

Burby, Harold F.

Burchards, Harold F.

Burdette, Joe L.

Burgett, Charles R.

Burgin, Richard A.

Burkhart, James F.

Burnham, Alunzo F.

Burns, Albert H.

Burns, Thomas D.

Burry, James E.

Burtle, Richard D.

Bush, Francis

Buss, Willard A.

Buzek, William W.

Byer, Samuel

Byers, Edgar M.

Calabrese, Pasquale A.

Caldwell, Key R.

Calire, James V.

Callaway, Charles R.

Cameron, Lauder C.

Campbell, Don L.

Campbell, John B.

Campman, Malcolm C.

Cantrell, Samuel T.

Cantwell, William J.

Capella, Bernard J.

Capps, Gordon, L.

Caputo, Anthony M.

Cardenas, Robert L.

Cariman, Harold L.

Carnahan, Edwin W.

Carpenter, Rex H.

Carraher, Robert P.

Carroll, Joseph R.

Carroll, Robert W.

Carroll, William E.

Carte, William D.

Carter, William R.

Cartmill, William J.

Caruso, Andrew J.

Carvour, George W.

Case, Marion A.

Casey, Howard E.

Cashio, Samuel J.

Cassidy, Charles F.

Cassinatis, Emanuel A.

Castelli, Bartolomeo

Cavanagh, Thomas F.

Cearley, Harold W.

Cercone, Bruno A.

Chapa, Amancio J.

Charochak, Joseph

Charrington, Ronald W.

Chase, Donald N.

Chatham, William L.

Chauvin, Hugh B.

Chavez, Saturnine

Cherry, Frank A.

Chianis, Andrew

Childs, Albert E.

Christenson, Donald O.

Christopher, Dominic J.

Cinibulk, Robert

Clare, Robert H.

Clark, Anthony

Clark, Edward L.

Clark, Forrest S.

Clark, George W.

Clark, Kenneth

Clark, Robert L.

Clayton, Joseph C.

Clayton, Wynfield S.

Cleary, William J.

Cleveland, Grover B.

Clevenger, William J.

Cliney, Thomas P.

Close, William K.

Cloutier, Herbert L.

Cobb, Willard D.

Cockrum, Nelson G.

Cole, Walter L.

Coleman, John N.

Colgate, Roland K.

Collins, Clyde V.

Comer, Roger M.

Conlan, Gerald V.

Connell, Robert K.

Connelly, Clarence C.

Connolly, James J.

Conrad, Richard F.

Conry, Thomas R.

Conselman, William H.

Cook, Dean F.

Cook, James W.

Cook, Robert A.

Cook, William T.

Cooper, Arthur

Cooper, Donald L.

Cooper, Roy D.

Copley, Howard H.

Coquat, Marcellos C.

Corbitt, James P.

Cosper, John H.

Costa, Jesse

Cote, Andrew P.

Coulson, Ralph L.

Councell, Marbury L.

Coune, Francis L.

Counts, George E.

Cowey, Albert E.

Cox, Dorris E.

Cox, Ermil T.

Craig, Robert P.

Crane, Bruce E.

Cranston, William R.

Craven, John L.

Crawford, Milton N.

Crenshaw, Ollie G.

Crews, William A.

Criswell, Calvin D.

Crow, Robert B.

Culbertson, Earl W.

Culkin, Myron L.

Culler, Daniel L.

Culley, Paul E.

Cumbia, Joseph L.

Cunningham, Edward G.

Curry, William H.

Curtis, Howard D.

Cusic, Glen W.

Cyr, Albert L.

Dalrymple, Thomas D.

Daly, Robert P.

Danella, Frank

Daniels, Kenneth E.

Danko, Charles G.

Danowitz, Arthur

Darragh, Charles D.

Dassow, Arthur W.

D'Atri, Joseph A.

Daves, Bob D.

Davis, Archie C.

Davis, Richard L.

Davison, James W.

De Camp, Virgil Y.

Decker, Chester D.

Delemar, Jewell W.

Dellerba, Paul A.

De Lozier, William R.

Deluca, Salvatore J.

Denbroeder, Adrian J.

Denere, Jake R.

Dengler, Walter E.

De Piano, Angelo W.

De Shazer, Lloyd V.

Desmond, Robert H.

Devoe, Charles N.

De Vincenzi, Arthur T.

Dewy, Robert W.

Dias, Ronald A.

Dickson, Kirk C.

Diener, Henry

Dienhart, Edward W.

Dillworth, Robert S.

Di Pietro, Guido

Disbrow, David W.

Dixon, Bruce F.

Dobaran, Louis

Dobbs, Eugene R.

Dodd, Francis C.

Donahue, James F.

Dooley, Robert J.

Doolittle, Wilfred G.

Dorsa, William A.

Dow, John J.

Dowd, John F.

Downey, William A.

Downs, Harvey R.

Dowse, Howard A.

Dox, Williard S.

Drake, Chester W.

Drawdy, Herman L.

Dreher, Russell L.

Drew, Everett D.

Dualsky, Rudolph J.

Dubail, Arthur W.

Dudla, John R.

Dufau, George L.

Duke, Basil L.

Duncan, George T.

Duncan, Sam P.

Dunn, John B.

Durant, Donald A.

Dustin, John P.

Dvorak, John J.

Dwyer, William F.

Dyer, Eugene N.

Dykstra, James

Dzedzy, John L.

Earle, Guy H.

Early, James B.

Ebert, Dale

Echstenkamper, Earl R.

Eckles, Sylvester
Eckman, James B.
Eddingfield, Russell D.
Edwards, Jack P.
Edwards, Jesse R.
Ehelebe, Richard A.
Eibs, Edward H.
Eich, Joseph M.
Eilers, George W.
Eisner, Eugene
Elber, George A.
Elder, George W.
Ellington, Dale C.
Elliot, Humphrey J.
Elliot, Ralph V.
Elliot, Richard R.
Ellis, Leighton R.
Ellsworth, Charles E.
Embree, Thaylus
Emerson, Billy
Emerson, Clayton A.
Emmel, Leonard H.
Engler, David J.
Englert, Paul R.
English, Burton C.
Enyart, Arthur G.
Epstein, Bernard
Epstein, Milton R.
Erdel, Albert
Ertel, Raymond C.
Estes, James L.
Estes, Leon
Estes, Victor H.
Etheredge, William C.
Etherington, John R.
Etier, Lloyd W.
Eure, Spurgeon B.
Evans, Richard E.
Everart, Allan V.
Everett, John E.

Everhart, Herman
Fabiniak, Victor A.
Fagan, Vincent F.
Fairall, Alfred V.
Fairclough, Edward S.
Falk, Jack G.
Fanelli, John V.
Faron, John J.
Fatico, Frank
Faulkner, Thomas P.
Faust, Harry J.
Feibush, Ernest M.
Feltner, Kenneth N.
Ferguson, William S.
Ferreira, Joseph
Field, Earl
Fiene, William R.
Fike, Norbert A.
Fillman, Robert W.
Filush, George
Finley, Ray
Finneran, Leon
Finseth, Levi S.
Fischbach, Clement J.
Fishback, Donald M.
Fisher, Edward J.
Fisher, Henry T.
Fitzpatrick, John J.
Flammia, Joseph E.
Flanagen, James L.
Fleer, Howard C.
Fletcher, Donald H.
Fletcher, James W.
Flister, Henry O.
Flynn, Norman C.
Foley, Daniel
Fooks, Leslie E.
Ford, Homer L.
Forrester, Clyde A.
Fortune, Mark E.

Foster, Harry J.

Foster, Jesse T.

Fotheringham, Donald K.

Fowlkes, Richard D.

Fox, John M.

Fox, Wayne G.

Francis, Arthur J.

Frausto, Guemecindo J.

Frazee, Francis L.

Frederick, Robert P.

Fredrickson, Christian L.

Freeman, Joyce K.

Freund, William R.

Fridye, Stash J.

Friedberg, Mitchell R.

Friedman, Eugene M.

Friedman, Lester Z.

Frisbie, Bryce C.

Froment, Dorrance V.

Fulkerson, Melvin R.

Fuller, Norman D.

Furcolo, Michael P.

Furrow, Jesse R.

Gadek, William V.

Gagola, Edward T.

Gaide, Melvin E.

Gallagher, Thomas F.

Gallo, Carmine A.

Gallup, Robert A.

Gallupe, Donald E.

Gamal, Vincent A.

Gambaina, Paul J.

Garcia, Edward J.

Garcia, John H.

Garcia, Rudy

Garner, Eugene F.

Garrison, Lewis A.

Garrity, John M.

Gass, Charles R.

Gates, John S.

Gault, Raymond W.

Geiger, Aubrey H.

Genetti, John D.

Gentile, Albert J.

George, George S.

Gerdes, Leonard

Geron, Alva J.

Gertler, Isidore

Giammettie, Anthony A.

Gibbard, Norman P.

Gidley, John A.

Gilbert, Harry R.

Gill, William L.

Gilliam, Walter T.

Gilligan, James P.

Gilmore, John E.

Ginn, Robert J.

Girard, Francis J.

Gividen, Harold V.

Glasgow, Mark O.

Glasier, Arthur F.

Goings, James D.

Golden, Willie M.

Goldenbloom, Nathan

Goldman, Robert E.

Goldsmith, Stuart

Gordon, Robert G.

Gorman, William G.

Gormley, Edward O.

Gorski, Henry D.

Goyer, Leonard

Graham, James E.

Grauer, James E.

Graul, Robert J.

Grear, Howard M.

Gredicek, William J.

Green, James A.

Green, Jesse B.

Greenberg, Stanley L.

Greene, Robert P.

Greenebaum, Jesse L.

Gregory, William J.

Greim, John R.

Gribble, James A.

Griffin, Charles J.

Griffith, Rockford C.

Grimes, Donald J.

Grogan, Walter S.

Grooms, Ray M.

Gross, Walter H.

Grove, Paul S.

Grove, Ronald N.

Grover, Charles S.

Grubb, Dale E.

Grubka, John

Guertin, Robert P.

Gutmann, Henry R.

Haaland, Milton L.

Habich, Arthur L.

Haffermehl, George T.

Hagen, Stanley J.

Hague, Robert F.

Haley, William L.

Hall, Albert P.

Hall, Kerneth J.

Hallberg, Bengt R.

Hallenback, John W.

Halliburton, Edward W.

Halsne, Milton O.

Hamby, Charles W.

Hamilton, Charles H.

Hamilton, Gerald T.

Hamilton, James W.

Hamilton, John T.

Hamlin, Howland J.

Hammarlund, Lloyd A.

Hammer, Lloyd W.

Hammer, Robert J.

Hancock, James H.

Hancock, William M.

Hanrahan, Vincent M.

Hanson, Alfred A.

Happy, Oliver F.

Haraga, Wilford C.

Harbison, Robert J.

Harding, Charles S.

Hardt, Raymond G.

Hardy, Raymond H.

Harmon, Harold P.

Harney, Albert G.

Harper, Joseph C.

Harper, Richard W.

Harper, Ryan D.

Harris, Hiram E.

Harris, Russell

Harris, Secar J.

Harrison, Alfred B.

Harshbarger, William C.

Hart, Robert G.

Harte, David A.

Hartman, Uriah G.

Hartung, William R.

Harvey, Harry B.

Harvey, Marshall C.

Harwick, Michael G.

Hass, Raymond W.

Hatch, Howard L.

Hatfield, Harland D.

Hathaway, Milfred K.

Hatley, Clyde S.

Hattaway, Robert S.

Havlik, Karel

Hay, James F.

Hayes, Edwin A.

Hayes, Vincent V.

Haynes, Hagwood

Hays, Ralph E.

Hazelton, Bert

Hazelton, Frank H.

Hebron, Walter T.

Hedgelon, Robert P.

Hedrick, George L.

Hegedus, Ernest J.

Heintz, James E.

Heller, Jerome M.

Helms, Joseph E.

Helwig, Harold C.

Henderson, Leonard M.

Henderson, Lester J.

Hendry, Leonard L.

Hennesey, John E.

Henry, William

Henshaw, Boyd J.

Hensley, Frank E.

Hequembourg, Frank D.

Herendeen, Phillip G.

Hergesheimer, Henry E.

Hermann, Leask H.

Hewett, Allan D.

Hewitt, Edwin F.

Hewlett, James A.

Hickey, Thomas P.

Hicks, Walter R.

Higdon, Thomas R.

Higdon, Willard W.

Higginbotham, Kenneth A.

Higley, Glenn O.

Hilderbrand, Robert H.

Hill, Earl

Hiller, Robert D.

Hintz, George J.

Hobbs, Calvin C.

Hobt, Richard D.

Hoch, Frank L.

Hocking, Frank T.

Hodges, Colman R.

Hodges, John M.

Hoelzer, Robert C.

Hoerl, Norbert A.

Hoffman, Kenneth L.

Hoffman, Leo J.

Hofmann, Raymond

Hogue, Fred T.

Holder, Charles A.

Holeton, Strickland J.

Hollingsworth, Richard R.

Holloway, Elmer R.

Holmes, David H.

Holt, Morris E.

Homistek, Martin A.

Hommer, Roy A.

Hooker, Robert B.

Hooks, Maurice L.

Hoops, Christopher W.

Hopkins, Herbert C.

Horetski, Frank V.

Horne, Joseph R.

Horton, Charles G.

Horvath, William F.

Hostetter, Ralph L.

Hotter, Edward J.

Houston, Leonard S.

Howard, James H.

Howe, Sidney E.

Howell, Frank L.

Howell, William W.

Hubbard, Clare W.

Hubbard, Robert H.

Huber, Richard A.

Hucker, Henry C.

Hughes, John J.

Hughes, Luther O.

Huising, Robert W.

Humphry, Loy

Hunt, Claud W.

Hunt, Thomas P.

Hunter, George T.

Hunter, Howard O.

Hunter, James

Hurst, Caleb B.

Hurwitz, Sidney
Huston, William W.
Hutchinson, Robert L.
Hutchinson, Roger W.
Hutchinson, Rupert I.
Hymnas, Dowie J.
Iacona, Richard P.
Infurna, Michael S.
Irwin, Winston C.
Isaacson, Harold C.
Israelson, Elmer P.
Italia, Santo
Jackson, Lorance N.
Jackson, Ralph B.
Jacob, Louis P.
Jacobs, Don R.
Jacobs, Robert M.
Janczak, Benedict F.
Janiszewski, Arthur I.
Janos, George A.
Janowiak, Erwin P.
Januszewski, Joseph C.
Jaquis, John R.
Jaspers, Alvin W.
Jeffries, Ralph W.
Jennings, Edward J.
Jennings, John T.
Jeroski, Edward B.
Joeckel, Charles R.
Johnson, Arthur J.
Johnson, Carl A.
Johnson, Clifford
Johnson, George W.
Johnson, Harvey A.
Johnson, Jackson C.
Johnson, James E.
Johnson, Lorenz G.
Johnson, Paul L.
Johnson, Robert E.
Johnston, Donald M.

Johnston, Robert F.
Jonas, Fred A.
Jones, Charles H.
Jones, Clarence H.
Jones, Gene R.
Jones, George E.
Jones, Johnnie F.
Jones, Rex L.
Jones, Talmidge R.
Jones, Walter B.
Jones, Warren L.
Jorgenson, Donald G.
Joseph, Louis
Jost, Clarence J.
Joyner, Robert W.
Kale, William A.
Kalioness, Harry A.
Kaminski, Bruno
Kane, Kent K.
Katainen, Rudolph A.
Katz, Bernard H.
Kaub, Robert W.
Keefer, John P.
Kelleher, Edwin F.
Keller, Oliver F.
Kelly, William J.
Kendall, Earl F.
Kenneally, Robert J.
Kennedy, Earl R.
Kenney, George E.
Kennon, Clifford L.
Kent, Amos
Kerr, Gerald L.
Kester, William E.
Key, William E.
Kibler, Jack W.
Kiefer, Henry W.
Kiehn, Harold J.
Kimmel, Charles E.
King, Archie W.

King, Eddie R.

King, James E.

King, Norris W.

King, Raymond J.

Kintana, Frank T.

Kirchner, Donald E.

Kisinger, Maynard W.

Kissell, John L.

Kizer, Lawton E.

Kleber, Harry W.

Klein, George E.

Klein, Larry

Kliss, Donald J.

Knapp, Frederick R.

Knapp, Martin J.

Knauer, William W.

Knize, Edwin A.

Kobiernicki, John

Koenig, Lawrence P.

Koenig, Raymond A.

Koeppel, Oscar J.

Koester, William H.

Kogut, John P.

Kolb, William P.

Kollman, Frank R.

Konkel, William O.

Kornacki, Edward T.

Kosinski, Hipolis P.

Kovacs, Frank W.

Kowalozyk, Felix

Kozel, Edward

Koziol, Adam C.

Kozlowski, Walter A.

Kraft, Roger L.

Krajewski, Joseph Z.

Kravitz, Lester

Kreuzer, Harold L.

Kristen, William J.

Krucek, John O.

Krummel, Oscar F.

Krus, Donald M.

Kurz, Anthony L.

Lacombe, Raymond C.

La Faitte, Raymond C.

Laing, Randall C.

Laird, John C.

Lambert, Douglas W.

Landry, Gerald E.

Landry, Louis H.

Lang, William E.

Lanigan, Arden O.

Lanman, Frank L.

La Penna, Alexander V.

Laperriere, Urvin J.

Larsen, Carl J.

Larson, Robert P.

Lasco, Melvin

La Seur, William V.

Laskowsky, Andrew

Lasskow, Maxwell J.

Lattimer, Albert V.

Launius, John E.

Lauro, Michael A. J.

Laux, Paul M.

Lavin, Thomas J.

Law, John M.

Lawler, Lawrence T.

Lawson, Grover R.

Lawson, Tracy W.

Leach, Reginald G.

Leaphart, Robert E.

Leatherman, Glen C.

Lee, Robert G.

Lee, Thomas R.

Leesley, Robert F.

Legg, Jarrell F.

Leggett, Thomas A.

Lehman, Robert E.

Leiser, William M.

Leitsch, Vernon P.

Le June, Alexander J.

Lenovich, William A.

Leonard, Edward S.

Lessig, Joseph W.

Lester, James J.

Levine, Melvin L.

Levinson, Paul

Lewis, James M.

Lewis, Ned E.

Lewis, Victor H.

Libell, Robert N.

Liedahl, Richard J.

Lienning, Louis B.

Limb, Byron

Lindenbaum, Russell L.

Lindskoog, Arthur H.

Linner, Harold L.

Liscomb, Russel P.

Lisenby, Spencer B.

Livermore, John W.

Llewellyn, Edman E.

Lloyd, William N.

Lockard, Robert W.

Loftiss, Louis E.

Loh, Phillip H.

Long, Byron K.

Long, Paul H.

Long, Robert A.

Longchamps, Alfred L.

Looker, Rollin C.

Love, William V.

Lowery, William H.

Lucas, John B.

Lucas, Robert R.

Luebke, Harold W.

Lukas, Emil J.

Lunte, Raymond V.

Luther, Ernest C.

Lydon, Martin J.

Lynn, Bert H.

Lyons, James J.

Lysek, Peter J.

Lyskawa, Chester F.

MacDonald, Gordon W.

Machovec, Glenn W.

MacIntyre, Archie A.

MacIntyre, Donald K.

Mack, Glenn R.

MacKoul, Nicholas

MacMullen, Donald H.

MacSpadden, Floyd E.

Maddox, Jessie G.

Mahaffey, James D.

Mahar, Ronald J.

Mahon, James F.

Maino, Alfred B.

Malavich, Charles

Malchiodi, Peter B.

Malcolm, Frank J.

Malin, Harry G.

Malloy, Donald W.

Maloney, Joseph F.

Maloney, Robert A.

Manbeck, Roland K.

Manning, Robert E.

Manolio, Dominick J.

Manzi, Anthony E.

Mardeuse, Alfred K.

Marion, Sid T.

Markowitz, Isidore

Marks, Morton L.

Marks, Norman G.

Marotta, Michael M.

Marra, William

Marshall, Jewell K.

Marshall, Joseph F.

Martin, Earl M.

Martin, Ferris S.

Martin, Glenn R.

Martin, Joseph W.

Martin, Robert M.

Martinez, Louis M.

Martini, Howard N.

Martucci, Angelo

Maruk, John

Mason, Horace R.

Mason, Richard C.

Massengale, Arnold L.

Massey, Glenn L.

Mathewson, Ralph J.

Matthews, Edward E.

Matthews, Harold H.

Mattinghy, Scott J.

May, Sheldon

Maynor, Harry W.

Mazor, John

McArdell, Herbert G.

McBey, Donald J.

McCafferty, Curtis I.

McCallum, Roy A.

McCanna, John J.

McCarrell, Carl C.

McClellan, Pat N.

McClure, Thomas R.

McConnell, Benjamin R.

McConnell, Donald H.

McCormic, John

McCune, John A.

McDonald, Carl D.

McDonald, Leo F.

McDonough, Robert W.

McEncroe, Paul R.

McFarland, John W.

McFarland, Leebert W.

McGann, James P.

McGee, Thomas D.

McGoldrick, William

McGovern, James M.

McGown, Robert L.

McGrath, Vincent K.

McGuire, Lawrence R.

McGurr, Bernard C.

McKain, Armor L.

McKee, Richard J.

McKee, Robert E.

McKee, When L.

McKeever, Jack F.

McKinney, Jack N.

McKinney, Louis K.

McKinnon, Albert J.

McLaughlin, Vincent P.

McNamara, John S.

McNeil, Edward N.

McNeil, John A.

McNulty, Edward J.

McReynolds, Robert L.

Means, Harry K.

Mears, George W.

Melazzi, Anthony T.

Melson, Howard E.

Menzl, Raymond A.

Mercado, Robert L.

Merisotis, Peter E.

Merletti, Nicholas P.

Merrigan, William J.

Merritt, Loren L.

Mersereau, Robert C.

Metz, Eugene J.

Meyer, Robert W.

Meyers, Lawrence C.

Michael, Arthur L.

Michel, George W.

Miles, Thomas D.

Miller, Clarence E.

Miller, Edward J.

Miller, Harry G.

Miller, John G.

Miller, Richard G.

Million, Willis, E.

Milojecvich, John H.

Miltner, Robert F.

Miner, John C.

Miner, Robert E.

Minkowitz, Samuel

Minor, Charles C.

Miranda, Charles A.

Mirt, Charles C.

Misuraca, James I.

Mitchell, Elbert E.

Mitchell, Jewell W.

Mitchell, Michael D.

Mitton, Randolph L.

Modell, Robert L.

Moeller, Wayne G.

Molina, Frank W.

Monfort, William D.

Monroe, George K.

Moody, Robert E.

Moore, Charles C.

Moore, Donald H.

Moore, George E.

Moore, Olin H.

Moore, Preston T.

Moore, Stanley

Moore, William F.

Moore, William J.

Moran, James V.

Morat, John B.

Morehead, Claude R.

Morgan, Leonard E.

Morin, Robert N.

Morison, Robert B.

Moritz, Paul F.

Morse, Loyd F.

Moss, Alva H.

Moulton, Reed L.

Moultrie, Homer H.

Mount, Dick W.

Mours, John D.

Mucek, Walter A.

Muise, George A.

Munsey, Roy G.

Murray, Robert M.

Murray, William H.

Muscari, Joseph V.

Myles, Thomas E.

Nadeau, Leslie D.

Nagle, Donald T.

Nagle, Gilbert C.

Nance, Envoy F.

Neal, Blair C.

Nedrow, James E.

Neely, Hugh A.

Neigler, Forrest C.

Nelle, William G.

Nelson, Edward N.

Newall, Raymond A.

Newhouse, Richard V. S.

Newhouse, William E.

Newport, Ora E.

Newton, Granville

Nichols, Hollis R.

Nichols, Robert E.

Nicodemus, Walter B.

Niedzialek, Stanley B.

Nobles, Roger G.

Noce, Jack S.

Norby, Clinton O.

Nordgren, Herbert V.

Northcott, Clyde A.

Northfelt, Wallace O.

Norton, Richard E.

Noyer, John L. E.

Nuber, Robert E.

Oakes, Donald K.

Oates, David K.

O'Brien, Earl J.

O'Brien, John G.

Obsharsky, Theodore P.

O'Connell, John P.

O'Connell, Maurice G.
Ogden, Earnest C.
O'Hara, John J.
O'Hare, John P.
Olds, George D.
Olinik, John P.
Olson, Keith R.
O'Neil, John F.
O'Neil, John M.
Oravec, Joseph J.
Orman, Verdon E.
Osborn, Thomas E.
O'Shields, William P.
Ossiander, Jay D.
Otto, Frederick P.
Overton, Roscoe L.
Owen, Thomas B.
Pac, Walter J.
Pace, Jessie V.
Padula, Dominick R.
Page, Charles W.
Palmer, Billie D.
Palmer, Harris M.
Palumbo, John
Paolucci, Umberto
Parker, Earl S.
Parker, James C.
Parks, Kenneth C.
Parramore, William W.
Parrish, Earl
Parsons, Hoyt D.
Patrick, Lindsey A.
Patten, Irving B.
Patton, William E.
Pawleczak, Chester D.
Peacock, Clyde E.
Pearce, Clarence F.
Pearson, Keith L.
Peck, Wesley H.
Pedigo, Millard F.

Pemberton, Randolph C.
Peraggine, Louis A.
Peskin, Samuel D.
Peters, Harold M.
Peterson, Carl F.
Peterson, Hobart P.
Peterson, Wayne M.
Petrick, George A.
Petrie, Charles R.
Petrie, William D.
Petruzzi, Evo J.
Pettit, Richard J.
Phares, Alvie J.
Phillips, Murray R.
Piederowicz, Edward J.
Piekarski, Henry J.
Piel, Donald E.
Piemonte, Guiseppe M.
Pierce, Peter C.
Pinkerton, Paul E.
Pinkney, Harold
Pitcock, Milburn
Pizzi, Frank B.
Platinsky, Saul
Polizzotti, Gastano S.
Pollard, Frank B.
Pollock, Bert D.
Pollock, John F.
Poplawski, William T.
Poppel, Samuel B.
Porter, Maurice D.
Pothier, Delbert J.
Potter, Eugene R.
Potter, William C.
Potter, Wilmer E.
Powell, William A.
Powers, George
Pratt, Disney J.
Pratt, Marion D.
Prentice, Donald M.

Pressey, Richard T.
Pribek, Edward L.
Proctor, Donald M.
Prodger, Allen P.
Promen, Robert N.
Pulley, Darrell G.
Pustelnik, Stanley J.
Putiri, John S.
Putnam, Charles L.
Quarve, Walter G.
Quillan, Harry D.
Quinn, Louis F.
Radin, Norman I.
Raff, Lawrence C.
Rains, Sidney A.
Rakes, Guiy E.
Raley, Cecil
Rapport, Stephen P.
Rashid, Farris R.
Rasmussen, Frederick A.
Ratchick, Selig
Ravlin, Robert J.
Rawhauser, Wesley A.
Reagan, Penrose W.
Reed, James W.
Reeves, Robert C.
Register, Ellis W.
Reid, Raymond W.
Reinhart, Donald G.
Rekart, Jerome U.
Reneau, Clifton J.
Reno, Robert R.
Resovsky, Edward G.
Reves, Jouis E.
Rhew, James I.
Rhodes, Raleigh H.
Rhodes, Robert F.
Rhodes, Roland H.
Rich, Charles
Rich, Dante A.

Rich, Keith W.
Richards, William W.
Richardson, David M.
Richardson, Noel L.
Richmond, Alva P.
Richmond, Cecil L.
Rickenbacker, Henry B.
Riddel, William C.
Rients, Vernon W.
Riester, Robert W.
Riley, Hugh O.
Riolo, Pete V.
Ristom, George A.
Ritter, Ralph T.
Roach, Lloyd H.
Robber, William T.
Robbins, Norman V.
Roberts, Charles S.
Roberts, Chester H.
Roberts, Kenneth A.
Roberts, Lewis M.
Robertson, James R.
Robertson, Siegvart J.
Robinette, Howard C.
Robledo, Ricardo
Robson, Gerald H.
Roddey, John B.
Roderique, Benjamin H.
Rodman, Michael L.
Rodriguez, Eusebio
Rogers, Harold E.
Roland, Gerard B.
Roscetti, Elvio
Rosema, John H.
Rosen, Leonard T.
Rosencutter, Archie G.
Rosenfeld, Bernard
Rosenfeld, Julius
Rosenthal, Leon
Rossi, Frank

Rossi, Joseph R.

Rounds, Finis L.

Rouse, Donald E.

Rowen, Bruce R.

Rowley, Donald T.

Rudolph, Robert A.

Ruggerio, Rocco J.

Rummage, Luther D.

Rundquist, Ralph G.

Runyan, Howard W.

Russell, Joseph W.

Rutherford, Bill H.

Ryan, Charles O.

Ryan, Richard G.

Ryba, Edward S.

Rynier, Kenneth, R.

Saari, Lloyd A.

Sabalaske, William E.

Sakmar, Ervin M.

Sampson, Oscar C.

Sander, Robert T.

Sanders, William A.

Sangas, John

Sanner, Harold C.

Sarantos, Demo D.

Sarkovich, Lewis M.

Saroney, Robert S.

Saviski, Stanley V.

Savitski, Leonard S.

Sawyer, Norrell B.

Scarbrough, Francis W.

Scefonas, Felix J.

Schaller, Hubert P.

Schaub, George F.

Schenkelberger, Gordon

Scherzer, Louis

Schibler, George J.

Schiefelbein, Melvin F.

Schilling, Edward A.

Schnaebel, Ernest F.

Scheetz, Elvin N.

Schraner, Wilbur I.

Schreck, John C.

Schroeder, Henry B.

Schultz, Harry

Schultz, Lawrence J.

Schuster, Raymond H.

Schwedock, Irwon

Schott, James P.

Schott, John P.

Schott, John S.

Scott, Henry J.

Scott, Robert C.

Scott, Stanley V.

Scott, Venton H.

Scott, Wendell O.

Seaman, John S.

Secor, Howard J.

Seery, James B.

Sefton, Jean H.

Segal, Bernard

Seidel, William E.

Seifert, Morris

Seilheimer, John R.

Seipold, Eugene O.

Seippel, William H.

Sellar, Donald C.

Selover, Frank L.

Sendleback, Richard M.

Senheiser, George A.

Serine, Harold E.

Sfarnas, George O.

Shank, Paul W.

Shanks, Oscar E.

Shattuck, Ira

Shaw, Marvin E.

Shearer, Alfred M.

Sheffield, Woodrew W.

Shepard, Robert S.

Shephard, Monroe E.

Sherbourne, Russell K.
Sherlock, Paul E.
Sherry, Richard D.
Shidek, Anthony J.
Shive, Howard
Shoebottom, Robert L.
Shorten, Frederick J.
Shoup, William T.
Siemens, Harry J.
Siemer, Otto F.
Siirila, Ted B.
Silag, William J.
Siles, Joseph P.
Simington, William M.
Simms, Samuel R.
Simons, Langdon S.
Simpson, Curtis
Simpson, Elmo C.
Simpson, Robert V.
Singer, Arnold B.
Sinitsky, Joe
Sink, Robert E.
Sipser, Morris
Sirkis, Jonah
Sizemore, Ray F.
Skarania, Stephen M.
Skoba, John E.
Skurka, Clem J.
Slaughter, Aaron C.
Slovacek, Adolph
Smallwood, Arthur G.
Smith, Alvin F.
Smith, Arthur J.
Smith, Castleton D.
Smith, Charles B.
Smith, Charles E.
Smith, Doyle R.
Smith, Harold W.
Smith, Harry D.
Smith, Hurley D.

Smith, Jack R.
Smith, James R.
Smith, Jesse T.
Smith, Jimmy A.
Smith, Leonard
Smith, Milford A.
Smith, Roger C.
Smith, William O.
Snapp, Myron P.
Snyder, George E.
Snyder, Myles A.
Snyder, Robert W.
Sobel, Leon H.
Souther, Max L.
Sparacio, Salvatore J.
Speakman, James E.
Spencer, Herbert R.
Sprenger, Paul F.
Springer, Arnold D.
Springer, Walter H.
Spurlock, Raymond J.
Spurr, Joseph J.
Stafford, Jacob A.
Stallings, Warren D.
Stambaugh, Jacob F.
Stamm, Neal E.
Stanley, James R.
Starek, Joseph B.
Starr, Frank J.
Stavast, James A.
Stear, Kenneth J.
Steichan, John W.
Stelzer, Bernard
Stemac, Frank
Stetson, Carl D.
Steurer, Robert W.
Stevens, Cleo F.
Stevens, John O.
Stevens, Nolan D.
Stewart, Seth R.

Stine, David E.

Stokes, Ralph R.

Stoller, Ray L.

Stoller, Roy H.

Stolz, John J.

Stone, Robert N.

Stotts, James D.

Stover, Gilbert E.

Strader, Noel R.

Stringer, Lelan H.

Strutz, George J.

Struzynski, Benjamin

Stuempfle, Robert A.

Stultz, Glen E.

Styers, Charles W.

Sullivan, John J.

Sutters, Elmer J.

Swanson, Dwight F.

Sweet, Elliot B.

Swift, Herbert E.

Swindell, Gerald W.

Sykes, John

Syroid, Walter A.

Syverson, Burton M.

Szafranski, Joseph E.

Tapia, Luis H.

Taylor, Vee L.

Taylor, William H.

Telford, George D.

Tennant, John W.

Terry, Paul

Testa, Francis J.

Tharpe, John F.

Theis, Earl L.

Thoma, John J.

Thomas, Earl M.

Thomas, Frank S.

Thomas, Martin J.

Thompson, Abraham

Thompson, Albert L.

Thompson, Bernard

Thompson, Earl G.

Thompson, Earnest L.

Thompson, John H.

Thompson, William L.

Thornbury, Joseph R.

Thornton, Carter F.

Thursby, George E.

Tilley, James R.

Tinney, Jack R.

Tinsman, William

Tobias, Julius

Todd, Robert E.

Tofte, Donald F.

Toler, Needham

Tollman, Lewis A.

Tomlinson, Franklin E.

Tompkins, Lonnie E.

Tompkins, Robert V.

Tonnesson, Tonnes E.

Tracey, John C.

Trautner, John J.

Travis, Meredith W.

Trendell, Albert T.

Trice, Richard L.

Tritle, Robert C.

Trotter, Perry V.

Truitt, Brooks K.

Tsairis, Constantine

Tucker, Jack B.

Tunstall, Garnett T.

Turk, Richard E.

Turley, Harold N.

Turner, Billie L.

Turner, Robert G.

Turner, Sam R.

Turner, Wayne G.

Underwood, Walter I.

Ura, George J.

Urquhart, Wesley

Vail, Robert B.

Vandenberg, Willie

Vanderstek, Henry M.

Vanderveen, Stewart L.

VanderWeide Edward B.

Vann, Thomas P.

Van Noy, Ferril W.

Vaubourg, Edmond

Vaughn, Winston E.

Veldhuizen, John C.

Vessichelli, Vito G.

Vinson, John E.

Vittiello, James J.

Vochatzer, Ralph L.

Vorek, Bernard T.

Vuchechevich, Philip J.

Waddell, Carroll

Wagner, Frederick J.

Walker, Ira E.

Walker, Robert B.

Walker, Samuel M.

Walker, Virgil F.

Walker, William M.

Wall, Joseph K.

Wallace, James G.

Wallach, Charles D.

Walser, Walter A.

Walsh, Robert W.

Walter, Arnold H.

Walters, Calvin A.

Ward, John N.

Ward, Marshall M.

Ward, Russell E.

Warns, Raymond H.

Warsavage, Edward J.

Wartman, Franklin T.

Waska, Charles D.

Wasmer, Frank G.

Wasserman, Bernard

Waters, Donald A.

Watkins, William

Weaver, Lester F.

Webb, Frank W.

Weber, Theodore L.

Weeks, Roy L.

Weinberg, Morris

Weir, DeWitt J.

Weisberg, Jerome I.

Wellnitz, Howard N.

Wells, John E.

Welsch, Robert H.

Wessinger, James O.

Wesson, William H.

West, Grover C.

West, Marshall F.

Weyer, Edwin T.

Whatley, Hubert L.

Wheadon, Elmer D.

Whiston, Edward G.

Whitbeck, Harold B.

White, James G.

White, Ralph L.

Wiggins, Willard A.

Wightman, David L.

Wikle, Earle P.

Wilcox, Albert L.

Wilcox, Edward T.

Wilcox, Raymond J.

Wiley, Robert A.

Wilkey, William

Wilkins, Albert K.

Wilkins, John R.

Wilkinson, William H.

Willeford, Joe J.

Willemin, William W.

Williams, Homer W.

Williams, Ralph O.

Williams, Robert L.

Willingham, Nelson H.

Willis, Arthur W.

Willis, Vincent C.
Willoughby, Martin L.
Wilson, Bennie D.
Wilson, Bernard O.
Wilson, George W.
Wilson, Max E.
Winborne, Thomas B.
Windes, Honor G.
Windle, Edward M.
Wingfield, Tazwell R.
Winkler, Thomas H. Z.
Winner, Roy B.
Wiren, Gordon R.
Wise, Lorran E.
Wiseman, Dorsey E.
Wisniewski, Walter J.
Wolinsky, David S.
Womacks, S. C.
Woodruff, Donald C.
Woodward, Edgar F.

Wootten, Herbert D.
Wright, Joseph
Wright, Lucian
Wright, Melvin M.
Wright, Richard O.
Wutkiewicz, Walter E.
Yager, Woodrow W.
Yaskas, Leo J.
Yeoman, Jack
Young, Thomas J.
Younger, Samuel P.
Youngren, Kenneth G.
Youst, Kenneth E.
Zarafonatis, Peter
Zermeno, Roy
Ziemba, Aloysius P.
Zisco, William
Zittrauer, Wilbur E.
Zullo, Christy
Zupan, Don J.

NOTES

Abbreviations Used in the Notes

RG   Record Group

SFA   Swiss Federal Archives, Bern, Switzerland

SIA   Swiss Internees Association

Chapter 1. Switzerland on the Brink

1. Dieter Fahrni, *An Outline History of Switzerland: From the Origins to the Present Day.* At the Battle of Sempach in 1386, Duke Leopold III of Austria sent four thousand armed knights against a thirteen-hundred-man Swiss peasant force armed with halberds and wooden pikes. The Austrians invaded, and were again defeated, in the 1388 Battle of Nafels.

2. Edgar Bonjour, *Swiss Neutrality, Its History and Meaning,* 12–13.

3. "Switzerland and the Second World War: A Clarification," speech delivered for the Campaign for an Independent and Neutral Switzerland by Dr. Christoph Blocher, Swiss People's Party representative, 1 March 1997, Hotel International, Zürich-Oerlikon, Zürich.

4. Bonjour, *Swiss Neutrality,* 11.

5. Cyril Black et al., *Neutralization and World Politics.*

6. Rene Albrecht-Carré, *Diplomatic History of Europe since the Congress of Vienna,* 14–15.

7. John McPhee, *La Place de la Concorde Suisse.*

8. Fahrni, *Outline History of Switzerland.*

9. Neutral rights and obligations as outlined in treaties such as the Declaration of Paris (1856) standardized certain laws of neutrality. The Declaration of Paris agreement concerning the rules of maritime warfare, issued at the Congress of Paris, was the first major attempt to codify the international law of the sea. The Declaration of London (1909), which codified certain principles of neutrality with regard to maritime law, grew out of an attempt at the second Hague Conference to set up an international prize court with compulsory jurisdiction. The declaration comprised seventy-one articles dealing with many controversial points, including blockade, contraband, and prize.

10. H. K. Meier, *Friendship under Stress: U.S.-Swiss Relations 1900–1950.*

11. Bonjour, *Swiss Neutrality,* 106.

12. Alan Morris Schom, "A Survey of Nazi and Pro-Nazi Groups in Switzerland: 1930–1945."

13. Ibid.

14. Jerrold M. Packard, *Neither Friend nor Foe: The European Neutrals during World War II,* 10.

15. Ibid.

16. Ibid.

17. Ewald Banse, *Germany, Prepare for War,* 357.

18. Ibid., 360.

19. Ibid., 361.

20. Packard, *Neither Friend nor Foe,* 71.

21. Ibid.

22. Gerhard L. Weinberg, *A World at Arms: A Global History of World War II,* 23.

23. Packard, *Neither Friend nor Foe,* 75.

24. Urs Schwarz, *The Eye of the Hurricane: Switzerland in World War II,* 22.

25. Packard, *Neither Friend nor Foe.*

26. William A. Luck, *A History of Switzerland,* 797.

27. Jon Kimche, *Spying for Peace: General Guisan and Swiss Neutrality,* 28.

28. Ibid.

29. Switzerland is one of Europe's smallest countries, but it has the largest army on the continent with approximately 400,000 men, most of them in reserves. Today conscripts do service for three weeks a year, gradually decreasing to one week. Soldiers, whether alone or in groups, are trained to attack with ruthlessness foreign parachutists, airborne infantry, and saboteurs. If no officers or noncommissioned officers are present, each soldier is mandated to act on his own initiative.

30. Packard, *Neither Friend nor Foe,* 74, 146.

31. Hans-Heiri Stapfer and Gino Künzle, *Strangers in a Strange Land,* vol. 2: *Escape to Neutrality,* 3.

32. Ibid.; Weinberg, *A World at Arms.*

33. In 1938 the Swiss Air Force bought ten Bfl109Ds; in 1939 it bought fifty Bf109E-1s and thirty Bf109E-3s; in 1940 it bought license to build 290 MS-406s; in 1943 it bought some Ju-52s and also interned a few Bf109Fs that were then added to active squadrons; and in 1944 it bought about a dozen Bf109G-6s. The Swiss built some of their own designs as well, the EKW C.3600 series of single-engine light reconnaissance bombers among them. In September 1939 the Swiss Air Force had seven Me-109 squadrons: one with Bf109Ds and six with EKW biplanes. These were replaced in 1940 with Me-109Es.

34. *New York Times,* 11 May 1944.

35. Stapfer and Künzle, *Escape to Neutrality,* introduction.

36. Don A. Waters, *Hitler's Secret Ally, Switzerland,* 41.

37. Bonjour, *Swiss Neutrality,* 125.

38. Stapfer and Künzle, *Escape to Neutrality.*

39. Information obtained during an interview with Geoffrey von Meiss, a retired Swiss colonel who flew in the Swiss Air Force during World War II, 6 May 1997, Zürich.

40. Weinberg, *A World at Arms,* 397.

41. Jean Ziegler, University of Geneva, *La Suisse, l'or et les morts* (Paris: University of Geneva, 1997), 162–69.

42. Packard, *Neither Friend nor Foe,* 153.

43. Schwarz, *The Eye of the Hurricane,* 8.

44. Schom, "Survey of Nazi and Pro-Nazi Groups in Switzerland." Bircher was president of the Swiss Officers' Society from 1931 to 1937 and was also the editor of the official Swiss Army newspaper from 1934 to 1942.

45. Ibid.

46. Bonjour, *Swiss Neutrality.*

47. Ibid.

48. Ibid.

Chapter 2. The Policy of Internment

1. As recounted in *Swiss Internee* 39 (August 1992), SIA Archives, Lakewood, N.J.

2. Bonjour, *Swiss Neutrality,* 29.

3. Ibid., 93.

4. Werner Rings, *Life with the Enemy,* 212; and T. Jeff Driscoll, "Bourbaki's Retreat to Switzerland."

5. Thomas Sanction, "A Painful History," *Time,* 24 February 1997, 41.

6. Memo, June 1940, SFA, RG E5791.

7. Ibid.

8. Christopher Blocher [conservative member of Swiss Peoples Party], "Switzerland and the Second World War: A Clarification," speech given at the Hotel International Zürich-Oerlikon on 1 March 1997.

9. John V. H. Dippel, *Two against Hitler: Stealing the Nazis' Best-Kept Secrets,* 126.

10. Ibid., 126.

11. Schom, "Survey of Nazi and Pro-Nazi Groups in Switzerland."

12. Interview with G. von Meiss, 1997.

13. According to interviews with Roland "Rolly" Colgate, 24 September

1999; Jack Dowd, 24 September 1999; Lawrence "Larry" Lawler, 3 September 1997; Robert Long, 3 September 1997 and 12–13 August 2001; and Siegvart Robertson correspondence, April 2001–present.

14. Alfred Fairall memoirs; operational report regarding 18 March 1944, both in SIA Archives.

Chapter 3. Following the Silk Road

1. According to Roy A. Thomas in *Haven, Heaven, Hell: The United States Army Air Forces Aircraft and Airmen Interned in Switzerland during WWII*, the numbers are 117 aircraft from the 8th Air Force (115 fell inside Switzerland, 2 outside); 44 aircraft from the 15th Air Force; 4 aircraft from the 9th Air Force; and 5 aircraft from the 12th Air Force (3 outside Switzerland).

2. Roger A. Freeman, *The Mighty Eighth: A History of the Units, Men, and Machines of the US 8th Air Force*, introduction. Before the United States entered the war the Army Air Force was called the Army Air Corps.

3. Ibid., 267.

4. Richard G. Davis, "Carl A. Spaatz and the Air War in Europe," 376.

5. Gordon Daniels, *A Guide to the Reports of the United States Strategic Bombing Survey*, xviii.

6. Ibid., xviii.

7. Freeman, *The Mighty Eighth*, introduction.

8. Davis, *Spaatz and the Air War in Europe*.

9. Ibid., 361; information online at www.edp24.co.uk.

10. Geoffrey Perret, *Winged Victory: The Army Air Forces in World War II*, 128–31.

11. Stapfer and Künzle, *Escape to Neutrality*, 3.

12. Telephone interview with Siegvart Robertson, 21 April 2001.

13. Correspondence with Lester Kotlan, 26 November 2001.

14. Ibid., 4.

15. Richard G. Davis, *Carl A. Spaatz and the Air War in Europe*, 110–12.

16. John E. Helmreich, "The Diplomacy of Apology: U.S. Bombings of Switzerland during World War II"; and www.edp24.co.uk.

17. Waters, *Hitler's Secret Ally*, 91.

18. Stapfer and Künzle, *Escape to Neutrality*.

19. Ibid.

20. The information on Geron and his crew that appears in this chapter comes from an interview with Alva "Jake" Geron, 15 June 2001.

21. Interview with Leonard Schutta, 11 September 2001.

22. Davis, *Spaatz and the Air War in Europe*, 377.

23. Interview with John Rosenberg, 11 September 2001, Racine, Wisconsin.

24. Davis, *Spaatz and the Air War in Europe,* 378.

25. Letter from the U.S. legation to the Swiss Federal Political Department regarding 24 April 1944 Greifensee incident, SFA, RG E5791.E27/14.354.Bd. 3–4.

26. SFA, RG E5791.E27/14357.

27. Information regarding the crew of *Hell's Bells* is from the SIA Archives.

28. Interview with Norris King, 14 April 2001.

29. Memoirs of Marion "Dale" Pratt, 1 July 1990, SIA Archives.

30. Joe Carroll, operational report, 10 October 1944, SIA Archives.

31. Thomas, *Haven, Heaven, Hell,* vi.

32. Jack Falk, "Tragic Landing at Ponte Tresa," 6 March 1995, SIA Archives; and article in *Swiss Internee* 59 (December 1995).

33. Letter from Morris Sipser, 10 March 2000.

34. Stapfer and Künzle, *Escape to Neutrality,* 72.

35. Russell Sherbourne, operational report, 26 September 1944.

36. George Michel, correspondence with the author between April 2001 and the present.

37. James Hewlett, correspondence, 16 February 2000.

38. Davis, *Spaatz and the Air War in Europe,* 446.

39. Swiss newsreel footage, 1944–45, SIA Archives.

40. Memo from Legge to Spaatz and Eaker, 9 August 1944, SFA.

41. From James Mahaffey memoirs; and operational report, 26 September 1944, both in SIA Archives.

42. Norby memoirs, July 1980, SIA Archives.

43. Information from Louis Joseph, "One Experience," *Swiss Internee* 8 (June 1987), SIA Archives.

44. Interview with Donald Sellar, 20 October 1999.

45. Leon Finneran, *Swiss Internee* 57 (August 1995), SIA Archives.

46. Letter from Reagan to Hans Stapfer, 25 January 1988, SIA Archives.

47. War log, 20 July 1944–17 February 1945, SIA Archives; "Home from Europe," *Foley [Alabama] Onlooker,* 29 October 1945.

48. Thomas, *Haven, Heaven, Hell,* vi.

49. Ibid., 83.

Chapter 4. Like Angels from the Sky

1. The information in this chapter about *Sugarfoot* and its crew is from an interview with Norris King, 26 April 2001.

2. Geron letter and tape recording, 15 June 2001.

3. Mahaffey, operational report, 26 September 1944, SIA Archives.

4. Letter from Ron Freeman to Victor Fabimak, 21 March 1988, SIA Archives.

5. Packard, *Neither Friend nor Foe*, 251.

6. Edward Pribek, operational report, 26 September 1944, SIA Archives.

7. SFA, RG E5791.2/36.2.832, 1 September 1944.

8. Ibid.

9. SFA, RG E5791.2/36.2.832, 5 September 1944, from Col. Girard, chief of Federal Commission for Internment and Hospitalization, to U.S. military attaché, Prof. Dr. Dubois, hospital de L'Ile, Bern, and Dr. von Deschwanden.

10. Interview with Jack Dowd, 24 September 1999.

11. Diary of James Stotts, 18.

12. Testimony of Sgt. Robert Hiller, 448th Bomb Group, 713th Bomb Squadron, 8th Air Force, witness to the suicide, in letter to Debbie Dickson, summer 2001.

13. Testimony of Sgt. Hugh Riley, 448th Bomb Group, 713th Bomb Squadron, 8th Air Force, witness to the suicide, in Hugh Riley, memoirs, 1991, SIA Archives.

14. Postwar briefing of Gerald Swindell, 12 July 1945, SIA Archives.

15. Interview with Joseph Piemonte, 23 October 1999.

16. Interview with George Michel, 10 September 2001.

17. Interview with Roland "Rolly" Colgate, 24 September 1999.

18. Letter from Edward Winkle to Robert Long, May 1990, SIA Archives.

19. Arthur Glasier, operational report, 23 September 1944, SIA Archives.

20. See chapter 2.

21. Milton Epstein, operational report, 25 September 1944.

22. Bill Rutherford, 7 November 1944, SFA, RG E5791.2/23.2.11833, 7.

23. Fairall, operational report, 13 August 1945, SIA Archives.

24. SFA, RG E5791.

25. SIA. For example, a 26 July 1944 letter from the War Department to Mrs. Helen G. Sykes in Pompton Lakes, New Jersey, reads: "Dear Mrs. Sykes: A report has been received that the above captioned individual is safe and interned in Switzerland. You may send him personal messages via commercial radio or cable facilities. Letters may be sent by prisoner of war mail channels."

26. Interview with Margrit Thüller, 3 April 1997.

27. *Marking Time*, vol. 6 (April).

28. Text of menu posted in Nevada Palace Hotel, courtesy of George Michel.

29. Interview with Jürg Aellig, 3 April 1997.

30. Interview with Ernst Oester, 3 April 1997.

31. Telephone interview with Siegvart Robertson, 21 April 2001.

32. "Marriage–is it possible?" SFA, RG E5791.2/20.2.1655.

33. The Commission for Internment and Hospitalization approved the marriage on 9 November 1944.

34. Letter from Jim Hewlett to author, 16 February 2000.

35. SFA, RG E5791.8/43.

36. Piemonte interview, 23 October 1999.

37. General Tomlinson to Ajudance 8 section, SFA, RG E5791.2120.2. 1659.

38. Memoirs of S.Sgt. Bernard Segal, 8th AF, 305 BG, 364 BS, SIA Archives.

39. First Sgt. William Aeschacher, October 1944, SFA, RG E5791.2/20.2.1659.

40. Russell Sherbourne, operational report, September 1944, SIA Archives.

41. Letters from Lewis Sarkovich to author, 17 and 19 April 2000.

42. Copy of memo as it appeared in *Swiss Internee* 41 (December 1992).

43. Wallace Northfelt, briefing for War Crimes Office, 28 June 1945, declassified 1973, SIA Archives.

44. John Hughes, "Beyond My Dreams," *Swiss Internee* 60 (February 1996), SIA Archives.

45. Lavder Cameron, operational report, 28 September 1944; and article in *Swiss Internee* 66 (February 1997), both in SIA Archives.

46. Jack McKinney, "My Swiss Miss Adventure," *Swiss Internee* 41 (December 1992), SIA Archives.

47. SFA, RG E5791.2/29.2.2293.

48. As told by Clinton O. Norby in *Swiss Internee* 28 (October 1990), SIA Archives.

49. Mahaffey, operational report, 26 September 1944.

Chapter 5. Escape and Espionage

1. The information about Martin Andrews and his crew in this chapter is from a September 1997 interview with Andrews, Port Jefferson, Long Island.

2. Freeman, *The Mighty Eighth.*

3. Information in this chapter regarding Von Meiss is from an interview on 6 May 1997.

4. Waters, *Hitler's Secret Ally,* 137.

5. Allen Welsh Dulles, *Germany's Underground: The Anti-Nazi Resistance,* xvii.

6. Letter from Legge to FCIH, SFA, RG E5791.2/212.1582.

7. Geron tape, 15 June 2001.

8. Robert Vail, "Liberty Run," *Swiss Internee* 42 (February 1993), SIA Archives.

9. King correspondence with author, 20 April 2001.

10. Pratt memoirs, reprinted in *Swiss Internee* 25 (December 1989), SIA Archives.

11. George Telford, operational report, 11 and 26 December 1944, SIA Archives.

12. Francis Coune, operational report, 25 September 1944, SIA Archives.

13. Helmreich, "The Diplomacy of Apology."

14. Albert Burns, memoir, reprinted in *Swiss Internee* 73 (April 1995).

15. Robertson, correspondence with author, 13 June 2001.

16. Communiqué regarding second inspection of commandant, Colonel Lederrey, 29 August 1944, SFA, RG E5791.8(43).

17. Final Report of the Swiss Commission for Internment and Hospitality on the Internment of Foreign Military Personnel from 1940–1945, SFA, RG E5791.27.14927.16.

18. Aellig interview, 3 April 1997.

19. Memo from Brig. Gen. B. R. Legge, Military Attaché, Bern, to all USAAF internees, 29 August 1944, SIA Archives.

20. Segal, untitled article in *Swiss Internee* 70 (October 1997), SIA Archives.

21. Fairall report, 18 March 1944.

22. Letter dated 19 October 1944, SIA Archives.

23. Dippel, *Two against Hitler*, 126.

24. Michel interview, 10 September 2001.

25. Dippel, *Two against Hitler*, 194. The Watson Papers, in the IBM Archives in Armonk, New York, include a letter from W. C. Lier to Thomas J. Watson dated 15 November 1942.

26. Dippel, *Two against Hitler*, 127.

27. Norman Gibbard, "Switzerland and Exodus," memoir, 6 April 1987, SIA Archives.

28. Memoirs of Peter Zarafonatis, SIA Archives.

29. Sarkovich correspondence, 17 and 19 April 2000.

30. Sherbourne report, September 1944.

31. Information from Siegvart Robertson and Robert Long correspondence, and interview with George Michel; memo from General Legge to Assistant Chief of Staff, War Department, 27 November 1944, box 1020, RG 319, National Record Center. A 6 August 1943 communiqué from the U.S. War Department noted: "Publication or communication to any unauthorized persons of experiences of escape or evasion from enemy-occupied territory, internment in a neutral country, or release from internment not only *furnishes useful information to the enemy* but also *jeopardizes future escapes, evasions and releases*" (AG 383.6 [31 July 1943] PB-S-B-M. KLS/el-2B-989-Pentagon).

Chapter 6. The Wauwilermoos Penitentiary Camp

1. Information in this chapter about Larry Lawler is from an interview on 3 September 1997.

2. Pratt memoirs.

3. Robertson interviews, 25 April 2001–present.

4. The 1929 Geneva Accords led to article 89 of the Geneva Convention.

5. SIA document 27-14927-16.

6. Ibid.

7. Memo dated 19 October 1944, SFA.

8. Northfelt briefing for War Crimes Office, 28 June 1945.

9. SFA, RG E5791.

10. Pratt memoirs.

11. James Misuraca memoirs, reprinted in *Swiss Internee* 21 (August 1989), SIA Archives.

12. Béguin Papers, SFA, RG E5330 1975/95.194598/2918/1.

13. Morris Siefert, memo, 5 September 1945, SIA Archives.

14. Northfelt briefing, 28 June 1945.

15. Dowd interview, 24 September 1999.

16. Memos in the Swiss Federal Archives document the events described below; specifically, see the final report of the FCIH, May 1945.

17. SFA, RG E5791.

18. Jacob Alpert, operational report, 13 August 1945, SIA Archives.

19. Peter Lysek, war log, 20 July 1944–17 February 1945; and operational report, 29 October 1945, both in SIA Archives.

20. Béguin Papers, SFA.

21. Ibid.

22. Letter dated 22 June 1945, SFA, RG E5791.

23. Information on Daniel Culler in this chapter is from correspondence with the author between 2000 and the present; letter to Pvt. Hugh McWhinnie, 21 June 1944, SFA, RG E57916/92.622; and Culler, *The Black Hole of Wauwilermoos.*

24. Report of the interrogation of Daniel Culler after his escape, SFA, RG E5791.

25. Culler is referring to South Africans.

26. Report by Dr. König, 27 June 1944, regarding complaints made by Culler, forwarded to Ajudance 8, SFA, RG E57916/92.622.

27. SFA, RG E57916/92.622/14.

28. Béguin Papers, SFA.

29. Affidavit of Georges Troesch for Béguin court-martial, SFA, RG E5330 1975/95 194598/2918/1.

30. Report to Grand Judge of Tribunal Division, 22 November 1944, SFA, RG E5791.

31. Letter from Major Imer, 18 May 1942.

32. Inspection report, 18 August 1944, SFA.

33. When Red Cross representatives visited Theresienstadt, now in the Czech Republic, they noted the orderly manner in which the camp was run and completely overlooked the atrocities being carried out there.

Chapter 7. Diplomacy and Bombs

1. Helmreich, "The Diplomacy of Apology."

2. Jackson Granholm, *The Day We Bombed Switzerland: Flying with the US Eighth Army Air Force in World War II,* 135.

3. Operational reports as noted in Helmreich, "The Diplomacy of Apology."

4. Helmreich, "The Diplomacy of Apology."

5. Ibid.

6. SFA RG E5791; Waters, *Hitler's Secret Ally;* and information from Don Waters correspondence, George Michel interview, Robert Long interview, and Siegvart Robertson interview.

7. Waters, *Hitler's Secret Ally,* 16.

8. Ibid., 176.

9. Convention Relative to the Treatment of Prisoners of War, 27 July 1929, Art. 86, 47 Stat. 2021, 2 Bevans 932.

10. *United States* v. *Balides/Sincock,* U.S.C.M. 291679.

11. Helmreich, "The Diplomacy of Apology."

12. Stapfer and Künzle, *Escape to Neutrality.*

13. The incident was described in the 8 September 1944 issue of *Marking Time,* headlined "Tragic End to Battle over Zürich."

14. *Marking Time,* 8 September 1944.

15. *United States* v. *Balides/Sincock,* U.S.C.M. 291679.

16. Schom, "Survey of Nazi and Pro-Nazi Groups in Switzerland."

17. Legge to Smith, 9 November 1944, as noted in Helmreich, "The Diplomacy of Apology."

18. Maddux to Commanding General, Army Service Forces, 14 November 1944, as noted in Helmreich, "The Diplomacy of Apology."

19. "Switzerland, International Law, and World War Two," 466.

20. Hague Convention respecting the Rights and Duties of Neutral Powers and Persons in Case of War on Land, 18 October 1907, Art. 7, 36 Stat. 2310, 1 Bevans 654.

21. Ibid., Art. 6, 36 Stat. 2415, 1 Bevans 723, to which Switzerland, a land-locked nation, was a party.

22. "Switzerland, International Law, and World War Two."

23. Packard, *Neither Friend nor Foe*, 78.

24. Ibid.

25. Dean Acheson, *Present at the Creation: My Years in the State Department*, 50.

26. Theodore Rousseau, Consolidated Interrogation Report no. 2: "The Goering Collection," OSS report, 15 September 1945, National Archives.

27. Acheson, *Present at the Creation*.

28. Ibid., 59.

29. Numerous, books, articles, documentaries, the report of the Eizenstat Commission, etc., describe how Switzerland methodically stored money and goods looted by the Nazis and tried to conceal their source.

30. Acheson, *Present at the Creation*, 59.

31. *United States* v. *Balides/Sincock*, U.S.C.M. 291679.

32. Ibid.

33. Helmreich, "The Diplomacy of Apology."

34. Ibid.

35. *United States* v. *Balides/Sincock*, U.S.C.M. 291679.

36. Granholm, *The Day We Bombed Switzerland*.

37. *United States* v. *Balides/Sincock*, U.S.C.M. 291679.

38. Granholm, *The Day We Bombed Switzerland*.

39. *United States* v. *Balides/Sincock*, U.S.C.M. 291679.

40. Davis, *Spaatz and the Air War in Europe*, 575.

41. Ibid.

42. *United States* v. *Balides/Sincock*, U.S.C.M. 291679.

43. Ibid.

44. Ibid.

45. Ibid.

46. Ibid.

47. Ibid.

48. Ibid.

Chapter 8. At War's End

1. Thüller interview, 3 April 1997.

2. Lysek war log, SIA Archives.

3. Stapfer and Künzle, *Escape to Neutrality*.

4. Ibid.

5. Ibid.

6. Ibid., 2.

7. Dowd interview, 3 September 1999.

8. Letter from Corcoran to Col. Rayens, 23 May 1944, communication no. 418, SIA Archives.

9. Davis, *Spaatz and the Air War in Europe.*

10. Ibid.

11. Ibid.

12. Ibid.

13. U.S. Code, Title 38, section 101 (3a).

14. Legge postwar accounting, SIA Archives.

15. Gary Hickman, "Prisoners of War Interned in Switzerland," white paper issued by Veterans Benefits Administration Compensation and Pension Service, U.S. Veterans Administration, 23 February 1996 [hereinafter VA 1996 White Paper].

16. Department of Veterans Affairs, Board of Appeals, citation no. 9626376, docket no. 93-01 864.

17. VA 1996 White Paper.

18. I apologize in advance for leaving out any names.

19. Stapfer and Künzle, *Escape to Neutrality.*

20. SFA RG E5791.98/2918.

21. SFA RG E5791.Bestands-Rr.27, Archiv No. 14927, Bd. 16.

22. Letter from Dan Culler to Bob Long, 29 September 1994, SIA.

23. Michel interview, 10 September 2001.

BIBLIOGRAPHY

Unpublished Sources

Interviews and Correspondence

Aellig, Jürg, interview, 3 April 1997, Adelboden, Switzerland

Andrews, Martin, interview, August 1997, Port Jefferson, N.Y.

Bammetter, Col. Josef, interview, 12 May 1997, Wauwil, Switzerland

Clark, Forest, e-mail correspondence, September and October 2002

Colgate, Roland "Rolly," interview, 24 September 1999, Sagamore, Mass.

Councell, Marbury L. Jr., letter, 27 February 2000

Culler, Dan, correspondence, 1997–present

Deschwanden, Peter von, interviews, 25 March 1997 and 3 April 1997, Bern, Switzerland; 2 May 1997, Wauwil, Switzerland

Dickson, Debbie, e-mail correspondence, summer 2001

Dowd, Jack, interview, 24 September 1999, Sagamore, Mass.

Geron, Alva "Jake," tape and letter, 15 June 2001

Granholm, Jackson, e-mail correspondence, 17 April 2001

Hewlett, James A., letter, 16 February 2000

King, Norris, e-mail correspondence, April 2000–present

Kotlan, Lester, correspondence, September–November 2001

Lawler, Lawrence "Larry," interview, 3 September 1997, Teeterboro, N.J.

Long, Robert, interviews, 3 September 1997, Teeterboro, N.J.; 12 and 13 August 2001, Lakewood, N.J.; correspondence, 1997–present

McKain, Keith [son of internee Armor Leroy McKain], e-mail correspondence, November 1999

Meiss, Geoffrey von, interview, 6 May 1997, Zürich

Michel, George, interviews, 10 and 11 September 2001, Racine, Wisc.; correspondence, April 2001–present

Oester, Ernst, interview, 3 April 1997, Adelboden, Switzerland

Piemonte, Joseph, interview, 23 October 1999, Brookline, Mass.

Radin, Norman, e-mail correspondence, November 1999

Robertson, Siegvart J., letters and e-mail correspondence, April 2001–present

Sarkovich, Lewis, letters, 17 and 19 April 2000

Schutta, Leonard, letter, 25 September 2001

Sellers, Dan, interview, 20 October 1999, Brookline, Mass.

Sipser, Morris, letter, 10 March 2000

Thüller, Margrit, interview, 3 April 1997, Adelboden, Switzerland

Waters, Dan, correspondence, March 2002

Documents

Final Report of the Federal Commission on Internment and Hospitalization of Foreign Military Personnel from 1940–1945. Swiss Federal Archives, RG E5791.27.14927.16. Bern.

Record groups E5791 and E5330. Swiss Federal Archives, Bern.

Swiss Internees Association Archives and the association's publication, *The Swiss Internee.*

United States v. *Balides/Sincock.* U.S.C.M. 291679. National Records Center, Suitland, Md.

Wartime log of James Stotts. In the possession of Debbie Dickson, Lubbock, Texas.

Published Sources

Acheson, Dean. *Present at the Creation: My Years in the State Department.* New York: W. W. Norton, 1969.

Albrecht-Carré, Rene. *A Diplomatic History of Europe since the Congress of Vienna.* New York: Harper and Row, 1973.

"Armons nos soldats de la paix." *L'Hebdo,* no. 44, 4 November 1999.

Bancroft, Mary. *Autobiography of a Spy.* New York: William Morrow, 1983.

Banse, Ewald. *Germany, Prepare for War! From the German Raum und Volk im Weltkrieg.* Translated by Alan Harris. London: Lovat Dickson, 1934.

Black, Cyril, et al. *Neutralization and World Politics.* Princeton: Princeton University Press, 1968.

Bonjour, Edgar. *Swiss Neutrality, Its History and Meaning.* Translated by Mary Hottinger. London: George Allen and Unwin, 1946.

Culler, Daniel. *The Black Hole of Wauwilermoos.* Green Valley, Ariz.: Circle of Thorns Press, 1995.

Daniels, Gordon, ed. *A Guide to the Reports of the United States Strategic Bombing Survey.* London: University College of London, 1981.

Davis, Richard G. *Carl A. Spaatz and the Air War in Europe.* Washington, D.C.: Center for Air Force History, 1993.

Dippel, John V. H. *Two against Hitler: Stealing the Nazis' Best-Kept Secrets.* New York: Praeger, 1946.

Driscoll, T. Jeff. "Bourbaki's Retreat to Switzerland." *Military History* 17, no. 6 (2001): 58.

Dulles, Allen Welsh. *Germany's Underground: The Anti-Nazi Resistance.* 1947. Reprint. New York: Da Capo Press, 2000.

Fahrni, Dieter. *An Outline History of Switzerland: From the Origins to the Present Day.* 4th ed. Pro Helvetia Arts Council of Switzerland Information, 1987.

Freeman, Roger A. *The Mighty Eighth: A History of the Units, Men, and Machines of the US 8th Air Force.* London: Cassell, 1970.

Granholm, Jackson. *The Day We Bombed Switzerland: Flying with the US Eighth Army Air Force in World War II.* England: Airlife Publishing, 2000.

Helmreich, John E. "The Diplomacy of Apology: U.S. Bombings of Switzerland during World War II." *Air University Review* 28, no. 4 (1977): 19–37.

Hickman, J. Gary. "Prisoners of War Interned in Switzerland." White Paper issued 13 February 1996. Veterans Benefits Administration Compensation and Pension Service. U.S. Veterans Administration, Washington, D.C.

Jost, Hans Ulrich. "Switzerland's Atlantic Perspectives." In *Swiss Neutrality and Security: Armed Forces, National Defence and Foreign Policy,* ed. Marko Miliovojevic and Peter Maurer. New York: Berg, 1990.

Kimche, Jon. *Spying for Peace: General Guisan and Swiss Neutrality.* London: Weidenfeld and Nicolson, 1962.

Luck, William. *A History of Switzerland.* Palo Alto, Calif.: Society for Promotion of Science and Scholarship, 1985.

McPhee, John. *La Place de la Concorde Suisse.* New York: Farrar, Straus and Giroux, 1983.

Meier, H. K. *Friendship under Stress: U.S.-Swiss Relations 1900–1950.* Zürich: Peter Lang, 1970.

Packard, Jerrold M. *Neither Friend nor Foe: The European Neutrals during World War II.* New York: Maxwell Macmillan International, 1992.

Perret, Geoffrey. *Winged Victory: The Army Air Forces in World War II.* New York: Random House, 1993.

Petropoulos, Jonathan. "Co-opting Nazi Germany: Neutrality in Europe during World War II." *Dimensions* 11, no. 1 (1997): 15–21.

Rings, Werner. *Life with the Enemy: Collaboration and Resistance in Hitler's Europe 1939–1945.* Translated by J. Maxwell Brownjohn. New York: Doubleday, 1982.

–––. *L'Or des Nazis, la Suisse, an Relais Discret.* Lausanne, Switzerland: Payot, 1995.

Schom, Alan Morris. "A Survey of Nazi and Pro-Nazi Groups in Switzerland, 1930–1945." Manuscript on file at the Simon Wiesenthal Center, 1998.

Schwarz, Urs. *The Eye of the Hurricane: Switzerland in World War II.* Boulder: Westview Press, 1980.

Shirer, William L. *The Rise and Fall of the Third Reich: A History of Nazi Germany.* New York: Simon and Schuster, 1960.

"Small Switzerland Has a Large Citizen Army." *Washington Times,* 20 January 2000.

Stapfer, Hans-Heiri, and Gino Künzle. *Strangers in a Strange Land.* Vol. 2: *Escape to Neutrality.* Carrollton, Tex.: Squadron/Signal Publications, 1992.

"Swiss on the Front: Air Defense 1939–1945." *Our Militia,* no. 102, January 1994.

"Switzerland, International Law, and World War Two" [Editorial Comment]. *American Journal of International Law* 91, no. 3 (July 1997): 446.

Thomas, Roy J. *Haven, Heaven, Hell: The United States Army Air Forces Aircraft and Airmen Interned in Switzerland during WWII.* Monroe, Wisc.: Puka Press, 1991.

"War Trade between Switzerland and the Axis Powers: Exchange of Letters at London December 19, 1943." The Avalon Project at the Yale Law School.

Waters, Don A. *Hitler's Secret Ally, Switzerland.* La Mesa, Calif.: Pertinent Publications, 1992.

Weinberg, Gerhard L. *A World at Arms: A Global History of World War II.* Cambridge: Cambridge University Press, 1994.

Ziegler, Jean. *Une Suisse au-dessus de tout soupçon.* Paris: Seuil, 1976.

Web Sites

The following sites offer information regarding war trade, internment of individual airmen, Swiss-U.S. relations during WWII, international law, and the 8th Air Force.

www.aeroflight.co.uk/waf/switz/swisaf2.htm

www.edp24.co.uk/Content/Features/USAAF/asp/USAAFdefault.asp

www.44thbombgroup.com

www.geocities.com/cadet1.geo/AV1.html

www.heavybombers.com

www.jmi.com/WWII

www.wiesenthal.com/swiss/survey/noframes/index.html

INDEX

About the Author

Cathryn J. Prince has a B.A. from George Washington University's Elliott School of International Affairs and an M.S. from The Graduate School of Journalism, Columbia University. After working as a reporter in Boston, she moved to Switzerland where she covered the United Nations in Geneva and Swiss politics for *The Christian Science Monitor*. Upon returning to the United States she covered the United Nations in New York City. Ms. Prince has also worked as an adjunct professor of journalism at Columbia University and at Boston University. She lives in Connecticut.

The Naval Institute Press is the book-publishing arm of the U.S. Naval Institute, a private, nonprofit, membership society for sea service professionals and others who share an interest in naval and maritime affairs. Established in 1873 at the U.S. Naval Academy in Annapolis, Maryland, where its offices remain today, the Naval Institute has members worldwide.

Members of the Naval Institute support the education programs of the society and receive the influential monthly magazine *Proceedings* and discounts on fine nautical prints and on ship and aircraft photos. They also have access to the transcripts of the Institute's Oral History Program and get discounted admission to any of the Institute-sponsored seminars offered around the country.

The Naval Institute also publishes *Naval History* magazine. This colorful bimonthly is filled with entertaining and thought-provoking articles, first-person reminiscences, and dramatic art and photography. Members receive a discount on *Naval History* subscriptions.

The Naval Institute's book-publishing program, begun in 1898 with basic guides to naval practices, has broadened its scope to include books of more general interest. Now the Naval Institute Press publishes about one hundred titles each year, ranging from how-to books on boating and navigation to battle histories, biographies, ship and aircraft guides, and novels. Institute members receive significant discounts on the Press's more than eight hundred books in print.

Full-time students are eligible for special half-price membership rates. Life memberships are also available.

For a free catalog describing Naval Institute Press books currently available, and for further information about subscribing to *Naval History* magazine or about joining the U.S. Naval Institute, please write to:

Membership Department
U.S. Naval Institute
291 Wood Road
Annapolis, MD 21402-5034
Telephone: (800) 233-8764
Fax: (410) 269-7940
Web address: www.navalinstitute.org